Empathy in Counseling and Psychotherapy

Perspectives and Practices

Empathy in Counseling and Psychotherapy

Perspectives and Practices

Arthur J. Clark
St. Lawrence University

LAWRENCE ERLBAUM ASSOCIATES, PUBLISHERS
2007 Mahwah, New Jersey London

Lawrence Erlbaum Associates, Inc., Publishers
10 Industrial Avenue
Mahwah, New Jersey 07430
www.erlbaum.com

Cover design by Tomai Maridou

Library of Congress Cataloging-in-Publication Data

Clark, Arthur J.
Empathy in counseling and psychotherapy / Arthur J. Clark
p. cm.
Includes bibliographical references and index.
ISBN 0-8058-5366-9 (hardcover : alk. paper) —
ISBN 0-8058-5950-0 (pbk. : alk. paper)
1. Counseling. 2. Psychotherapy. 3. Empathy. I. Title.
BF637.C6C4533 2006
158'.3—dc22 2005055503

Books published by Lawrence Erlbaum Associates are printed on acid-free paper, and their bindings are chosen for strength and durability.

Printed in the United States of America
10 9 8 7 6 5 4 3 2 1

For more than 30 years it has been my abiding good fortune to have been given the gift of empathy in the company of my wife, Marybeth, and my friend, William P. Brown. It is to them that I dedicate this book.

Contents

Preface

In the fall of 1977 I attended a public lecture in Boston presented by Carl Rogers. The address by the eminent psychologist was given in a large auditorium that was filled to capacity. Toward the conclusion of his well-received presentation, Rogers invited questions from members of the audience. At the end of a lively exchange, an older man asked Rogers about the most prominent aspect or legacy of his life's work. In response, Rogers, pausing for a moment, stated that in his view, perhaps his most important contribution to the lives of others was his observations and writings on empathy. Rogers related further that he wished he had more time to think and write about empathy, but he was currently involved in a number of endeavors that precluded this possibility.

During the few minutes that Rogers talked about empathy, I realized that I was already relatively knowledgeable about the topic. I had recently completed graduate studies in counseling where empathy and the client-centered therapy of Rogers were emphasized. My early career background also included direct service positions where I had come to value the importance of empathically understanding clients. At the time, my sense of empathy was that it primarily involved the technique of reflection, wherein a practitioner restates to a client something about that person's feelings and perceptions. When I thought further about empathy, I was curious about Rogers's interest in devoting even more time to an approach in which he seemed so well versed. Indeed, Rogers had already achieved acclaim for writing extensively about the construct as one of the facilitative conditions that foster therapeutic change in a treatment situation. I also wondered why Rogers felt the need to study empathy further because reflection, as the basis for empathic understanding, did not seem conceptually complex to the point that it required extended research.

As the years passed and I gained further treatment experience with a diverse range of clients, I realized that I had too easily taken empathy for granted in my earlier view of the construct. As my perspective of empathy evolved from a narrow and simplistic conception, I began to more deeply appreciate the profound effect that empathic understanding has on individuals in a treatment situation beyond the technique of reflection. During this period, I also became familiar with the extensive literature that, in addition to client-centered therapy, addressed empathy from a broader and more comprehensive context. At the same time, I often found the empirical and conceptual material hard to assimilate and to put into practice. In part, my difficulty seemed related to the widely varying assumptions among theorists on the nature and definition of empathy. In the vast research on the topic in counseling and psychotherapy, empathy has multiple meanings that have been conceptualized variously as an experiential condition, a communication skill, and as an observational method.

With a further passage of time, I entered academia as a professor and found scholastic conditions for teaching about empathy in a treatment context constricted and ambiguous. Most introductory and advanced counseling and psychotherapy texts reflect the sustained interest in empathy, yet discussion is typically limited to a client- or person-centered theoretical perspective or is delegated to the circumscribed function of reflection as a technique. As a result, empathy is frequently underestimated or misunderstood in terms of its therapeutic potential and range of application in a treatment situation. Although there are ample writings available on empathic understanding in the therapeutic process, the material frequently lacks a coherent and practical focus. Existing texts on empathy are primarily edited volumes compiled by multiple authors with varying theoretical orientations. As a consequence, students and practitioners in mental health capacities often lack an awareness of the significance and potential for understanding empathy from a more comprehensive and intelligible perspective. Furthermore, individuals exposed to the literature on empathy are rarely introduced to the limitations and cautions that relate to the effective application of the construct.

This book focuses on theoretical positions and research on empathy and the use and application of empathic understanding in counseling and psychotherapy. In Part I of the text, discussion begins by examining the lengthy history of the divergent and often vague conceptualizations of empathy in a therapy context. Empathy as a concept originated from an appreciation of aesthetics in the late 19th century and has evolved into a major psychological construct. A distinction is made between empathy and the frequently confused terms of sympathy, identification, and projection. Consideration of the value of empathy in the treatment process recognizes how an attunement with an individual's experience is indispensable for increasing client understanding, enhancing the therapeutic relationship, and enriching the therapeutic process.

Part II shifts to analyzing formulations and practices of empathy across theoretical systems of counseling and psychotherapy. Thirteen contemporary psychotherapies were found to provide varying degrees of emphasis with respect to empathy in each of the orientations. Separate chapters address the central role of empathy relating to the traditions of person-centered, psychoanalytic therapy, and self psychology. From a person-centered perspective, consideration is given to clarifying misunderstandings about attitudes and techniques in the application of the human dimension of empathy. Within the persuasion of psychoanalytic therapy, discussion focuses on empathy's long and controversial history that may be unfamiliar to many practitioners. Attention then shifts to the role of empathy in self psychology both as an observational method and as a tool for client understanding.

Part III introduces a substantially new framework relating to empathy in counseling and psychotherapy. Empathic understanding in a treatment situation encompasses three ways of knowing: subjective, interpersonal, and objective. Empathy is operational at three levels, and hypotheses are interwoven through a contextural or a multiple perspective approach. The employment of multiple knowledge channels provides a comprehensive means for using empathy and empathic understanding in therapeutic interactions. Discussion then relates to the integration of empathic understanding in the technical domain of individual counseling and psychotherapy. Empathy, as a mode of understanding, potentially enables a practitioner to become attuned to a client's experience through all phases of the therapeutic experience. In the context of group treatment, attention is given to a practitioner's role in empathizing with an individual, members of a subgroup, or to the group as a whole. A group counselor or therapist is also in a position to model the use of empathy and to stimulate its development among group participants. In the concluding chapter, a case study emphasizes the use of empathy across three stages of the treatment process.

Empathy in Counseling and Psychotherapy: Perspectives and Practices is written to address the clear need to organize the voluminous literature on empathy into a coherent and practical text for students and practitioners. The text focuses on understanding empathy from a broad range of perspectives and developing strategies for effectively employing the construct in treatment practice. The volume is designed for use in courses in counseling and therapy techniques, theories of counseling and psychotherapy, and the counseling internship. I have also written the book for counselors, psychotherapists, psychologists, psychiatrists, social workers, and other direct service providers.

ACKNOWLEDGMENTS

A number of people deserve my appreciation for assisting me in completing this book. Allen Ivey has been steadfast in his support of my writing endeavors for a number of years and has encouraged me to write this text. William P. Brown has been the "editor" of all of my publications, from the first articles in a local town newspaper to the culmination of this text. I also wish to express my gratitude to the reviewers of my book. Al Mahrer at the University of Ottawa and Les Greenberg at York University provided thoughtful and incisive critiques. Thanks to my graduate assistants at St. Lawrence University—Denise LaBar, Christine Winston and Kathleen Marsh—for their contributions. Bonnie Enslow and Naomi Ten Eyck, University Senior Secretaries, were particularly helpful in the manuscript preparation. Finally, Steve Rutter, Senior Editor, Debbie Ruel, Senior Book Production Editor, Nicole Buchmann, Editorial Research Coordinator, and other members of the capable staff at Lawrence Erlbaum Associates saw the project through to its end.

PART I

Empathy: Historical and Contemporary Perspectives and Practices in Counseling and Psychotherapy

Chapter 1

The Meaning of Empathy in Counseling and Psychotherapy

Wouldst thou the others know well, look thou within thine own heart.

—Schiller (1795/1985, p. 329)

My search for refinement of the meaning of empathy and an appreciation of its potency in the therapeutic experience has evolved over the past 30 years. As a graduate student in counseling in the early 1970s, I thought that empathy was largely about perceiving a client's internal frame of reference and striving to convey this understanding back to the individual. It was also my belief that empathy should be expressed in a caring and accurate manner. In practice, this meant that I would listen attentively to a client and attempt to reflect back the essence of what I had heard. I can recall my numerous efforts to achieve the highest level of perceptivity with my client in my role as a "grand empathizer." Thinking back on my early views of empathy, I realize that, although I may have grasped essential elements of the construct, I also held an oversimplified conception of empathy and a too narrow perspective of its potential role in counseling and psychotherapy.

As the years passed and my experience in working with a diverse range of clients grew, I became aware that my conception of empathy had become increasingly diffuse and ambiguous. I soon realized that it was essential to include a cognitive component or framework in empathic understanding in order to more fully assess the functioning of clients. I also began to clarify the difference between expressing empathy as a mode of communication and experiencing empathy as an attitudinal engagement. This distinction took on added importance as questions arose in the literature about the operational definitions of empathy, and criticism proliferated relating to the adequacy of measuring empathy as a construct in research designs. It also became apparent to me that closely related concepts, including sympathy, projection, and identification, were also subject to semantic confusion in the therapeutic practice of employing empathy. Finally, as my knowledge of the theoretical conceptualizations of empathy increased beyond client-centered therapy, I began to recognize the importance of expanding my views on the meaning and application of empathy in a treatment situation within a broader context.

THE ORIGIN OF THE MEANING OF EMPATHY

The modern usage of empathy has roots in German aesthetics when Robert Vischer, in 1873, coined the term *einfühlung* (Hunsdahl, 1967; Pigman, 1995). In his discussion of aesthetics and form perception, Vischer made reference to einfühlung as a means of coming to know a particular work of art through the projection of human feelings (Watson, 2002; Wispé, 1987). For example, when a person observes a piece of art, he or she may experience an inclination to merge or fuse with the object on a physically felt level and lose a sense of self-awareness (Katz, 1963). The German word derives from an individual's psychological aesthetic experience of "feeling oneself into" or to "feel within" (Jenkins, 1997). In 1897, the German psychologist Theodor Lipps began to discuss einfühlung as a means of perceiving and appreciating art forms, but he subsequently developed a theory that extended the construct into the realm of interpersonal functioning (Wispé, 1987). Through his extensive writing on einfühlung, Lipps conceptually broadened its meaning into the area of understanding others from a psychological vantage point. Lipps conceptualized the response of a person by detailing a process of projection and imitation (Deutsch & Madle, 1975), whereby a person "feels into" the experience of another individual as a means of knowing. The systematic work of Lipps led to a broader understanding of the term as a relational experience in common use and in the professional literature.

Interest in the concept of einfühlung continued to increase into the 20th century. In the United States, Edward Titchener translated einfühlung into *empathy* from the original German (Katz, 1963). In his 1909 rendering of empathy, Titchener emphasized the aesthetic aspects of the term as they related to projection of feelings into perceived objects (Pigman, 1995). In his later writings, Titchener discussed the process of "feeling oneself" into situations that individuals experience as an imaginative aspect of empathy (Post, 1980; Wispé, 1987). With respect to etymology, Titchener's translation of empathy originates by way of the Greek word *empatheia,* which means to enter or to be with a person's suffering or passion (Schmid, 2001; Wispé, 1987).

MODES OF EMPATHY IN COUNSELING AND PSYCHOTHERAPY

Although there is ambiguity and debate relating to the meaning of empathy in the psychotherapeutic literature, it is possible to conceptually organize the construct into three modes in a treatment context. Experiential, communication, and observational modes represent broad categorizations across diverse theoretical orientations. Carl Rogers recognized empathy as a way of being or an attitude that is a critical variable in therapeutic change. Rogers, and others who expanded on his ideas, emphasized an *experiential* mode of empathy wherein a counselor or therapist assumes a transitory engagement with a client in an attempt to grasp the inner experience and meanings of a person. The practitioner resonates in a bodily felt response to a client's functioning and conveys aspects of this interaction to the individual.

As a mode of *communication,* extensive efforts of researchers have focused on developing operational definitions of empathy for use in practice and for training purposes. With an explicit goal of conceptualizing empathy as a communication skill, criticism grew regarding the quality of the research relating to the construct and its subsequently diminished attitudinal role in counseling and psychotherapy. At the same time, it is widely recognized that for empathy to engender therapeutic gain, it must be communicated to an individual. Contemporary research efforts continue to refine models for evaluating the communication of empathy in a therapeutic situation. With respect to an *observational* mode, a practitioner may utilize empathy as a means of acquiring psychological data relating to a client. It is then possible for a counselor or therapist to transform the knowledge into an interpretation or related interventions. This process of observing and explaining suggests a deeper quality of empathic understanding as a client achieves a broader perspective relating to his or her experience. The interaction requires the practitioner to simultaneously function in a role that is emotionally involved with a client and in a qualitatively different pursuit that is more detached and objective.

Empathy as a Mode of Experiencing

Throughout the lengthy period when Rogers wrote about the topic of empathy, he was insistent that the construct be viewed as an attitude in counseling and psychotherapy. In his early work with client-centered therapy, Rogers (1949) proposed a set of attitudes that become implemented by various methods and techniques that are consistent within the treatment approach. Rogers (1966) ultimately determined that the presence of empathy was one of the definable variables that, in addition to congruence and unconditional positive regard, affect progress and success in counseling and psychotherapy. In this respect, Rogers's intent was to convey a comprehensive definition of empathy as a posture or a position of a therapist rather than a repertoire of particular interventions and strategies (Bozarth, 1998). As a fundamental aspect of an empathic attitude, Rogers (1951) felt that it was essential for a practitioner to attempt to grasp the internal frame of reference as a client perceives it and then endeavor to communicate key aspects of this experience to the individual. In this subjective and immediate interaction, an experiential condition of empathy occurs between a counselor and a client. It is the nature of this empathic experience in the therapeutic process that subsequently became a major focus for Rogers and other client- or person-centered therapists.

By distinguishing an attitudinal focus of empathy, Rogers wished to convey a steadiness of purpose on the part of a counselor or therapist. Rogers felt that an effective practitioner needed to consistently manifest an empathic stance in the presence of a client. For Rogers, a sustained attitude on the part of a therapist was crucial in attaining emotional growth and healing (Bennett, 2001). In this respect, empathy involves a way of being with a client and a commitment to a treatment approach that engenders a predictable and therapeutic supportive climate. In particular, an empathic attitude requires that a counselor attempt to capture and stay within a client's perceptual field in an immediate context (Bozarth, 1998). In order to do this, a practitioner typically expresses empathic responses to a client in order to verify or affirm the experience of the individual. This interactive aspect of understanding emphasizes the experiential quality of empathy. Experiential empathy occurs in the immediate moment in response to a client's verbal and nonverbal disclosures. A client's tone of voice, gestures, and manner and content of expression reveal aspects of the individual's experiencing (Gendlin, 1961). In therapeutic interactions with a client, a practitioner attempts to grasp the explicit and implicit meanings of the person (Rogers, 1966).

The work of Rogers was instrumental in establishing a prominent position with respect to empathic experiencing in counseling and psychotherapy. His focus on empathy largely involved trying to understand the inner experience of an individual in terms of what it would be like if one were the other person. Rogers did attend to aspects of his own experiencing, such as intuitive responses, in the immediacy of counseling, and he began to give more attention to this functioning as his theory evolved. Expanding on the ideas of Rogers, other researchers gave increased emphasis to the experience of the therapist within the counseling relationship. Gendlin (1961, 1962) and Vanaerschot (1990, 1997) wrote about the counselor engaging in empathic resonance and bodily felt responses in reaction to what a client is experiencing. In an intentional way, a practitioner attunes his or her subjective reactions to those of the client. This becomes a visceral process as a therapist experiences transitory feelings similar to those of the client (Chismar, 1988; Feiner & Kiersky, 1994). In practice, a therapist momentarily identifies with a client in order to imagine what it might be like to be the person (Bachrach, 1976). This endeavor calls on a counselor to be openly engaged and responsive to one's own internal reactions and sensibilities in the service of understanding individuals.

In a treatment example relating to experiential empathy, Justin, a 15-year-old adolescent, is referred to a therapist due to acting-out behavior in his school and community. In the initial session, Justin is sullen and withdrawn and largely refuses to participate in the counseling endeavor. From an experiential perspective, the therapist subjectively reacts by briefly identifying with Justin and fleetingly imagines what it is like to be mandated to attend therapy. The practitioner also experiences a visceral response of tightness in her chest when interacting with Justin. As the therapist attempts to understand Justin's phenomenological or subjective experiencing, she is aware of Justin's strong feelings of resentment and alienation. In this context, the practitioner intuitively senses that Justin's negative feelings must be immediately addressed in order to engender any hope for therapeutic movement.

It may be apparent that when a counselor or therapist identifies with a client through an experiential mode of empathy, there is always a potential for confusion of psychological boundaries. A practitioner may become enmeshed in the experiencing process and fail to maintain a sufficient degree of emotional detachment (Mearns, 2003). As a counselor experiences the feelings and perceptions of a client, even on a momentary basis, the vicarious contact may be intense and engrossing. A therapist is particularly vulnerable to an excessive level of identification with another individual when personal issues and conflicts are unresolved and subject to merging with the material of the client. Rogers (1957) was aware of the possibility of enmeshment when he emphasized the importance of a therapist being able to perceive the experience of a person, but to do so without losing the condition *as if* the counselor were the client. In practice, it is essential for a practitioner to avoid allowing conflictive personal issues to encroach on the counseling relationship (Boy & Pine, 1982). At the same time, if a therapist maintains only an emotionally distant level of engagement with a client, communications and understandings that are forthcoming from an experiential mode of empathy may be diminished or precluded.

Empathy as a Mode of Communication

Although experiential empathy involves an active resonance, it does not necessarily imply that a therapist communicate this experiencing back to a client (Marcia, 1987). Most often, however, in the context of the therapy process, empathy is understood by a client with respect to its verbal and nonverbal components as expressed by the practitioner (Haase & Tepper, 1972). Rogers (1975) wrote about the therapist sensing the client's inner experiencing and communicating something about this understanding back to the person. In this regard, empathy involves a commitment to grasp the internal state of an individual as accurately as possible (Cochran & Cochran, 2006; Egan, 2002). It is the sustained interpersonal stance of the counselor in perceiving and responding to the private meanings of the client that is central to the healing and change process (Barrett-Lennard, 1976; Bennett, 2001; Rogers, 1975). In order for an empathic response of a therapist to affect a client, it must be expressed or made visible in some form (Barrett-Lennard, 1981). Rogers (1951, 1961, 1980) provided numerous examples of empathic understanding in his written and recorded sessions with clients in order to identify and clarify experiencing and communication endeavors.

As researchers and practitioners increased their interest in empathy as a therapeutic variable, efforts were extended to operationalize the function of the counselor or therapist with respect to empathic understanding. The perception and communication of empathy as an interpersonal skill became a major focus of research in the late 1960s through the 1970s. Evaluating the accurate communication of empathy through observable criteria largely replaced the sensing of a client's experience from an attitudinal perspective (Hackney, 1978). During this period, scales were developed that measured the ability of an individual to demonstrate empathy in terms of predictive accuracy (Carkhuff & Berenson, 1977; Jacobs & Williams, 1983; Truax & Carkhuff, 1967). Typically, brief segments of counseling interviews were conducted, and scaled ratings of the interviewers' ability to express empathy were compiled. After a period of time, many of these research findings were criticized due to what were perceived as serious conceptual and methodological flaws (Barkham, 1988; Gladstein, 1977, 1983; Marks & Tolsma, 1986). Participants in the studies were typically undergraduate students with minimal levels of training, and commentary in the interviews was frequently isolated from a broader treatment context. Definitions of empathy were operationalized in terms of behavioral components, and the meanings of empathic understanding often differed among researchers (Duan & Hill, 1996).

From Rogers's initial conception of empathy as an attitude and a way of being, the construct subsequently began to assume primarily technological qualities as a communication skill or technique. The essence of empathy became transposed from an experiential state involving the client and counselor to an observable interpersonal process. In particular, the technique of reflection came to be equated with empathic understanding (Bohart & Greenberg, 1997). Other modes of expressing empathy beyond reflecting the feelings and perceptions of clients were subject to far less research interest. The conceptual confusion between empathy and reflection particularly affected client-centered therapy, as the orientation was becoming primarily associated with the technique of reflection. It is understandable that Rogers found the focus of empathic understanding as a communication skill disturbing, and he said that it "led to appalling consequences and complete distortion of client-centered therapy" (Rogers, 1980, p. 139).

The focus on explicit communication methods and the equating of reflection with empathy restricted consideration of a broader range of empathic counseling interventions within theoretical orientations and in practitioner training programs (Bozarth, 1984; Feller & Cottone, 2003). In numerous instances, attitudinal and experiential aspects of empathy were relegated to more narrow operational methods. At the same time, attempts to conceptualize empathy with respect to measurable and observable criteria have enabled trainees and practitioners to clarify what can be a vague and abstract conception (Clark, 2004a). Furthermore, research and training efforts are advanced when constructs are explicitly described. In this direction, although definitions of empathy in counseling and psychotherapy remain ambiguous, in recent years empathy research has improved in terms of providing increased participation of counselors and therapists as subjects, while expanding the contextualization of counseling topics (Avenanti, Bueti, Galati, & Aglioti, 2005; Crutchfield, Baltimore, Felfeli, & Worth, 2000; Duan & Hill, 1996). Additionally, the later work of Rogers and recent trends in the writings of other person-centered therapists have formulated broader ways of conceptualizing and communicating empathic understanding.

To continue the earlier treatment example relating to the adolescent Justin, the therapist recognizes that it is essential for her to attempt to communicate an understanding of Justin's aversive feelings:

Therapist: It doesn't make much sense to you to have to be here for counseling.
Justin: You got that one right. I get sick of people always being on my case.
Therapist: A lot of times you resent being told what to do by other people.
Justin: Yeah. It's either my mother or my teachers who are constantly after me.
Therapist: It seems to you that adults in your life are always letting you know what's best for you.
Justin: They think so and they never let up. The other day I was in school and . . .

In this brief exchange, the practitioner utilizes the technique of reflection in an effort to initiate communication with Justin. In an early stage of counseling, the therapist emphasizes communication that focuses on Justin's phenomenological experiencing and internal frame of reference.

Empathy as a Mode of Observation

From a perspective that is fundamentally different from experiential empathy, an observational mode of empathy provides a method for a counselor or therapist to acquire psychological data with respect to a client. This information-gathering activity is subsequently transformed and communicated to the client through an interpretation or related interventions (Poland, 1984). In a two-part conceptualization, the acquisition of knowledge about a client enables a practitioner to provide informed therapeutic interventions that serve to broaden and deepen the individual's self-insight (Kahn, 1985). Kohut (1991) conceptualized the interrelated process of understanding and explaining as a means of moving from a lower form of empathy to a higher form. As a therapist observes and increases his or her understanding of a client, it also becomes possible for relevant data to be transposed into theoretical formulations. Unlike experiential empathy, which tends to focus on the immediate functioning of a person, observational empathy more often involves a prolonged immersion in a broader perspective of a client's life (Ornstein, 1979). In this regard, a practitioner is able to build a model of a patient that provides a developmental context as a basis for deeper understanding (Greenson, 1960; Lichtenberg, 1981). This tentative patient or client model evolves over a period of time and serves as a functional guide for treatment directions.

Through an enhanced knowledge of a client, a counselor or therapist is in a position to express an increased understanding in an empathic form. In turn, the therapeutic alliance is strengthened as an individual experiences a deeper sense of empathic understanding. In order to acquire information from the immediate experience of a client, however, it is necessary for a practitioner to become emotionally involved with the person. Kohut (1977) refers to this process as an *experience-near* function of the therapist. In this position, a counselor assumes a stance manifesting participatory qualities of experiential empathy, including a transitory and vicarious identification. In a major departure, however, from experiential empathy, a therapist evokes a more objective observer perspective while simultaneously retaining a participant role (Greenson, 1967; Kohut, 1984; Sullivan, 1954). Kohut (1977) identified the more detached role of the therapist as *experience-distant,* as the function includes both evaluative and conceptualization endeavors. As an example, a practitioner may evaluate a client in terms of defensive functioning or consider diagnostic impressions. This experience-distant posture then serves to guide the more immediate interactions of a counselor in the service of empathic understanding.

To conclude the example involving Justin, treatment has continued on a weekly basis for over 2 months. Justin and the therapist have established an open degree of communication and rapport within the therapeutic relationship. Through a prolonged immersion in attempting to empathically understand Justin, the therapist has developed a working model of a client. While oscillating from an experience-near role, the practitioner was able to conceptualize Justin's functioning from an observational or experience-distant capacity. Over a sustained period of time, the therapist recognizes that Justin perceives himself as a deficient and flawed person. In the context of discussing this inference, the therapist relates, "You seem to say that you feel different from other people, perhaps not measuring up." In response to this initiation of an interpretation, Justin states, "For a long time I have felt kind of overlooked and not particularly important." The practitioner continues with, "Could it be that you have found it necessary to emotionally cut yourself off from people so that you won't be hurt even more?" As Justin explores the implications of this inferential statement, discussion continues to emphasize a broader perspective of empathic understanding.

COUNTERPRODUCTIVE REACTIONS AND EMPATHY

As a therapeutic modality, the potential effectiveness of empathy may be diminished by counterproductive reactions of a practitioner. Sympathy is often confused with empathy as both conceptions are viewed as conveying a sense of caring or compassion. In practice, however, there are clear differences between these processes that may either potentially impede or enhance the treatment experience. Identification and projection represent defense mechanisms that can distort a counselor's ability to communicate and maintain an empathic posture with a client. The defenses relate to conflictive issues in a therapist's functioning that emerge during threatening interactions in treatment. Although identification and projection were originally conceptualized in the psychoanalytic tradition, the constructs are prominent in the contemporary practice of counselors and psychotherapists from diverse orientations (Clark, 1998a). Countertransference is another construct with origins in the psychoanalytic persuasion, and relates specifically to unresolved conflicts of a practitioner that potentially have a negative impact in the therapy process (Gelso & Hayes, 2002). Because it involves distortion of perceptual functioning, countertransference results in the diminished ability of practitioners to focus on the needs of a client.

Empathy and Sympathy

Although empathy and sympathy both involve feelings that resonate from an individual in response to the experience of another person, there are distinctions between the two terms that have important implications in counseling and psychotherapy. In the therapeutic process, as in everyday life, confusion often exists between empathy and sympathy, and it is possible to mistakenly view the two conceptions as interchangeable (Chismar, 1988; Dymond, 1950; Strunk, 1957). Qualities of empathy and sympathy are susceptible to blurring, and failure to differentiate the unique aspects of each term potentially contributes to misdirection and misunderstanding in therapy. In counseling, empathy typically engenders therapeutic advance, whereas sympathy may more often be a hindrance. It is possible to identify critical variables that provide relatively distinct ways of differentiating empathy from sympathy through such comparative dimensions as purpose, similarity, accuracy, agreement, and approval.

Distinguishing the linguistic difference between empathy and sympathy enables a practitioner to determine an appropriate use of each entity. The primary intent of empathy is to understand a person and the focus of sympathy is the well-being of an individual (Black, 2004; Halpern, 1993; Wispé, 1986). In practice, if a client expresses emotional distress, a counselor employing an empathic stance tries to understand the individual's functioning and convey a sense of the experience back to the person. In contrast, if a therapist sympathetically responds to a client's distress, he or she may attempt to alleviate the client's plight. As an example, in a therapy session, a young-adulthood client begins to cry about her inability to maintain intimate relationships in her life. Suddenly, the client states, "I don't want to talk about it anymore." In an empathic response, a therapist states, "It's hard to talk about something that hurts so much." In a contrasting reaction proceeding from a sympathetic stance, a counselor quickly decides to change the topic of discussion in order to immediately relieve the client of further distress.

In a therapeutic context, empathy and sympathy present contrasting positions relating to the similarities between a therapist and a client. Sympathy involves an active sharing of a client's pain on the part of the counselor and an expression of compassion (Beck, Rush, Shaw, & Emery, 1979; Olinick, 1984), with the focus directed more frequently to the needs of the therapist than to the needs and issues of a client (Katz, 1963). This may be apparent in such simple sympathetic expressions as "I feel so bad for you" or "You sure have it rough." With sympathy, a practitioner's identity may begin to merge with a client's feelings and situation (Kalisch, 1973). As psychological boundaries between the client and therapist blur, and the sharing of feelings intensifies, the expectation that a counselor will be able to assume an objective or detached perspective becomes more remote. A manifest pattern of similarity with a client's behavior may indicate the operation of identification as a defense mechanism on the part of a counselor

(Clark, 1998a). In contrast to sympathy, empathy implies a sense of detachment and separateness. A practitioner's identity is maintained except for momentary periods of active resonance with a client (Wispé, 1986). With empathy, a counselor directs attention more to the needs and issues of a client and attempts to maintain a focus on the individual's perspectives.

Empathic understanding implies a sense of detachment and objectivity that enables a therapist to appraise the accuracy of a client's experiencing. In the absence of an emotional distancing, a practitioner's assumption of being in a similar position to that of the client may be erroneous and lack therapeutic effectiveness. A counselor is subject to being psychologically drawn into the experience of a client, and the interaction can lead to a distortion of perspectives. As an example, an adolescent reports that he has been a target of constant ridicule in a school situation. The client relates with a sense of despair, "I have tried everything that we have talked about so the kids will like me. It hurts so much when they pick on me." In response, the counselor sympathetically states, "I know exactly how you feel. I also know that if you keep trying and don't give up, everything will work out in time." Although the likely intent of the counselor is to provide hope, the sympathetic statement does not accurately reflect the client's perceptions and feelings.

Sympathetic expressions of condolence or pity on the part of a practitioner may also imply a sense of unintended agreement with a client (Greenson, 1960; Meier & Davis, 2005; Rud, 1993; Wispé, 1986). Although sympathy has a legitimate and helpful role in everyday life, sympathetic reactions may imply an accord that affirms a client's position. The intent of a counselor to recognize an individual's suffering through sympathy may also have a discouraging effect (Dinkmeyer & Sperry, 2000). Consider the statement of a therapist in response to a middle-adulthood client who has lost his job due to a reorganization within his company. As he cries softly, the client relates, "I've let my wife and my whole family down. This puts my oldest daughter's plans to go to college in jeopardy." In response, the therapist states: "Oh, that's terrible that all of this has happened. And in the middle of it all you are able to think about your family when your own heart is breaking. This demonstrates so well your strength of character." In a comment that expresses sympathy, the therapist tacitly agrees with the client's perspective.

The approval of a client's experience may also be sympathetically conveyed in a therapeutic relationship. A practitioner's expression of sympathy connotes a type of endorsement that is not communicated with empathic reactions (Wispé, 1986; Wolf, 1988; Young, 2005). As a form of approval, a therapist may sympathetically praise or acknowledge a client for particular actions or functions. From an empathic stance, a counselor attempts to minimize praise by enabling a client to evaluate his or her own behavior. To continue with the example of the individual who recently lost his job, the client defiantly states, "The bastards called me on the telephone and asked if I would consider taking another position that involves a relocation to another state. I immediately said no and began to tell them off." In response, the therapist says, "They are being totally unrealistic. You can't uproot your whole family and move just like that." Although the practitioner is sympathetic, his evaluative comment precludes a more balanced consideration of the client's actions and likely forecloses an in-depth discussion of a potentially viable offer. The forceful one-sided reaction of the therapist also makes it more difficult for the client to reverse his position at a subsequent point and reexamine the possibility of relocation without losing face.

Empathy and Identification

An essential function of empathy is the capacity of an individual to emotionally put oneself in the place of another, and an enhanced understanding of a client rests on the ability to identify with a person on a momentary or transient basis (Arlow, 1979; Beres, 1968; Beres & Arlow, 1974). The task of a practitioner is to attempt to achieve an optimum level of identification with a client that will strike a controlled and reversible therapeutic balance (Olinick, 1969). A limited or insufficient degree of identification may result in a practitioner's inability to perceive or acknowledge the experience of a client. In contrast, an excessive level of identification may convince a therapist that his or her experiencing is the same as the client's, regardless of markedly different circumstances (Shapiro, 1974). It is also essential that identification with a client be transient or short-lived. A counselor may then assume a perspective involving a psychological distance in order to more objectively evaluate felt-level experiencing (Stewart, 1955, 1956). When identification with a client extends beyond momentary periods in the service of empathic understanding, there is a risk that the therapist will become emotionally overinvolved and lose the capacity to shift to a more objective perspective. In such instances, when a practitioner adopts a sympathetic posture, a client's issues may take on a quality of being personally daunting and burdensome (Aring, 1958; Brammer & MacDonald, 2003).

When a pattern of identification occurs with a counselor or therapist, the process may give rise to responses characterized by defensive qualities (Clark, 1998a; Meissner, 1972). This function implies a desire to be like the client and a wish to establish a close emotional tie (Goldstein & Michaels, 1985). It is possible that a practitioner may identify with a client to the extent that he or she assumes certain behavioral qualities of the individual. Although these instances may be less frequent, the potential exists for the psychological boundaries between a client and therapist to become blurred and confused (Strunk, 1957). As a consequence, a counselor's ability to provide a therapeutic direction through a more emotionally detached, observer role is potentially compromised. As a defense mechanism, identification is a response to feelings of perceived threat and a sensitivity to conflictive issues on the part of the therapist. Inevitably, the readiness of the counselor to be emotionally available to the client for empathic understanding is diminished because of preoccupations evoked by threatening issues. As an example, a therapist, working with a young-adulthood client with a diagnosis of borderline personality disorder, frequently listens to the client discuss instances where he acts in impulsive and provocative ways. The therapist experiences a personal conflict over overtly expressing aggression and begins to identify with the client's behavior and experiences a level of emotional gratification. As the therapist identifies with the individual as a function of his own unresolved issues, he fails to therapeutically process the narrative material of the client.

Empathy and Projection

The capacity of an individual to attribute particular qualities to others as a result of one's subjective functioning is a common means of establishing mutual perspectives in human relationships. In the therapy process, a practitioner is in a position to use his or her personal reactions as a therapeutic tool in order to enhance an understanding of a client. As with identification, the projective use of personal experiencing provides a vehicle for empathic understanding. At the same time, projection on the part of a therapist may result in distortions in communication when the therapist's preoccupations interfere with making accurate judgments (Strunk, 1957). In these instances, attributions of a client's behavior emanate primarily from the internal state of the counselor. In a one-way reaction, a practitioner believes that the client experiences similar motivations. A therapist may naively assume that a client applies the same meaning to experiences and feels and reacts in the same way as the practitioner (Murstein & Pryer, 1959).

A pattern of projection may entail defensive elements when intolerable behavior is attributed to a client that is characteristic of the counselor or therapist (Clark, 1998a). The practitioner, after ascribing the behavior to the client, denies its existence in him- or herself (Shapiro, 1974). Through this interaction, the therapist reduces threatening and conflictual feelings by attributing them to the client. Although projection occurs more often in a client population, a representation of the defense mechanism by a practitioner produces distortions in communication and understanding. As with identification, a defensive engagement of projection by a counselor focuses on unresolved issues, which diminishes an empathic understanding of a client. In an example demonstrating a practitioner's employment of projection, a therapist meets with a client who is in treatment for an anxiety disorder. The client discusses her reluctance and inability to ask her supervisor for an extension of time to complete a project at work. The therapist, who also experiences feelings of threat and intimidation toward authority figures, forcefully responds to the client, "Well, why don't you stand up for yourself for a change and demand that you must have the extension?" Not only is the therapist's reaction unempathic, the client finds the comment insensitive and destabilizing.

Empathy and Countertransference

Countertransference is a broad and complex conceptualization that involves the manifestation of personal conflicts of a counselor or therapist (Gelso & Hayes, 2002; Mitchell & Black, 1995). Since Sigmund Freud's introduction of the term in 1910, acceptance and use of the construct has extended beyond the psychoanalytic model to a contemporary view that recognizes that countertransference reactions occur in all counseling and psychotherapy persuasions (Gelso & Carter, 1985; Gelso & Hayes, 2002). The classical definition of countertransference is widely conceived as encompassing all of a therapist's feelings or attitudes toward a client. A more clinically useful conceptualization limits countertransference to "internal and external reactions in which unresolved conflicts of the therapist, usually but not always unconscious, are implicated" (Gelso & Hayes, 2002, p. 269). Although there have been various meanings of countertransference proposed for nearly 100 years, researchers and practitioners generally agree that a lack of understanding and control of the construct can have adverse consequences in the counseling process by compromising a practitioner's ability to maintain a balanced and empathic posture (Gelso & Hayes, 2002). At the same time, countertransference has the potential, when managed effectively, to facilitate and enhance effective treatment by functioning as a powerful tool for understanding a patient's experience (Mitchell, 1988, 1993, 1997).

Conflictive issues and needs that preoccupy a practitioner may intrude on his or her ability to be emotionally responsive to a client. Frequently, a counselor or therapist may not be conscious of provoking factors that contribute to countertransference reactions, which in turn can inhibit empathic understanding of clients (Reich, 1951, 1960). A counselor's countertransference responses may involve excessively positive or negative feelings and actions toward a client. Strong positive affect may find expression in various behaviors such as oversolicitousness or sexually provocative activity. The negative affect of a therapist may become operative in certain instances that are characterized by the emotional withdrawal or rejection of a client. In the theoretical and empirical literature on countertransference, a distinction is made between the internal states of a practitioner and his or her overt behavior (Gelso & Hayes, 2002). Countertransferential behavior is generally viewed as having a negative impact on treatment because the therapist acts in psychologically harmful ways toward a client. Conversely, internal reactions of a counselor that relate to countertransference may serve to inform treatment when processed therapeutically.

In their extensive research relating to countertransference, Gelso and Hayes (2002) found that therapists who maintained strong positive or negative affect towards clients frequently experienced perceptual distortions relating to the experience of the individuals. Therapists who experienced strong positive affective reactions toward clients rated the individuals' personality more similar to themselves than was the case. In contrast, therapists with strong negative reactions toward clients evaluated the individuals' personality as dissimilar to themselves, and this view also was not upheld. In research directly relating to countertransference and empathy, Peabody and Gelso (1982) and Gelso and Carter (1985) found that counselors with higher levels of empathy experienced less frequent countertransference behavior. Furthermore, with an increase in empathic capacity, the counselors were more responsive to controlling their countertransference feelings.

From my early experience in counseling, I recall a case involving countertransference with an adolescent named "Dan." As a Grade 8 student, Dan rarely completed class or homework assignments, and his major focus in school seemed to be to irritate his teachers or to spend lengthy periods daydreaming. In our weekly sessions, Dan seemed to delight in provoking me by repeating my words, making silly faces, or insisting that we talk about skateboarding or horror movies. When I tried shifting our discussion to his school behavior, Dan would either become sullen or assume a demanding stance and ask why we had to meet for counseling. My discomfort level with Dan began to escalate, and the prospect of regularly seeing him became painful. On one level it seemed appropriate for me to feel tense about meeting with Dan because he was difficult to take, and my reactions had become increasingly intense. I began to think about Dan during times when we were not together and felt disgust and anger toward him. At times in our meetings, I found myself lecturing to him about the importance of school and making an effort in life. Although I knew that this was not at all helpful, I did it anyway. One morning when Dan was scheduled to come to my office, I felt that I simply could not tolerate seeing him. When Dan arrived, he banged on the locked door as usual and yelled my name. I was inside at my desk and remained silent and still. Suddenly, Dan's voice lowered and he plaintively called for me. It seemed like he was about to cry when he began to walk away. I did not know what to do, but I felt bad about what I had done. After a few moments, when I thought Dan had left, I opened the door and saw that he was just leaving the outside office. I called to him and we began to talk.

As I reflect on this case recalled from over 30 years ago, I recognize that my negative reactions were a form of a countertransference. Although Dan was not the easiest client to work with, he seemed to trigger in me unresolved issues from my own adolescence. In part, I felt negatively toward Dan due to the conflictive feelings that I experienced toward learning and school. Like Dan, I also wasted a great deal of time in school and was disciplined on numerous occasions. When Dan and I began our session after I invited him into my office, I told him about some of my difficulties in school. For the first time, I felt more like myself in meeting with Dan, and he seemed to respond with interest. As I started to make sense of my emotional reactions, my capacity for empathic understanding toward Dan began to intensify.

SUMMARY

The modern usage of empathy originated in the late 19th century in the perception of aesthetics, and over a period of time the term has conceptually broadened to include the realm of interpersonal functioning. Although there is ambiguity and varied opinion about the meaning of empathy, it is possible to identify at least three modes of empathy in counseling and psychotherapy. In the experiential mode, a counselor or therapist may assume a way of being or an attitude in empathic understanding. In response to a client, a practitioner empathically resonates in a bodily felt experience. The concept of empathy as a mode of communication has produced considerable controversy with respect to the quality of research relating to the construct in therapeutic practice. Concerns have also been raised about empathy being primarily viewed as a counseling skill, thus diminishing its attitudinal role. Yet, there is substantial agreement that unless empathy is communicated, the construct has limited utility in the treatment process. Empathy as a mode of observation involves acquiring knowledge about a client. The information generated is then transformed into an interpretation that is communicated to a client. This two-phase process of understanding and explaining potentially deepens empathic understanding of clients.

Sympathy, identification, and projection are terms that are frequently confused with empathy in the therapeutic experience. Empathy and sympathy may be semantically differentiated on the basis of the comparative dimensions of purpose, similarity, accuracy, agreement, and approval. The process of understanding the experience of others involves the operations of identification and projection. Conversely, the conceptions can assume defensive proportions and inhibit and distort communication. Countertransference may be distinguished on the basis of a practitioner's antitherapeutic feelings and actions. Recognizing and controlling countertransference reactions contributes to the enhancement of empathic understanding and treatment progress in counseling and psychotherapy.

Chapter 2

Value of Empathy in Counseling and Psychotherapy

> *Through empathy the therapist participates in the two-person relationship; and empathy is the single most important human and technical tool at the therapist's disposal.*
>
> —Strupp (1996, p. 137)

As I walked slowly down the corridor to the office of the assistant high school principal, Mr. King, I felt extremely disappointed in myself. A few minutes before, I had been sent out of the classroom by my art teacher and told to report to the office. I had made a murky mess with a watercolor painting and gleefully insisted on showing it to my classmates. It was well known in the large city school that Mr. King was a strict disciplinarian, and I had virtually no rationale with which to excuse my actions in the class. In my previous years in school, I had a reputation for making life difficult for my teachers, and my face was familiar to school administrators. Yet, this time my feelings were different from those I experienced in earlier trips to the principal's office. When I started the academic year, just a few days before my banishment from class, I was determined to improve my record and begin to take work seriously. When I entered Mr. King's office, he was sitting behind what seemed to be a particularly large desk, and he quietly asked me to sit in a chair in front of him. He looked stern, and I knew that I was in serious difficulty.

After Mr. King asked me why I had come to see him, I did not attempt to use my usual excuses, such as my confusion over the assignment or my lack of artistic skills. Instead, I told him that I was disappointed in myself because I did not want to start off in a new school this way. Mr. King was still for a moment, then he leaned forward and said in a kind voice, "What I am hearing you say is that you feel you have let yourself down." A sense of relief came over me, but it was not based on the possibility that he was "buying" my story, and that I might not be dealt with harshly. The relief that I felt related far more to his words and his tone, which emotionally connected to my experience. Almost immediately, I began to tell Mr. King that over the summer I had made a decision that when I entered the tenth grade, I would make more of an effort in school and stop wasting my time. I cannot remember more of Mr. King's words, but he did listen to me with an intensity that stays with me decades later.

THE VALUE OF EMPATHY: CLIENT UNDERSTANDING, THE TREATMENT RELATIONSHIP, AND THE THERAPEUTIC PROCESS

In counseling and psychotherapy, the utilization of empathy has the potential to increase client understanding, enhance the treatment relationship, and enrich the therapeutic process. In combination, experiential and observational empathy provide avenues for communicating an understanding to a client from an immediate and extended perspective. It is also possible to advance client understanding by utilizing culturally informed knowledge. As clients experience a sense of being understood, almost invariably there is an expansion of trust and rapport within the treatment relationship. In a climate of understanding, clients often reduce their defensiveness and begin to communicate more openly. As a counselor or a therapist acquires a deeper understanding of a client through an empathic immersion, this sensibility may inform the judicious employment of a range of therapeutic interventions. At the same time, an awareness of qualitative aspects and limitations of empathy enables a practitioner to more purposefully employ the construct in a treatment context.

EMPATHY AND CLIENT UNDERSTANDING

In order to engender empathic understanding, a counselor or therapist attempts to sense the feelings and personal meanings that a client experiences on a moment-by-moment basis in the therapy process (Rogers,

1966). This awareness is then communicated verbally and nonverbally to the client in the immediacy of a human encounter. In this interaction, there is a vitality to the exchange because both the client and the practitioner experience emotional reactions in the present or the "here and now." This does not mean, however, that past events in the life of a client are not given attention. Instead, considerations from the past may become subjects of discussion, but the material is processed in terms of how it affects the individual in the present. As an example, a middle-adulthood client diagnosed with an anxiety disorder recounts at length a painful experience that had occurred several years earlier, when he was overcome by anxiety and could not finish a presentation at a sales meeting. In order to shift the incident into the present on an emotional basis, the counselor states, "This is a scary thing for you. As you talk the tension in your voice is increasing, and your hands are trembling." This empathic response of the practitioner brings a focus to the client's immediate feelings and emphasizes how the experience continues to affect the individual. Although experiential empathy gives prominence to the moment-by-moment reactions of a client, the process has also been subject to criticism because there is a lack of emphasis on conceptualizing a comprehensive pattern or a context relating to a person's functioning.

From another perspective, observational empathy implies a broader conception of empathic understanding that extends beyond the immediate experiencing of a client. Rather than primarily acquiring a collection of insights, a counselor or therapist conceptualizes the obtained data into an overall view of the client in the context of particular aspects of the individual's life (Eagle & Wolitzky, 1997; Greenson, 1967). As a counselor or therapist continues an empathic immersion with a client over an extended number of therapy sessions, it becomes possible for the practitioner to conceptualize a hypothetical model of a patient or client (Greenson, 1967; Patton & Meara, 1992; Pepinsky & Pepinsky, 1954). By empathically understanding the experience of a client, a counselor begins to develop a coherent and integrated framework that organizes what is processed with the individual (Berger, 1984, 1987; Levy, 1985). The working model is developed from a wide variety of potential knowledge sources such as memories, fantasies, resistances, defenses, dreams, associations, dispositions, evaluations, and explanations (Brodley, 1996; Fox & Goldin, 1964). Although this litany may seem conceptually unwieldy and diffuse, it is intended to suggest the kinds of knowledge that are often acquired after spending a reasonably lengthy period interacting with a client and thoughtfully reflecting about the person on a conceptual level. The sources may be viewed as representative of a client in the present but also involve anticipations for the potential development of the individual (Greenson, 1967). Importantly, the suggested knowledge sources are not to be considered a systematic and determined number of client characteristics and experiences.

As the treatment process proceeds, a therapist interacts from a subjective and experiential vantage point of thinking and feeling along with a client and periodically shifts to the more objective stance of an "outside listener" (Schwaber, 1981). There is a continuous oscillation of participant and observer roles as each perspective informs and confirms the other. As patterns of client functioning emerge, the hypothetical model of a client evolves and functions as a resource for conceptual empathic understanding. Through the model, it becomes possible to anticipate client expectations and reactions (Patton & Meara, 1992). In turn, this anticipatory awareness potentially serves as a process guide for employing strategic interventions and evaluating client development and potentialities (Clark, 2002b; Greenson, 1967). In a therapy example, a school psychologist has met with Jed for three counseling sessions. A 9-year-old child, Jed, has recently been demonstrating withdrawn behavior at school and at home. Jed resists discussing any topic that relates to his isolating actions and assumes a perspective that "nothing is wrong." As the psychologist interacts with Jed, she resonates a sense of threat at any juncture that relates to his withdrawn behavior. From an observer stance, the psychologist conceptualizes the operation of denial as a defense mechanism. As counseling continues, she uses her knowledge of denial as a theoretical construct to strategically process Jed's reactions. From a broader perspective, Jed's defense pattern becomes integrated with additional client data, and that in turn contributes to the development of a model of a client.

Experiential and observational empathy primarily emphasize an understanding of the unique aspects of an individual's functioning. A more comprehensive awareness of a client's experiencing is attainable by considering broader cultural forces that influence the person (Ivey, 1987). It is possible to enhance awareness of a client's functioning by combining knowledge from experiential and observational empathy with understandings relating to the cultural aspects of a person. A culturally informed perspective relates to a practitioner's ability to accurately understand the experience of clients from diverse cultures (Ridley & Udipi, 2002; Robinson, 2005). In this regard, a practitioner's cultural competencies may be enhanced through the pursuit of training efforts that focus on cultural data and traditions and personal experiences (Constantine, 2001). Schmid (2001) points out that cultural empathy can serve as a "bridge" to ameliorate differences between a client and a counselor without ignoring or minimizing diversities. It is also important to recognize that although cultural forces influence an individual's behavior, they do not determine it.

In the multicultural and cross-cultural literature, the conceptualization of universal and individual perspectives of persons contributes to a more comprehensive empathic understanding (Jenkins, 1997; Sciarra, 1999). From a universal or *etic* stance, all persons have common needs or behaviors regardless of cultural origin. In contrast, from a particularlist or *emic* view, individuals have needs or behaviors that are culture specific. In an example of a universalist stance, a need for being cared about by others may be recognizable across diverse cultures. An illustration of a particularlist function may be found in the tendency of Euro-Americans to seek individual autonomy. With respect to empathic understanding, it may prove helpful for a practitioner to comprehensively respond to a client by maintaining an awareness of a person's functioning from multiple cultural perspectives. In a counseling example, a young-adulthood Native American client holds a collective orientation toward her tribe or nation that represents a particularlist perspective. At the same time, she has a desire to be understood and affirmed, which involves a universal stance.

In working with clients from diverse backgrounds, a counselor or therapist may demonstrate cultural biases and prejudices that diminish empathic understanding (Ridley & Udipi, 2002). The continuing development of interpersonal and intercultural awareness enables practitioners to recognize barriers that restrict open communication and trust (Ivey, 1987). As an example, in research with implications for empathic understanding, Dana (2000) and Jenkins (1997) found that minority clients in America tend to resist or reject a service delivery style that is relatively impersonal and task-oriented. In general, such individuals initially prefer a personal and relational approach to treatment and are not ready to immediately pursue instrumental therapy goals. Other researchers have shown how communication and understanding are constricted when differences between a counselor and a client are minimized or ignored (Kottler, Montgomery, & Marbley, 1998).

In a personal counseling example relating to unexpressed cultural differences, a number of years ago I was working with an African American adolescent named Rob. Rob lived in the inner city and was a middle school student participating in a diversity program in the sponsoring school district where I was employed. In our first two sessions, our communication was limited and strained, with the exception of an occasional derogatory comment toward me or toward the school. Yet, even in these instances, when I tried to follow up on his statements, Rob would refuse to talk further. He was resistant to almost any discussion topic, and we were at a therapeutic impasse. At this point, it occurred to me that I had to address the obvious differences between the two of us that were left unstated. With some hesitation and unease, I said to Rob that as an "older White guy" living outside of the city, I probably did not have much of an understanding of what he goes through each day. Almost immediately, Rob began to scornfully point out our differences. He told me that I could not understand what it is like for him when he has to run to catch the bus in the morning and run from the bus to his apartment in the afternoon for fear of being assaulted. After this "discussion," Rob started to talk more about personal issues, and a therapeutic relationship began to develop. I began to recognize at the time that demonstrating an interest in a client by learning more about his or her culture in a treatment situation can be affirming to the individual while promoting empathic understanding (Chung & Bemak, 2002).

From a clinical perspective, cultural differences have been shown to bias the accuracy of a therapist's diagnostic impressions of clients from diverse cultures. In a recent study, a group of Anglo-American clinicians tended to perceive Chinese clients as anxious, confused, and reserved. In contrast, Chinese American clinicians, evaluating the same individuals, did not observe these behaviors in the same group of clients (Dana, 2000). In another study relating to gender, Garb (1997) found that females were more likely to be diagnosed with a histrionic disorder than males, and males were more likely than females to be diagnosed with an antisocial personality disorder, even when the symptomatology was the same for both genders. Inaccuracies in clinical judgment can affect empathic understanding on the part of the practitioner, and an awareness of biases reported in the literature and the utilization of diagnostic criteria may decrease potential bias (Garb, 1997).

In an analogue study, Burkard and Knox (2004) found that therapists who scored in a high range on ratings of *color-blind* racial attitudes were reported to have significantly less empathy in comparison with those therapists scoring in the low range for color-blindness. Persons maintaining color-blind racial attitudes tend to deny the manifestations of racism in various contexts and believe that race has little meaning in the lives of individuals. In counseling, therapists' minimal awareness of racial issues, in the form of color-blindness, may impede their ability to empathize with clients. Finally, in a study relating to the role of gender in the empathic process, Petro and Hansen (1977) found that male and female counselors were equally accurate in their empathic judgments. Both male and female counselors also demonstrated significantly more affective sensitivity to males.

EMPATHY AND THE RELATIONSHIP IN COUNSELING AND PSYCHOTHERAPY

Across diverse theoretical orientations, the therapeutic relationship constitutes a salient factor in effecting constructive client change and securing beneficial treatment outcomes. In terms of research findings, empathic understanding has been shown to be a prominent aspect in the development of a positive working alliance between a client and a counselor or therapist. In the counseling experience, clients frequently employ defensive or evasive response patterns as a means to prevent the exposure of conflictual material and protect their self-esteem from perceived threat. Empathic understanding often reduces psychological threat through the development of trust and increased communication. Because a practitioner's conflicts and preoccupations can also interfere with the establishment of a sound treatment relationship, there is a continuing need to seek a level of self-awareness that will enhance the capacity to more accurately perceive a client's functioning and reduce potential distortions.

Empathy and the Relational Domain

The quality of the relationship in counseling and psychotherapy is a significant determinant of therapeutic progress and responds to the need of individuals to experience a sense of being understood (Bachelor & Horvarth, 1999; Free, Green, Grace, Chernus, & Whitman 1985; Schmid, 2001). As a significant factor in a quest to achieve therapeutic success with clients, the qualitative aspects of the treatment relationship have been a topic of intense scrutiny among researchers and practitioners. Empathic understanding is a primary variable in the counseling relationship and has been a focus of extensive investigations. A review of psychotherapy research suggests that as much as 30% of client improvement can be attributed to the therapeutic relationship (Ridley & Udipi, 2002). A comprehensive study reports that the quality of the therapeutic relationship is more predictive of positive treatment outcome than other discriminating factors including the practitioner's theoretical orientation, experience level, or professional designation (Bohart, Elliot, Greenberg, & Watson, 2002).

An individual's experience of being understood gives prominence to empathy in the context of the therapeutic relationship (Myers, 2000; Redfern, Dancey, & Dryden, 1993). In a study that examined the phenomena of being "deeply understood," van Kaam (1959, 1969) found that subjects expressed a feeling of relief when experiencing deep understanding. Other reactions that individuals experienced included feelings of relaxation, tension reduction, a sense of self-respect and importance, and a condition of being taken seriously. At times, a sense of being understood may be the most important process and outcome goal in treatment. As an example, in my early experience as a school counselor, I recall working with an early adolescent, Becky, who felt extremely embarrassed by her home situation. Becky's father collected discarded materials, such as washing machines and automobiles, and covered the yard surrounding the family home with the "junk." Becky would come into my office on a regular basis and her emotional reactions typically alternated between periods of softly crying and mild anger. Becky was particularly concerned that because of her fear of embarrassment she could not invite her girl friends to her house and did not wish people to know where she lived. During our sessions, for the most part, I quietly and attentively listened to Becky and acknowledged her feelings. I was not sure about what else to do or say. Becky did successfully complete the school year, and on the last day of classes she gave me an appreciative note about our time together and she signed it, "Becky, A Somebody."

The state of being understood generally increases a client's satisfaction in therapy and consequently contributes to the likelihood of compliance and involvement in the treatment process (Bohart, Elliot, Greenberg, & Watson, 2002). The relational dimension of counseling typically promotes a supportive emotional climate for client change (Fox & Goldin, 1964). At the same time, the therapeutic process also consists of a technical domain in which a practitioner utilizes a variety of interventions and techniques. In this respect, Kelly (1997) conceptualizes the counseling and therapy process as involving two major domains: relational and technical. Both dimensions are interrelated, but also relatively distinct in terms of practitioner response. Consider the example of a therapist's use of the technique of reflection of feelings with a client. From a relational dimension, the counselor attempts to engage a client through an emotional connection that is mutually shared and understood. In terms of a technical stance, the therapist attempts to identify the client's feelings and makes a coherent verbal observation about the individual's functioning. In the absence of a relational expression of empathic understanding, it is possible that the delivery of therapeutic techniques can be sterile and remote from a client's experiencing (Fox & Goldin, 1964). Yet, without the sustained employment of technical and intentional processing, material may remain unclear to the client in terms of what seems comprehensible to the therapist.

Empathy and Client Threat

In counseling and psychotherapy, conditions within the therapeutic relationship may evoke defensive and evasive reactions from the client as responses to perceived threat. Individuals tend to ward off disturbing conflicts and protect their self-esteem through emotionally protective functions. Since Sigmund Freud (1894/1962a, 1896/1962b) initially conceptualized defense mechanisms, numerous constructs have been detailed in the literature, but a smaller number of particular defenses are most frequently represented (Clark, 1991, 1998a, 2002a). As a client employs various defenses, a counselor may find it increasingly difficult to empathize with the person and establish a therapeutic bond (Snyder, 1992). It is understandable that a client who expends energy in order to avoid examining self-functioning is also likely to resist an empathic understanding of these efforts. A client largely lacks awareness of the defensive processes, and they occur through automatic and undifferentiated responses. Furthermore, the defenses distort client perspectives and entail avoidant behaviors both in therapy and in interpersonal encounters outside of the treatment situation. At the same time, the mechanisms serve the individual by providing a relative degree of identity, predictability, and stability (Erskine, Moursund, & Trautmann, 1999).

If a therapist initially challenges a client's defensive posture, the individual typically increases the intensity of his or her assertions or emotionally withdraws. Yet, if a practitioner fails to adequately process a client's defenses, an opportunity is lost to address the individual's subjective distortions. An alternative to premature challenge or acquiescence is the possibility of the practitioner's maintaining an empathic engagement while attempting to address a client's defensive functioning. As a therapeutic relationship evolves over a period of time, trust and more open communication typically develop. In a supportive and understanding emotional climate, a client frequently perceives or anticipates less threat and is more receptive to examining his or her experiencing (Snyder, 1992).

In a counseling example relating to defensive functioning, a middle-adulthood client named Bob is in mandated treatment as a result of a conviction for driving while intoxicated. Initially, Bob refuses to acknowledge his culpability in the offense and denies that he has a drinking problem. The counselor empathically acknowledges the "unfairness" of the charges from Bob's point of view. Bob also justifies recent incidents involving excessive drinking as being due to mounting pressures in his life. In this early phase of treatment, the counselor responds to Bob's rationalization at face value and avoids questioning the veracity of his statements. In time, Bob begins to perceive that the therapist does not appear to pose a significant threat and tentatively starts to express feelings of doubt and uncertainty. As treatment proceeds, the counselor utilizes the developing therapeutic relationship and begins to clarify the manner in which Bob appears to respond to conflictive feelings through defensive reactions. Subsequently, discussion expands into disturbing issues that Bob has masked through his defense pattern. Throughout the treatment process, the practitioner attempts to empathically acknowledge Bob's perspectives, even when challenging him with alternative points of view.

In comparison to defense mechanisms, the constructs of *safeguarding tendencies* are less well known but are also therapeutically useful in responding to client threat and evasive behavior, which require empathic understanding. Safeguarding tendencies were conceptualized by Adler (1929/1969, 1935) as a means by which individuals conceal assumed deficiencies by evading perceived problems. Safeguarding tendencies serve to protect an individual's self-esteem through evasive processes. Through a largely self-deceptive means, a person avoids or limits functioning in particular experiences that evoke feelings of inferiority (Clark, 1999a, 2000). An individual may also incur a range of sufferings in order to prompt sympathy from others while retreating from life challenges and responsibilities. Although Adler did not comprehensively delineate the operation of safeguarding tendencies, he did observe four movements of individuals that either avoid, restrict, divert, or hinder active problem solving (Adler, 1935).

In a therapy example, a middle-adulthood client employs the safeguarding tendency of hesitating attitude. Eunice is in treatment for an anxiety disorder, and she frequently complains about her inability to complete a number of assignments at her new place of employment. Eunice offers numerous reasons why particular tasks remain largely unfinished, and constantly refers to health issues and the time demands of her elderly parent. Eunice's colleagues at work are sympathetic about her personal problems but are also beginning to question her professional competencies and work ethic. Through interactions that are similar to defense mechanism processing, the therapist expresses an empathic understanding of the pressures that Eunice experiences in her life and acknowledges her inability to complete assigned projects at work. As a supportive relationship develops and treatment continues, Eunice begins to recognize that her avoidance of completing tasks seems to primarily relate to how she feels they will be evaluated when ultimately finished. Eunice assumes that her productions will likely receive a negative evaluation, and this will constitute another emotional blow to her already low self-esteem. As with defense mechanisms and other conceptualizations that relate to client threat, a practitioner's familiarity with the operation of safeguarding tendencies contributes to an empathic understanding of clients.

Empathy and Therapist Self-Awareness

At times, personal concerns and needs in the life of a counselor or therapist can divert attention from a focus on client issues and limit empathic understanding. In other instances, patterns of a practitioner's conflictive material may interfere with effective treatment in the therapy process. From an even broader perspective, a counselor's outlook on life has the potential to introduce bias into therapeutic practice and impede client progress. In each of these circumstances, a therapist's self-awareness involves the ability to recognize and address conditions that can restrict or inhibit the manifestation of an empathic stance with clients. To the extent that a practitioner is able to minimize the prevalence of his or her needs in the counseling relationship, the individual's capacity for empathy increases. A therapists' self-insight may also be instrumental in clarifying client issues and making sound treatment decisions and interventions.

Demonstrating a capacity for empathic understanding throughout the therapeutic process requires effort and concentration on the part of a counselor or therapist. Consistently attending to client issues is a challenging task over the duration of treatment, particularly when inevitable demands of life converge on a practitioner. It may become necessary for a counselor to acknowledge and respond to pressing personal issues that interfere with his or her ability to maintain empathic contact with a client. Addressing private matters outside of the therapy sessions enables a therapist to minimize distractions or preoccupations during treatment. Occasionally, it may be a judicious choice for a practitioner to share with a client the existence of an immediate personal concern that has the potential to intrude on the communication process. As an example, a therapist mentions to members of a family, who are present for therapy, "My 5-year-old daughter is recovering from the flu. She is doing better, but my attention may drift a little today in our session if I think about her." From a different perspective, the process of engaging clients empathically frequently has a paradoxical effect as a practitioner becomes absorbed in the treatment effort and experiences a temporary respite from personal demands and responsibilities. I can recall numerous instances when seemingly urgent matters on my mind at the start of a counseling session began to recede when I assumed an empathic posture with a client.

At times, personal issues of a practitioner may reach an intense and compelling level and are more representative of countertransference. Although conflictive reactions of a counselor or therapist can impede therapeutic progress, knowledge gained from countertransference may also provide valuable treatment information (Hayes, McCraken, McClanahan, Hilt, Harp, & Carozzoni, 1998; Rosenberger & Hayes, 2002). Behaviorally, countertransference materializes when a therapist either is overinvolved or emotionally withdraws from a client. A counselor's awareness of the dynamics relating to his or her behavioral tendencies and feelings decreases countertransferential responses (Tobin, 2003). As an example, a therapist has been experiencing difficulties with the management of her adolescent son. In her sessions with a client with two young children, the therapist had become increasingly directive and controlling. She became increasingly aware of her feelings of frustration and anger toward the client, particularly when topics of discipline and child management were discussed. After a period of self-reflection, the therapist began to recognize her need to control as the possible source of her negative feelings toward the client. With this awareness, the practitioner was able to reduce her excessively directive stance and limit her assumption of responsibility for the client. At the same time, from a more balanced perspective, the therapist was now able to draw on her experience and insights in order to enhance her empathic understanding of the client.

Various investigations reveal findings with implications for the quality of the therapeutic relationship and empathic understanding. In a study focusing on countertransference, Van Wagoner, Gelso, Hayes, and Diemer (1991) found that "reputedly excellent" therapists had a greater capacity for empathy in terms of being able to identify with a client's emotional experience and acquire a deeper cognitive understanding of client emotions. The therapists were also more able to differentiate client needs from their own needs and were more highly integrated in terms of personality than therapists in general. In a related study, Singer and Luborsky (1977) reported that countertransference reactions prevented the therapist from identifying with a client, and, consequently, the practitioner's therapeutic interventions were less empathic. In this regard, by adhering to inaccurate perceptions, a practitioner may determine that there is no apparent need to engage clients further in the treatment process or to provide them with more direction and support. In such instances, the practitioner's lack of client empathic understanding may restrict sound treatment decisions and the engagement of more challenging interventions.

In another direction, an emotional overinvolvement with clients can contribute to personal distress in the life of a counselor or therapist. In a study with rehabilitation counselors, Day and Chambers (1991) examined empathy and its relationship to the burnout syndrome. Key aspects of burnout are increased feelings of emotional exhaustion and disillusionment associated with excessive job-related demands on energy, strength, and resources. The authors found that individuals in the human services who report higher levels of empathic concern and perspective taking are less susceptible to burnout. In contrast, professionals reporting higher levels of personal distress and an increasing self-oriented emotional experience with clients are more likely to experience burnout. In this respect, excessive personal involvement in the problems and issues of the client is inclined to elicit the burnout phenomenon (Miller, Stiff, & Ellis, 1988).

Beyond personal issues and countertransference, another function may introduce the potential for perceptual distortion when a counselor or therapist works with clients. Convictional bias occurs when a practitioner overemphasizes his or her belief system when evaluating the functioning or needs of a client (Clark, 2002b). Convictional bias relates to the proposition that each person maintains an outlook on life that is relatively stable and enduring. Formed in early childhood, ingrained convictions include schemas relating to self, others, and events (Dinkmeyer & Sperry, 2000). A practitioner's outlook on life creates a bias when his or her assumptions unduly influence the understanding of a client and treatment decision making. In practice, this may occur when a counselor fails to sufficiently take into account perspectives of a client in a broader context and instead allows his or her subjective convictions to dominate clinical judgments. Consider the example of a therapist who maintains the view that life is bountiful and fulfilling. When the practitioner works with clients with a diagnosis of an affective disorder, she frequently has difficulty understanding or accepting client perceptions that life is bleak and hopeless. The therapist repeatedly finds herself bringing to the attention of clients the numerous possibilities for activity and stimulation. Because of her lack of awareness of convictional bias, the therapist may fail to understand fully that some individuals find life burdensome and the prospect of undertaking activities of any kind oppressive.

Professional development initiatives in the human services recognize the importance of practitioners increasing their level of self-understanding. Gaining a deeper awareness of one's outlook on life can be beneficial for the counselor or therapist, particularly when it serves to limit the occurrence of convictional bias. As a practitioner reflects on personal values and motivations, it is possible to gain an increased insight into convictions about life. Beyond self-reflection, supervisory experience and personal counseling are other venues that enable a practitioner to gain deeper insight into his or her own subjective perspectives (Gladstein & Associates, 1987). Another source of increased counselor self-understanding is available through the experience of providing counseling and psychotherapy. When a therapist reflects on treatment interactions with clients, such scrutiny can be enlightening in terms of how the practitioner integrates personal convictions into the therapeutic process and recognizes their effect on empathic understanding.

EMPATHY IN THE THERAPEUTIC PROCESS

It is possible to consider empathy in terms of a higher order frame of reference in which it assumes a central role in guiding a practitioner to formulate and execute a range of counseling and therapy techniques. Various interventions, such as reflection, self-disclosure, and confrontation, may be informed through a therapist's empathic understanding of a client. Although empathy has the potential to effect sound treatment directions, the construct is also subject to misunderstandings and misuses. In the service of empathic understanding, a practitioner may lose a sense of objectivity and become enmeshed in a client's experiencing. In another major misapplication of empathy, a counselor or therapist inappropriately may attempt to maintain an empathic posture with a client at all times, restricting the possibility of providing an alternative point of view.

Empathy and Therapeutic Dimensions

The treatment process may be conceptualized in terms of both relational and technical dimensions (Kelly, 1997). The relational component entails the qualitative nature of the interactions between a client and a practitioner. Identifiable conditions, such as the level of support, trust, and communication, characterize aspects of the relational domain. From a technical stance, various interventions and strategies comprise the instrumental activity of the counselor or therapist. This dimension involves numerous intentional functions, such as a decision to touch a client, the use of silence, and the implementation of a variety of other interventions. There is also an interactive effect between the therapeutic dimensions that can enhance or diminish the effectiveness of therapy. In this regard, the establishment of a sound therapeutic relationship fosters a supportive emotional climate that enhances the employment of technical operations. In the absence of a relational bond between a practitioner and a client, even a discriminating use of techniques and strategies may fail. Only in the presence of a stable and predictable psychological climate can there exist the facilitative conditions essential to stimulate client involvement.

From a relational perspective, empathic understanding has been widely recognized as a vehicle for establishing an attachment bond between a client and a therapist (Paivio & Laurent, 2001; Trusty, Ng, & Watts, 2005). At the same time, client information derived from the engagement of empathy potentially serves as a guide for a range of interventions across diverse theoretical orientations. A purposeful training direction in counseling and psychotherapy is to maintain an emphasis on relationship aspects of treatment while broadening technical dimensions beyond empathic listening toward more challenging therapeutic processes (Pearson, 1999). This endeavor becomes increasingly complex as a practitioner begins to employ treatment approaches that are outside of the frame of reference of a client.

In order to clarify the distinction between the utilization of empathy as it pertains to relationship and technical dimensions, the following therapy example focuses on the therapeutic techniques of reflection and confrontation. In a treatment illustration, an adolescent client, Ellen, has been referred to therapy due to symptoms of an eating disorder. In an initial session, Ellen states, "I'm sick of people being on my case and telling me that I'm too thin. All I'm doing is trying to get in shape and watch what I eat." In employing reflection, the therapist relates, "You feel angry when people interfere with your life, when you know what to do in order to take care of yourself." In this response, the practitioner stays within Ellen's frame of reference and does not question or challenge her perspectives. Subsequently, as counseling continues and a working alliance develops, the therapist assumes a more challenging stance. In the middle stage of counseling, Ellen states, "I'm so sick of people telling me what to do. I know how to take care of my health." In using a confrontation, the therapist responds, "Ellen, when you say that you are taking care of yourself, I hear something in your voice suggesting doubt and uncertainty." In whatever way Ellen reacts to the confrontation, from outright rejection to possible acceptance, the therapist attempts to empathically communicate an understanding of her response.

In instances when a counselor or a therapist challenges, questions, or confronts a client, it is possible for a practitioner to empathize with the individual in terms of what it is like to experience such exchanges (Josephs, 1995). In this regard, a counselor does act outside of the role of an empathic response for particular interventions but maintains an empathic connection relating to how a client receives or processes the approaches. The alternative of not communicating beyond a client's personal awareness forecloses the possibility of a therapist's creative or independent contribution. An expression of empathic understanding of a client's reaction to an alternative point of view enables a practitioner to hold his or her ground while taking the perspective of the individual seriously. As a therapist employs empathy in a flexible way with respect to challenging interventions, it is still possible to maintain an attitudinal consistency in the application of empathic understanding throughout the treatment process.

Misapplications of Empathy

In counseling and psychotherapy, erroneous conceptions and uses of empathy potentially restrict the therapeutic effectiveness of the construct. An awareness of inappropriate perspectives relating to the applications of empathy enables a practitioner to minimize or avoid treatment misdirections. In an initial consideration, semantic confusion exists with respect to the distinctions between empathy and the related terms of sympathy, identification, and projection. In part, this may be attributed to a lack of consensus in the professional literature relating to the meaning and function of empathy. In the pursuit of an increased understanding of empathy, however, it is important to clarify related processes that can blur similarities and differences, and subsequently lead to unsound treatment initiatives. Expressions of kindness and approval, and acting compliantly constitute certain behaviors that many have come to associate with an "empathic counselor" or an "empathic psychotherapist" (Book, 1988, 1991). This misunderstanding largely limits a practitioner's role to that of being only a participant in a client's experiencing and does not encompass a more detached and evaluative function. A misapplication of empathy also occurs when a practitioner dogmatically maintains an empathic stance by excessively identifying with a client. In these instances, a counselor attempts to operate from a position that involves psychological contact at all times in a forced attitudinal process that Bolognini (1997) refers to as *empathism*. When this occurs, empathy assumes an idealistic quality that becomes impossible to achieve, and, equally important, makes it difficult for the therapist to participate in an authentic and spontaneous way (Wolowitz, 2002).

With a continuous attempt to provide empathic understanding to a client, the communication endeavor minimizes the expression of a therapist's personal observations or views. In an effort to avoid intrusion with information outside of a client's experiencing or frame of reference, a practitioner may withhold a substantial amount of valuable knowledge or alternative perspectives without encountering the client in a meaningful way (Moses, 1988). Consider a counseling example that illustrates this constricted approach that also serves to "protect" the therapeutic relationship. A college freshman, Jerry, is in treatment in a university counseling center for unsatisfactory grades and conduct violations in his dormitory. Initially, Jerry repeatedly blames other students for his problems and insists that he is innocent of any wrongdoing. After several sessions with a counseling intern, there is little change in Jerry's views or in his behavior. At the same time, the counselor believes that she has developed a relatively positive sense of trust and rapport in the treatment relationship. Although the counselor has formal reports from the dormitory director that substantiate Jerry's continuing irresponsible activity, she decides not to confront him with the material because this tactic seems to lack empathic understanding.

Another misconception in the use of empathy in counseling and psychotherapy is that all individuals seek to be understood in a treatment situation. Although most clients do wish to gain a sense of understanding, some find the emotional closeness of the therapeutic relationship threatening and invasive (Modell, 1979; Williams & Irving, 1997). In other instances, the development of closeness and acceptance by a therapist may eventually be rebuked, and this prospect is intolerable (Fromm-Reichmann, 1950). What may be seen as penetrating insights by a therapist can be perceived by a client as painful and representing submission to a vulnerable state of psychological exposure (Buie, 1981; Marcia, 1987). Even the development of trust, which is valued in client understanding, is a condition to be avoided by some individuals. In these instances, clients typically evoke defensive or evasive means to avoid being understood (Clark, 1998a, 2000). It then becomes therapeutic for a practitioner to recognize the individual's adverse reaction to being more deeply understood. In a counseling example, an early-adulthood client with a diagnosis of histrionic personality disorder expresses strong emotions and a dramatic style of behavior. As treatment progresses, it becomes apparent that the client experiences feelings of emptiness and self-doubt that belie her engaging and evocative manner. As the therapist begins to clarify the client's feelings, she becomes emotionally distant and avoids exploring her more basic functioning. At this point, it is not advisable for the practitioner to pursue a deeper level of client awareness until the individual develops a psychological readiness through the treatment process. In this regard, the level of empathic understanding remains consistent with a client's capacity to consolidate affective functioning and emerging self-insight.

SUMMARY

The value of empathy in counseling and psychotherapy becomes manifest in understanding clients, advancing the treatment relationship, and integrating therapeutic interventions in the treatment process. Misapplications of empathy may also occur that impede the effectiveness of the counseling experience. Understanding a client is a prominent focus in experiential and observational empathy. The modalities, however, posit different conceptions and processes in the development of empathic understanding. A cultural context augments experiential and observational empathy by contributing to a comprehensive perspective of the functioning of individuals from diverse backgrounds. Empathy has the potential to be a central factor throughout the therapy process in terms of promoting constructive client change. Empathic understanding may be expressed through relational and technical dimensions within the working alliance. A counselor or therapist's self-awareness promotes the treatment relationship and positions the practitioner to be receptive to communicate with a client more openly. A therapist's personal issues, countertransference, and convictional bias involve material that can impede client advancement by producing inaccuracies in clinical judgment.

PART II

Empathy: Theoretical Orientations in Counseling and Psychotherapy

Chapter 3

Theories of Counseling and Psychotherapy and Empathy

Various schools of thought have arisen to explain how and why counseling works, but a common thread in most seems to be empathic understanding.
—Hartley (1995, p. 13)

During the fall semester of each academic year, I teach a graduate course entitled "Theories of Counseling." Among the dozen or more theoretical systems that I include for study is the person-centered therapy of Carl Rogers. In my early experience as an instructor, I thought that Rogers's views on empathy, in terms of its conceptualization and therapeutic application, largely covered the topic. However, as time progressed and my experience increased, I became aware that this perspective was inconsistent with my treatment practice and teaching. It became apparent to me that empathic understanding extended beyond the conceptions of the person-centered approach into a number of other therapeutic orientations. At the outset, I found it difficult to consolidate these positions because I lacked a systematic analysis of empathy and its relation to diverse psychotherapies. Over a period of time, I became familiar with the function of empathic understanding across various other modalities. In particular, the perspectives of self psychology with respect to empathy expanded the depth of my understanding. Through my continuing study of empathy, I have found that, with important and varying degrees of emphasis, the construct is represented in a broad range of traditions. In my research on the topic, I was able to identify 13 contemporary theories of counseling and psychotherapy that provide a relative degree of focus on empathy in the treatment process.

QUALITATIVE ASPECTS OF EMPATHY IN CONTEMPORARY PSYCHOTHERAPIES

Empathy is acknowledged by diverse theoretical approaches for its contribution to the development of a positive therapeutic relationship (Ivey, D'Andrea, Ivey, & Simek-Morgan, 2002; Lambert & Barley, 2002; Watson, 2002). Research evidence suggests that a practitioner's employment of empathy and related facilitative qualities within the working alliance promotes successful treatment outcomes (Bachelor & Horvath, 1999; Feller & Cottone, 2003; Lafferty, Beutler, & Crago, 1989). However, even though the importance of empathy is widely endorsed, the focus and function of the construct differs widely among therapy orientations (Cochran & Cochran, 2006; Nystul, 2003; Watson, 2002). In this regard, there are differences in the conceptualization and application of empathy and empathic understanding with respect to each theoretical approach.

Within a small number of psychotherapies, specifically person-centered therapy and self psychology, empathy is a significant and critical function. In these modalities, sustained empathy is applied throughout the treatment process, and reference to the construct is frequent in the literature pertaining to each theoretical model. In other orientations, including Individual Psychology, existential therapy, cognitive-behavioral therapy and cognitive therapy, and psychoanalytic therapy, empathy is prominent in the context of treatment interactions and interventions. Yet, within these specific traditions, there is only occasional reference to empathy or empathic understanding as operational terms in the professional literature relevant to each psychotherapy. With a larger number of theoretical approaches, empathy is recognizable in the therapeutic process, but direct reference to the construct in the literature respective to each particular orientation is relatively infrequent. Table 3.1 provides an outline of contemporary psychotherapies and empathy.

SIGNIFICANT ASPECTS OF EMPATHY IN CONTEMPORARY PSYCHOTHERAPIES

Person-centered and self psychology are major approaches to therapy that both emphasize sustained empathy in their treatment models (Tobin, 1991). Empathy has been a central focus in person-centered therapy for decades,

TABLE 3.1
Contemporary Psychotherapies and Empathy

Significant Aspects
Person-centered therapy
Self psychology
Prominent Aspects
Individual Psychology
Existential therapy
Cognitive-behavioral therapy and cognitive therapy
Psychoanalytic therapy
Recognizable Aspects
Rational emotive behavioral therapy
Transactional analysis
Solution-focused brief therapy
Gestalt therapy
Constructivist therapy
Feminist therapy
Family systems therapy

and the work of Carl Rogers has been highly influential in generating wide acceptance of the construct among theorists and practitioners (Bohart, 1991). In more recent years, Kohut's writings brought distinctive attention to empathy within the psychoanalytic tradition through his school of self psychology. Although the therapies of Rogers and Kohut share commonalities in their emphasis on empathy, each approach clearly differs in terms of conceptualization and practice with respect to the construct (Bohart, 1991; Emery, 1987). Rogers thought that empathy was one of the facilitative conditions that contribute to therapeutic movement, and these processes were sufficient in themselves for engendering positive client change. In contrast, for most of his career Kohut believed that empathy was a method of observation for laying the groundwork for interpretations that ultimately lead to a strengthening of the structure of the self (Silverstein, 1999). From a person-centered perspective, empathic understanding focuses more on the immediate frame of reference of a client, and self psychology generally emphasizes how clients or patients characteristically construe experiences from a broader perspective (Bohart & Greenberg, 1997).

In a study relating to theoretical orientation and empathy, Carlozzi, Bull, Stein, Ray, and Barnes (2002) found that humanistic/experiential and psychodynamic practitioners were more likely to endorse and utilize the construct in the treatment process. Their investigation points to the relatively more frequent use of empathy in therapeutic treatment when compared to other major theories by the humanistic/experiential orientation of person-centered therapy and the psychodynamic approach of self psychology. Although various therapies make reference to empathy, the meaning of the construct carries a distinct resonance with person-centered therapy and self psychology (Thorne, 2003). Given the salience of empathy within person-centered therapy and self psychology, each approach is featured in subsequent chapters after a brief introduction to the orientations in the following section.

Person-Centered Therapy

It would be difficult to overestimate the importance of Rogers's influence in bringing recognition to empathy as a critical factor in counseling and psychotherapy. Although empathy has been periodically mentioned in the therapeutic process since early in the 20th century (Teich, 1992a), Rogers, in his client-centered and later person-centered therapy, was the first theoretician to explicitly cite the centrality of empathic understanding across the body of his writings (Mearns & Thorne, 1988). In addition to congruence and unconditional positive regard, empathic understanding was identified as an attitudinal element that contributes to constructive client change in the treatment relationship. When Rogers (1957) first articulated the prominence of the facilitative conditions for therapeutic change, he set off a controversy in terms of the validity of his propositions that continued for years in professional quarters. Through his endeavors, Rogers formulated and popularized the meaning of empathy as a mode of understanding the frame of reference of another person (Teich, 1992c). His explications of empathy have stimulated extensive research on the effects of empathic understanding and possible means to operationalize the construct for treatment purposes. Other researchers continue to expand on his ideas, and the person-centered approach remains a vital and influential force in contemporary psychotherapy theory and practice.

Self Psychology

Within the framework of psychoanalytic psychotherapy, Heinz Kohut developed a self psychology approach that utilized empathy as a data-gathering activity that serves to inform therapeutic interventions that affect curative client or patient change (Tobin, 1991). In a departure from classical psychoanalytic treatment, a therapist attempts thereby to vicariously understand a client's experience in order to acquire psychological information about the individual (Wispé, 1987). In this regard, empathy initially serves as a method of observation and a mode of listening that enables a practitioner to make intelligible a client's communications (Silverstein, 1999). In a second or explanation phase, the practitioner applies client insights derived from empathic understanding as a requisite condition for the use of interpretations. Although self psychology emphasizes an empathic role of the therapist, the approach maintains the classical way of proceeding through observation and inference (Bohart & Greenberg, 1997). It was only in the final years of his life that Kohut (1991) recognized that empathy has a potential to be therapeutic and healing in its own right. Kohut also conceptualized a central function of empathy in the emotional development of individuals in early life stages and across the lifespan (Kohut, 1971, 1977, 1984). In particular, Kohut felt that the lack of a primary caregiver's expression of empathic understanding toward an infant or a young child had long-term implications in terms of psychopathology.

PROMINENT ASPECTS OF EMPATHY IN CONTEMPORARY PSYCHOTHERAPIES

It is possible to identify theoretical approaches in counseling and psychotherapy in which empathy is conceptually compatible and observable in a treatment context. With Individual Psychology, understanding a client's lifestyle and the expression of social interest involves a practitioner's use of empathy. An accurate evaluation of a client's early childhood recollections as a projective technique is only possible through the utilization of an empathic understanding in the assessment process. In terms of existential therapy, an engagement of empathy enables a counselor or therapist to acknowledge the uniqueness of an individual and also grasp a sense of a client's quest for meaning in life. The pursuit of a mutually empathic encounter with a client emphasizes the human dimension of the therapeutic relationship. From the perspective of cognitive-behavioral therapy and cognitive therapy, establishing a collaborative relationship and understanding a client's dysfunctional schemas or cognitive structures relate to the therapeutic use of empathy. Empathic understanding also facilitates the selective use of cognitive-behavioral techniques that promote adaptive functioning. Finally, various figures within the psychoanalytic orientation gave distinctive attention to empathy, and their contributions are comprehensively reviewed in a subsequent chapter.

Individual Psychology

In 1912, Alfred Adler named his newly formed theoretical orientation *Individual Psychology* in order to emphasize the value, uniqueness, and indivisibility of the person (Dreikurs, 1967; Mosak, 2005). In a number of his writings, Adler makes explicit reference to empathy, and he may be considered the first theorist to explicate its developmental and therapeutic expression. Adler equated empathy with the ability or capacity of a person to identify with and to understand others. Adler (1927) wrote, "Empathy occurs in the moment one human being speaks with another. It is impossible to understand another individual if it is impossible at the same time to identify oneself with him" (p. 60). Adler further extended his conceptualization of empathy and identification to the construct of social feeling. He thought that the faculty of an individual to empathize with others is an innate potentiality that needed to be nurtured in early life in order to develop (Adler, 1931/1958; Mosak & Maniacci, 1999). Adler (1927) stated, "If we seek for the origin of this ability to act and feel as if we were someone else, we can find it in an existence of an inborn social feeling" (p. 61). In this regard, social feeling is the capacity to be interested in others and to experience a sense of kinship with humanity (Ewen, 2003). Alienation and self-centeredness are opposites of the concept (Adler, 1931/1958).

Adler (1927) observed a developmental lack of social feeling and empathy in the behavior of particular individuals. "They think only of themselves, and lose all interest for the joys or woes of others. These are manifestations which are intimately related to a deficient degree of empathy" (p. 62). As Adler's thinking evolved, social feeling assumed a prominence in his theorizing in terms of an individual's pursuit of fulfillment in life by feeling part of a whole in the human community. In this regard, Adler (1931/1958) wrote, "Individual Psychology may claim as its contribution to have pointed out that empathy and understanding are facts of social feeling, of harmony with the universe" (p. 136). Through Adler's writings and various translations of his publications, the term *social interest* began to replace social feeling. As a personality dimension, social interest provides a direction to an individual's life in terms of meaning through an emotional bond with others and a contribution to society (Ansbacher, 1990). The construct is also a criterion for mental health as a person transcends personal concerns and preoccupations and finds a sense of well-being through involvement in human endeavors. In a relatively recent correction of an earlier translation, Ansbacher (1992) observed that from Adler's perspective, social interest is "the action-line of community feeling" (p. 405). In this respect, social interest relates to performance activities predicated on the broader term of *community feeling* involving a person's degree of identification with others and a sense of harmony with the universe.

From a therapeutic perspective, Adler largely based his understanding of clients on empathy (Ansbacher & Ansbacher, 1956). In an effort to define social feeling, Adler cited a phrase from an anonymous English author, "To see with the eyes of another, to hear with the ears of another, to feel with the heart of another" (Ansbacher & Ansbacher, 1956, p. 135). In another major construct of Individual Psychology, Adler theorized that an individual's social interest finds expression through his or her *lifestyle,* which provides the patterned and unified system by which an individual functions (Adler, 1927; Sonstegard & Bitter, 2004). Formed in early childhood, all experiences of a person are perceived or interpreted through the axiomatic lifestyle that is largely an unconscious process (Powers & Griffith, 1987). The lifestyle conception includes an individual's convictions or beliefs about the self, others, and events in a syllogistic framework (Manaster & Corsini, 1982). Once an individual's lifestyle is acquired, it remains the same unless the person gains an insight into his or her ingrained outlook on life (Adler, 1931/1958). A practitioner's sustained use of empathy in the treatment process contributes to an understanding of a client's lifestyle (Sharf, 2004). In working with clients, Adler (1929/1969) wrote, "In treating a case of this sort, identification—the ability to place oneself empathically in the situation of a person—is all-important" (p. 109).

Although it is possible for a counselor or a therapist to evaluate a client's lifestyle in various ways, early recollections provide an assessment tool that is relatively brief and incisive (Clark, 2002b). Adler originated the use of early recollections as a projective technique through which a practitioner typically elicits several memories that represent discrete experiences in childhood before a person is 8 years old (Adler, 1937; Mosak, 1958). In a therapeutic appraisal context, clients will typically recall instances from early childhood that are consistent with their fundamental convictions about life (Manaster & Corsini, 1982). Adler (1931/1958) wrote, "Early recollections have especial significance. To begin with, they show the style of life in its origins and in its simplest expressions" (p. 74). In this regard, in the context of a projective appraisal, persons recollect from countless early experiences those that relate to their outlook on life. These particular memories serve to warn, comfort, guide, or prepare a person with a tested perspective that is pertinent to his or her immediate situation (Adler, 1931/1958). In order to more fully grasp the meaning of a client's early memories, it is essential for a therapist to assume an empathic stance. Adler (1927) emphasized the importance of empathically eliciting early remembrances and accurately interpreting the memories in order to illuminate the pattern of an individual's convictions about life. In this respect, Adler (1929/1969) stated, "The art of understanding early recollections involves a high degree of empathy, an ability to identify with the child in his childhood situations" (p. 14).

After a practitioner evaluates a client's early recollections, it may also become apparent that the individual employs a pattern of safeguarding tendencies that serve a protective function within the lifestyle (Clark, 1999a, 2000; Oberst & Stewart, 2003). These safeguarding tendencies buffer a client's self-esteem by evading threatening conditions that pose a psychological threat to the person. When a client demonstrates safeguarding in response to perceived threat, within the treatment situation, a practitioner's empathic understanding of the behavior tends to lessen the intensity of the individual's defensive and evasive reactions. Adler (1936) wrote about the compulsive quality of one of the safeguarding tendencies, "The hesitating attitude finds expression in killing time, in seeking out and repeating a single routine, or expressive movement or idea which will preclude further contact with the terrifying problems of life" (p. 18). Through the therapeutic process, it is possible for a counselor or therapist to empathically respond to the manifestation of a client's safeguarding tendencies, and encourage the development of more adaptive and purposeful behavior.

Existential Psychotherapy

Existential psychotherapy shares commonalities with Individual Psychology in terms of emphasis of each orientation on the uniqueness and value of the individual and the pursuit of meaning in life (May, 1939). In both traditions, practitioners attempt to empathically understand the subjective or phenomenological experiencing of the person. In order to grasp the personal perspectives of a client from an existential stance, a therapist strives to empathize with the individual through a process of deep understanding (van Kaam, 1959, 1969). Even though there is a focus on the immediate functioning of the client, the counselor also maintains an emerging perspective on the potentiality of the individual. Through the treatment process, a practitioner endeavors to acknowledge or affirm the essence of a client's present functioning, while imagining the person that the individual may become (Schmid, 2001). The theologian Martin Buber (1957, 1958) referred to this process as *imagining the real* by confirming or affirming the whole potentiality and uniqueness of the other. A related aspect of the human condition is a search for meaning or purpose in life. Through a subjective quest, a therapist attempts to empathically focus on issues that foster a sense of meaning for the individual (Frankl, 1959).

The existential treatment method typically emphasizes a mutuality in interactions between a client and therapist that has implications for the conceptualization and utilization of empathy. In contrast to Rogers's belief that it is necessary to maintain an empathic focus on a client's frame of reference, Buber (1957) contended that a therapist should retain his or her separate identity in order to understand conditions that the client cannot perceive. Through an open exchange or dialogue, a counselor communicates perspectives to a client that convey what is empathically understood. The individual frames of reference of both the client and the practitioner are given legitimacy in a genuine existential encounter (Van Balan, 1990; Wolowitz, 2002). This is a validation that sanctions the perspectives of both individuals within the therapeutic relationship. Through a process that is anchored in a true reciprocity and dialogical exchange, a deeper level of empathy is possible in a human contact that allows for and respects commonalities and differences between persons (Havens, 1974; Schmid, 2001). Buber felt that only by honoring the unique positions of each person in the realm of interhuman relationships is it possible to engender a shared responsibility that reduces the isolation and manipulation of individuals (Jourard, 1959; May & Yalom, 2005). To this end, Buber (1957) spoke of the *I–Thou* relationship that emphasizes authenticity and mutual respect in human encounters.

In fairness to Rogers's views, his conceptualization of the core condition of congruence or genuineness and his later practice and theorizing reflect the importance of the therapist authentically expressing himself or herself in the person-centered approach. As one of the few treatment techniques associated with existential therapy, *therapist self-disclosure* conveys a human quality that can be therapeutic. When a counselor discloses personal experiences that relate to those of a client, a level of empathic understanding may be reached that is unsurpassed through any other intervention (Jourard, 1964). A client's sense of isolation or threat may also diminish when a practitioner transparently communicates the existence of common ground in their respective lives. Through this endeavor, a therapist intentionally evokes an identification with a client as a means of establishing an emotional connection at a basic level of human engagement.

Cognitive-Behavioral Therapy and Cognitive Therapy

In cognitive-behavioral therapy, a collaborative bond between a client and a counselor or therapist is typically viewed as a necessary condition to facilitate the application of specific techniques (Raue & Goldfried, 1994). Empathic understanding contributes to the development of the therapeutic relationship and assists in clarifying a client's cognitive structures in a treatment situation (Haaga, Rabois, & Brody, 1999; Keijsers, Schaap, & Hoogduin, 2000). In this regard, Watson (2002) wrote, "In cognitive-behavioral approaches, empathy is used in the service of identifying core conditions and accessing affective reactions" (p. 461). Rapport and open communication are sought in order to establish supportive conditions to challenge a client's dysfunctional cognitions and to follow through with behavioral interventions. In a study with a group of outpatients treated with cognitive-behavioral therapy for depression, Burns and Nolen-Hoeksema (1992) evaluated the quality of the treatment relationship. The patients treated by therapists with high ratings for empathy and warmth improved significantly more when compared to the patients of therapists with the lowest empathy ratings. The quality of collaboration was found to have a substantial impact on the clinical improvement in the depressed patients, and therapeutic empathy was robustly associated with the beneficial effects of the treatment relationship (Wampold, 2001).

As a cognitive-behavioral approach, cognitive therapy emphasizes the importance of accurate empathy for facilitating therapeutic collaboration, understanding patients' unproductive behaviors, and being less judgmental about them (A. T. Beck, Rush, Shaw, & Emery, 1979). Beck et al. (1979) stated, "By 'trying on' a patient's negative attitudes and cognitions, the empathic therapist can begin to develop an antidote or counter-argument to these negative ideas" (pp. 47–48). In this regard, a therapist empathizes with a client's negative emotional experiences and draws linkages between the individual's intensified feelings and dysfunctional cognitions. Through this endeavor, a practitioner more fully understands a client's experiencing and assumes a perspective from which to effectively scrutinize the person's faulty belief system through a collaborative interaction. This process rests on accurate empathy that Beck et al. referred to as "how well the therapist can step into the patient's world and see and experience life the way the patient does. In fact, the therapist will, to some degree, experience the patient's feelings" (p. 47). In recognizing the importance of empathic understanding in the treatment process, Beck et al. also cautioned against a therapist's overreliance on empathy with respect to being misled into accepting the "veridicality" of the patient's negative and self-defeating beliefs. Over a period of time, a practitioner may begin to believe that a patient's views represent accurate perceptions of life situations. It becomes necessary for the therapist to seek out alternative sources of objective information in order to balance the subjective reports of the patient.

In cognitive therapy, empathy and the exploration of a client's *cognitive distortions* involves an interdependent process (Persons & Burns, 1985; Safran & Segal, 1990). An empathic relationship fosters a type of collaboration that allows for the effective execution of cognitive-behavioral interventions. At the same time, empathic understanding is also to be considered a therapeutic entity that contributes to treatment progress and client change. Safran and Segal (1990) stated, "True empathy does more than provide a precondition for effective cognitive interventions; in and of itself, it can be one of the most powerful means of challenging a patient's dysfunctional interpersonal schemas" (pp. 188–189). From a counseling and psychotherapy perspective, *schemas* represent cognitive structures consisting of a person's core beliefs and assumptions developed early in life (A. T. Beck & Weishaar, 2005). A major focus of cognitive therapy is to challenge ingrained dysfunctional client beliefs and to develop more purposeful and adaptive schemas. In the event that a client becomes closed to discussion about alternative perspectives, it is helpful for a practitioner to empathically explore the individual's emotional reactions. The client may feel criticized or threatened, and only by empathically validating the individual's perspectives does it become possible to examine core processes (Safran & Segal, 1990).

In the pursuit of empathic understanding, a counselor or a therapist may tend to assume that a client's dysfunctional schemas and automatic thoughts are static and unchangeable (A. T. Beck et al., 1979). A more purposeful perspective is that a patient's negative views are only cognitions and are subject to change by being confirmed or disconfirmed through the therapeutic process. This observation requires the therapist to attempt to maintain an objective and less emotionally involved stance in order to complement his or her empathic posture. The balance of multiple frames of reference enables a counselor to be less judgmental toward a client's unproductive behavior. With this in mind, Safran and Segal (1990) stated, "The therapist walks in the patient's shoes, feels affected emotionally by what the patient says, and finds the patient's responses to the therapist's empathic comments invaluable in feeling understood" (p. 89). In this regard, a sound therapeutic relationship contributes to the effective processing of negative emotions and negative thoughts. In turn, enhanced client cognitive functioning fosters the purposeful implementation of cognitive-behavioral techniques.

Psychoanalytic Therapy

When introducing the term in psychoanalysis, Sigmund Freud made brief and sparse references to empathy across his voluminous writings (Pigman, 1995). Sándor Ferenczi, a pioneer in the psychoanalytic tradition, formulated a central role for empathy in the final papers of his life (Rachman, 1997). Several other prominent psychoanalytic figures also recognized the significance of the function of empathy in their works. As previously mentioned, Heinz Kohut, from the psychoanalytic perspective of self psychology, theorized about the role of empathy in the treatment process and in human development. In subsequent chapters, psychoanalytic therapy and self psychology are comprehensively considered with respect to their relationship with empathy.

RECOGNIZABLE ASPECTS OF EMPATHY IN CONTEMPORARY PSYCHOTHERAPIES

There are a number of theories of counseling and psychotherapy in which there is only an occasional mention of empathy in the literature pertinent to each modality. At times, reference to empathy or empathic understanding is explicit and in other instances, the construct is only implied as a component of the therapeutic process. Rational emotive behavioral therapy, transactional analysis, and solution-focused brief therapy include cognitive-behavioral or cognitive features. Gestalt therapy, constructivist therapy, and feminist therapy emphasize the perspectives of clients from broad contexts. Family systems therapy employs a systemic perspective relating to individual functioning.

Rational Emotive Behavioral Therapy

Albert Ellis, the founder of rational emotive behavior therapy (REBT), felt that a warm relationship is not a necessary or sufficient condition for personality change in psychotherapy (Ellis, 2005). Soon after Rogers

(1957) identified the necessary and sufficient conditions for therapeutic growth, Ellis (1959) stated that he was "most dubious" that it was absolutely necessary for any condition to be present in treatment for basic personality change to occur. Ellis cited instances in everyday life, such as through personal readings and environmental changes, in which individuals make basic changes in their behavior without the benefit of therapy. Although Ellis (2005) agreed that a therapeutic rapport is desirable, he primarily emphasized the importance of full and unconditional acceptance of a client as a part of a close collaboration in the treatment process. In a two-part conceptual framework, Ellis described a *general* form of REBT that closely relates to cognitive-behavioral therapy and a *preferential* REBT that stresses profound philosophic change in a client's perception of self and others (Ellis, 2005).

From an REBT perspective, Dryden (1990) conceptualized *affective empathy*, which focuses on client understanding in a vein similar to the person-centered approach. It may be assumed that in the general form of REBT, this process is instrumental in promoting client understanding in ways that approximate other cognitive-behavioral orientations. Dryden (1990) also proposed a *philosophic empathy* in REBT treatment that conveys to a client an understanding of the assumptions and convictions that underpin the individual's perceptions (Wilkins, 2003). In this respect, REBT goes beyond a focus on symptom removal and, at a philosophical level, attempts to effect change in a client's basic values that keep the person disturbed (Ellis, 2005).

Transactional Analysis

As a treatment process, transactional analysis includes numerous constructs that involve the scrutiny of interpersonal exchanges or transactions between individuals (Berne, 1961; Gladding, 2005). The analysis of various transactional constructs, such as games, scripts, and ego states, potentially involves an empathic stance on the part of a counselor or a therapist. In the context of transactional analysis, Erskine (1993) described an attunement that entails a two-part process of a therapist being fully aware of a client's functioning and subsequently communicating the awareness to the individual. Empathic responses of the practitioner reduce the intensity of psychological threat that often occurs during the painstaking analysis of a fixed Child ego state. A Child ego state that is fixed in early childhood reflects an unregulated affect and primitive developmental needs. In another direction, Guistolise (1996) observed that the processes of empathy and attunement enable therapists to gain an understanding of clients who have developed scripts about others and the availability of empathy. These individuals hold ingrained beliefs such as "no one is here for me" or "people only care about themselves" (Guistolise, 1996, p. 285). The scripts represent decisions made in childhood in response to the perceived failure of parental figures to meet the client's developmental needs for empathy and emotional attunement.

Solution-Focused Brief Therapy

Most solution-focused approaches are practiced within a time-limited framework that emphasizes the importance of the therapeutic relationship (Murdock, 2004; Nicoll, 1999; Presbury, Echterling, & McKee, 2002). This assertion possibly contrasts with the perspectives of some counselors and therapists who assume that brief therapy is technique-oriented, seemingly insensitive to the emotional needs of clients, and lacking in empathic understanding (Seruya, 1997). For many solution-focused therapists, however, a collaborative relationship provides encouragement to clients as the practitioner attempts to gain a phenomenological understanding of the individual's experiencing (Nystul, 2003; Watts & Pietrzak, 2000). In addition, a therapist empathically assesses a client's strengths and resources and becomes an active partner in goal-setting in order to enhance the pursuit of solutions and change.

It is also possible for a practitioner to utilize empathic communication without accentuating a client's pain and discouragement in a situational context (Presbury et al., 2002). As an example, a therapist states to a client, "You feel overwhelmed by everything that seems to be happening all at once." Immediately after the client reacts to the empathic statement, the practitioner says, "At the same time, you faced a similar situation a few years ago, and you successfully managed to get through it." In this component of the example, the therapist suggests that the client's emotional reactions are situational and time-limited and that finding solutions has a potential for a viable therapeutic direction.

Perspectives from other psychotherapies have also been integrated with solution-focused therapy in order to diversify and extend the effectiveness of treatment. Seruya (1997) melded the concepts and techniques of self psychology and cognitive-behavior therapy with short-term therapy, and LaFountain (1996) incorporated Individual Psychology principles within a brief therapy approach. In each integrated model, a strong working alliance and empathic understanding assume central positions in treatment.

In the conceptualization modality of LaFountain (1996), social interest contributes to a nourishing therapeutic climate and provides a constructive outlet for client development. In the context of an empathic brief therapy model, Seruya (1997) discussed the importance of empathy in stimulating the potentialities of a client. Seruya (1997) observed, "The experience of feeling understood deeply and in a sustained way leads to a greater sense of cohesion, continuity, and vitality of the self" (p. 59).

Gestalt Therapy

As a theoretical approach that emphasizes individual choice and responsibility, Gestalt therapy reflects existential qualities in its therapeutic practice (Fall, Holden, & Marquis, 2004). A key Gestalt assumption is that the meaning of a client's experience rests on the individual's subjective interpretation. In treatment, a counselor or a therapist attempts to promote a client's awareness of his or her functioning in order to facilitate the development of self-understanding and maturation. Day (2004) stated that client awareness of experiencing from moment to moment is critical for treatment success, and an emotional engagement is enhanced by the therapeutic conditions of accurate empathy and genuineness. The employment of empathic understanding offers a potential for enhancing the working alliance and for fostering psychological contact with clients (Sharf, 2004). In particular, Gestalt theory stresses the value of attempting to understand a client holistically rather than in an emotional isolation or in the abstract (O'Hara, 1984). O'Hara (1984) asserted that in order to expand a client's holistic thinking, it is essential for the individual to extend his or her consciousness of the practitioner in the treatment relationship. The greatest potential for therapeutic growth of a client occurs when the person's empathic stance extends toward the counselor. Empathic understanding on the part of the client and the therapist assumes a self-transcendent quality as both individuals broaden their awareness in growth-enhancing ways.

Constructivist Psychotherapy

Constructivist modalities involve a family of therapies that acknowledge divergent realities and share basic tenets and assumptions (Neimeyer, 1995). From a constructivist perspective, individuals actively create and acquire knowledge through collaborative human endeavors and relationships. A person is historically and culturally situated among groups of people in which these forces constitute significant developmental influences (Cox

& Lyddon, 1997; Gergen, Lightfoot, & Sydow, 2004). As a part of the constructivist approach, social constructionism affords particular emphasis to the importance of understanding the subjective perspectives of an individual in interpersonal exchanges (Mahoney, 2000, 2003). Each person creates and sustains personal meanings through social relationships with others. From a therapeutic perspective, the psychological growth of a client involves changes in those socially constructed patterns of meanings that are ingrained and dysfunctional.

In order to gain an empathic understanding of a client's maladaptive schemas or core ordering processes, a social constructivist therapist attempts to establish a collaborative relationship and downplay the role of an "expert" (Corey, 2005). In this regard, Corey (2005) stated, "Empathy and the collaborative partnership in the therapeutic process are more important than assessment or techniques" (p. 386). Treatment stresses an affirmative therapy style that is respectful and trusting. It is assumed that clients will experience a sense of disequilibrium when challenged with alternative ways of perceiving reality, and an empathic stance of a practitioner is essential for effective therapeutic processing. Neimeyer (1995) wrote that a constructivist therapist "adopts an empathic, collaborative, respectful, and at times almost reverential mode of relating to the client struggling with understandable 'resistance of change'" (p. 18).

In treatment practice, Corey (2005) makes the point that a social constructivist practitioner affirms the position of a client as possessing the most knowledge about his or her life. The counselor assumes a "not-knowing" stance that is characterized by efforts to empathically understand significant narratives or perspectives in the life of a client (Corey, 2005). In the process of working with a client, a constructivist therapist typically attempts to assess the magnitude of client change that seems therapeutically necessary in the context of the individual's life. In this sense, it is possible to strategically clarify treatment planning in terms of first- and second-order change (Lyddon, 1990). First-order change does not alter a client's fundamental belief system and focuses more on transitory symptom relief. Second-order change is transformative and attends to promoting change in dysfunctional core ordering processes. Finally, Watts and Shulman (2003) identified commonalities between the principles and processes of constructivist and Adlerian psychotherapies. In particular, Adlerian or Individual Psychology treatment emphasizes the centrality of the therapeutic relationship, recognizes the importance of understanding behavior in a social context, and identifies core ordering processes or schemas through the concept of the lifestyle.

Feminist Therapy

A feminist therapist attempts to foster an egalitarian relationship in the treatment process, and to recognize the uniqueness of the client in a broad contextual background (Evans, Kincade, Marbley, & Seem, 2005; Murdock, 2004). The client is assumed to be the person who is most knowledgeable about herself, and the individual's perspective is valued and affirmed. Feminist therapists strive toward being authentically themselves in the therapeutic experience and attempt to engender a mutual expression of empathy (Enns, 2004; Jordan, Surrey, & Kaplan, 1991; Miller & Stiver, 1997). This *mutual empathy* is a shared activity in which both the client and the practitioner participate as fully as possible. In this regard, as treatment evolves, empathic understanding becomes a reciprocal and collaborative interaction between a client and a practitioner. This conception has also been termed *relational empathy,* which involves empathy for oneself and for others in the context of the counseling process (Jordan et al., 1991).

As a *self-in-relation* model, the therapeutic process promotes a secure base for women to separate or distance themselves from oppressive relationships or conditions in the context of their lives (Jordan, 2001; Jordan et al., 1991). Gender-linked inequities in power is a prominent issue in feminist therapy, and a mutuality in the expression of empathy contributes to a balance of power within the treatment relationship (Miller, 1986; Worrell & Johnson, 2001). At the same time, engendering empathic exchanges affirms a woman's orientation toward relationship and caring, qualities that are frequently devalued in society (Murdock, 2004). From an affirmative perspective, Miller (1986) wrote, "Women, more easily than men, can believe that any activity is more satisfying when it takes place in the context of relationships to human beings—and even more so when it leads to the enhancement of others" (p. 49). The cultivation of relational consciousness also enables women to reduce a sense of isolation that may put them at risk to conditions of threat and violence in culturally embedded contexts (Miller, 1986).

Family Systems Therapy

Although there are various schools of family therapy, most contemporary treatment models utilize a systems perspective that guides theory and practice (Fall, Holden, & Marquis, 2004; Gladding, 2002). Systems theory reflects the principle of circular causality where each member's interactive behavior within a family mutually influences the functioning of all other family members (Nystul, 2003). In this conceptualization, individuals are perceived as being an integral part of a larger interrelated family. Consequently, a family therapist gives particular focus to qualitative aspects of relationships and communication patterns within the family. Furthermore, family members tend to demonstrate a consistency of behavior within a family in order to preserve a dynamic equilibrium, as change within the system can be destabilizing and disruptive. Even when problems continue in a family and individual member's needs are not met, the family typically seeks to maintain homeostasis or a balance (Nystul, 2003). In general terms, a family therapist's awareness of systems thinking can contribute to an empathic understanding of the actions of family members within a broader systemic context. With respect to this point, Domokos-Cheng Ham (1989) related that in a family therapy context, "the study of empathy can offer a framework for understanding a multiperspective view of human behavior" (p. 39).

In the presentation of a communication model that has implications for change in a family system, Warner (1989) discussed the operation of strategic family interactions that can impede or block empathic understanding and open communication. In order to empathically understand strategic family communication, a therapist should be aware that communication in a family represents two levels of meaning: strategic and surface. Strategic communication has an instrumental value for family members that is not overtly expressed. As an example, the acting-out of a family member may produce an emotional closeness among family members—even if the communication involves frequent arguments and disputes. Family members generally attain a sense of equilibrium and familiarity with strategic maneuvers, and the alternative of more open or surface communication is uncertain and potentially more painful. If a therapist prematurely and repeatedly directs his or her attention to strategic communication within a family, the family members may feel that the practitioner lacks an empathic understanding of the behavioral dynamics of the family and is insensitive to their individual needs. Even though family members may recognize that situations may be out of control, there is a fear that prematurely examining their intentions too closely may make matters worse and possibly subject individuals to exposure and vulnerability. At the same time, however, if a therapist maintains a surface level of understanding and does not challenge the strategic positions of family members, the possibility for change in a family system becomes remote.

In order to therapeutically address strategic positioning within a family, Warner (1989) stated, "If therapists can understand strategic maneuvers within the family and still maintain a sense of empathy and prizing for family members, an overall atmosphere of trust can develop in the family" (p. 337). A therapist may empathically understand that symptomatic behavior has a strategic value, and that family members are covertly expressing their needs. Specifically, Warner (1989) suggested that a therapist may empathically reduce the escalation of strategic interactions on the part of family members by minimizing intrusiveness and respecting the conflictive emotions of individuals as they approach therapeutic change. In another model that considers the influence of empathic understanding within a family system, Snyder (1992) suggested that family members be taught how to employ empathy in their mutual interactions. Through a process of explanation, demonstration, modeling, and feedback, individuals learn how to more effectively communicate feelings and personal views. As family members become more adept at expressing and receiving empathic understanding, they tend to become less defensive and are more open in their communication.

SUMMARY

Empathy as a therapeutic construct is accepted and practiced across a wide range of contemporary counseling and psychotherapy approaches. However, the goals and function of empathic understanding differ among the psychotherapies in a treatment situation. In person-centered therapy and self psychology, empathy is a significant and critical function in the theory and practice of each model. The literature of both traditions frequently makes reference to empathy as a pivotal influence in affecting client progress. Empathy is also prominent in Individual Psychology, existential therapy, and cognitive-behavioral and cognitive therapy. There is occasional reference to the construct in the written works of each of the therapies, and empathic understanding is observable in therapeutic practice. In various other psychotherapies, empathy is recognizable in the treatment process, but direct reference to the conception is infrequent, and empathic understanding within the professional literature is more often implied than explicitly documented.

Chapter 4

Person-Centered Therapy and Empathy

In the theory and practice of client-centered therapy, there is no concept more important than empathy.
—Raskin (2001, p. 1)

As a graduate student in the early 1970s, while I was studying one afternoon in the university library, I recall coming across Rogers's (1961) book, *On Becoming a Person.* I found the work so captivating that I read most of it over the next few hours. The text has a personal quality that seemed to speak directly to me and gave expression to Rogers's beliefs about the inherent value of persons and the vast range of human potentialities. During my years of training in the human services, I became further acquainted with the writings of Rogers and his client-centered therapy and was attracted to the clarity and sensitivity of its conceptions and treatment. Rogers's approach seemed relatively easy to grasp with its positive view of human nature and lack of emphasis on formal psychological evaluations, its minimal exploration of a client's past, and limited number of advanced treatment interventions. Reflection, as the major therapeutic technique of client-centered therapy, did not appear to be too complex to understand, nor did it seem difficult to develop some degree of proficiency with the intervention. In my early experiences in counseling, I also found that reflection was quite effective with clients and assisted me in empathically expressing an understanding of their experiencing through a procedure of mirroring back feelings and perceptions.

In the years since my early introduction to Rogers's ideas, I have come to appreciate even more his insights into the human condition and the sophistication of his treatment approach, which is often underestimated in the therapeutic community. Looking back at my initial grasp of client-centered therapy, I realized that I had a simplistic and narrow view of its theory and practices. I also mistakenly equated the technique of reflection with Rogers's conception of empathy or empathic understanding. Today, in my professional capacity as a professor in a graduate counseling program, I find that students generally view what is now called *person-centered therapy* in a manner that is similar to my experience as a student many years ago. Most students seem to be attracted to the positive and uplifting human quality of the theory and the accessibility of the treatment process. Typically, students-in-training find reflection to be an intriguing and purposeful intervention in counseling. At the same time, however, they sometimes express reservations about the technique due to its seemingly circular function of repeating back client verbalizations and the constricted limits imposed by attempting to stay within a client's frame of reference. Student criticisms also surface regarding the seemingly limited possibilities in person-centered therapy for affecting client change involving a range of more versatile and challenging treatment interventions. Furthermore, the practice applications of the theory to the treatment efficacy of long-term dysfunctional behavior is at times called into question. Yet, even with these reservations, students frequently rank person-centered therapy among the highest of all of the orientations that they study.

CARL ROGERS AND EMPATHY

No other individual has done more to bring prominence to the pivotal role of empathy in the psychotherapeutic relationship than Carl Rogers (Barrett-Lennard, 2003; Hackney, 1978; Wispé, 1987). Rogers and his colleagues have produced a substantial number of investigations with respect to the construct of empathy over a period of many years (Bozarth, 1997). Although empathy has been mentioned in a treatment context since early in the 20th century, Rogers succinctly defined its therapeutic meaning and popularized its operation in counseling and psychotherapy (Haugh & Merry, 2001; Teich, 1992c). Fifty years ago, Rogers (1957) identified empathy, in addition to unconditional positive regard and congruence, as essential variables for engendering client change in the therapy process. Since Rogers first introduced the facilitative or core conditions, they have been among the most frequently recognized and researched *common factors* relating to the treatment relationship (Bachelor & Horvath, 1999; Kirschenbaum, 2004). At various points in his writings, Rogers made specific observations about the value of empathy in the therapeutic experience. In this regard, Rogers (1980) wrote, "Empathic listening provided one of the least clouded windows into the workings of the human psyche, in all its complex mystery" (p. 50). In one of his last publications, Rogers (1986b) stated, "To my mind, empathy is in itself a healing agent. It is one of the most potent aspects of therapy, because it releases, it confirms, it brings even the most frightened client into the human race. If a person can be understood, he or she belongs" (p. 129). Rogers also extended the function of empathy beyond the treatment process as he expanded and pursued his interests through a person-centered approach into the broader domains of education, business, and the building of community (Barrett-Lennard, 1998; Kahn, 1989).

PERSON-CENTERED PERSPECTIVES ON EMPATHY

Over a period of decades, Rogers's definition of empathy evolved and became more comprehensive and precise. Rogers was constant in his views that empathy centers on the internal frame of reference of a client and manifests an attitudinal stance of a counselor or a therapist. Through his research, Rogers came to recognize that beyond a practitioner's expression of empathic understanding, the variable must be accurately perceived by the client. With his emphasis on the immediate frame of reference of a client, Rogers believed that a counselor's judgments and evaluations have the effect of diminishing and biasing client understanding and are often perceived as a form of psychological threat. Preconceived views of a client appear to compromise the capacity of a practitioner to understand the uniqueness and potentialities of the individual in a treatment situation. Rogers (1957) identified particular facilitative or attitudinal conditions in therapy that he regarded as necessary and sufficient for client growth. He viewed congruence, unconditional positive regard, and empathic understanding as constituting the definable conditions that are essential for a therapist to provide in the context of the therapeutic relationship. In a related direction, several major personality constructs in person-centered theory contribute to empathically understanding clients in counseling and psychotherapy. The concept of the self, the actualizing tendency, and congruence are central formulations of Rogers's therapeutic approach that have significant implications in the treatment process.

Defining Empathy

Rogers articulated and refined his thoughts on empathy in a number of publications (Raskin, 2001). Although he did not explicitly define empathy in a therapeutic context until 1957, Rogers made reference to related conceptualizations in his earlier writings. In 1949, Rogers stated that it is the counselor's function "to perceive the world as a client sees it, to perceive the client himself as he is seen by himself, to lay aside all perceptions from the external frame of reference while doing so" (p. 86). In his widely acclaimed *Client-Centered Therapy* (1951), Rogers repeated this same rendition, but added, "and to communicate something of this understanding to the client" (p. 29). At this point, Rogers was aware of the importance of communicating that which is perceived by the counselor with skill and sensitivity. In another direction, Rogers recognized distinctions and cautions relating to a practitioner's identification with a client. Rogers (1951) makes reference to an empathic identification, "where the counselor is perceiving the hates and hopes and fears of the client through immersion in an empathic process, but without himself, as the counselor, experiencing those hopes and fears" (p. 129). In this regard, Rogers (1951) further delineated the role of a practitioner in assuming an attitudinal stance, as opposed to an emotional identification, in understanding the experiencing of a client.

In 1957, Rogers published a highly influential article that provided defining qualities of empathy, and identified additional facilitative conditions in therapy. Rogers emphasized particular aspects of perceiving a client's experience, which had the immediate effect of stimulating extensive research and controversy within the traditions of counseling and psychotherapy. Rogers (1957) defined empathy in terms of a therapist being able "to sense the client's private world as if it were your own, but without ever losing the 'as if' quality—this is empathy, and this seems essential to therapy" (p. 99). From Rogers's perspective, in the absence of a focus on an "as if" condition, a state of identification may occur between a counselor and a client that is deleterious (Teich, 1992c). In this respect, Rogers recognized inherent difficulties with identification when the practitioner ignored or merged his or her psychological boundaries with a client (Schmid, 2001). In contrast, the "as if" quality serves to minimize the possibility of a therapist assuming an evaluative or judgmental stance toward a client. Through an emotionally distant posture inherent in an appraisal process, the therapist is susceptible to objectifying a client.

Building on earlier versions of defining empathy, Rogers (1959) articulated his most comprehensive and well-known definition of empathy in which he held that the therapist attempts "to perceive the internal frame of reference of another with accuracy, and with emotional components and meanings which pertain thereto, as if one were the other person, but without ever losing the 'as if' condition" (p. 210). As in his earlier definitions of empathy, Rogers believed that it is essential for a therapist to set aside one's perceptions from an external point of view (Bozarth, 1998). The efforts of the counselor to accurately perceive a client's internal frame of reference establishes a posture that provides an uncompromised degree of empathic understanding. Rogers also recognized the importance of a therapist both understanding a client's emotional and affective experiencing and comprehending the meaning of an individual's perceptions. Encompassing both affective and cognitive dimensions within his definition of empathy enabled Rogers to include a broad level of client functioning, while avoiding an emphasis on one quality or the other.

Rogers (1959) designated the "state of empathy or being empathic" as distinct from the communication exchange in a therapist's interactions with a client. In his view, being empathic focuses on accurately and sensitively perceiving the functioning of a client in the immediacy of the therapeutic relationship (Rogers, 1966). Rogers came to prefer the terms *empathic understanding, accurate empathic understanding,* or *understanding responses* as they relate to perceiving a client's frame of reference and subsequently communicating aspects of this experience to the individual (Schmid, 2001). Rogers also presented qualitative aspects of empathic understanding with respect to the relative depth or extent of client awareness. In this regard, Rogers (1957) stated that a therapist may "voice meanings in clients' experience of which the client is scarcely aware" (p. 99). Bohart (2004) observed that an empathic therapist introduces variations in what a client states by using different words or drawing out implications from a new or different angle. Through the interpersonal experience of empathic understanding as a source of knowledge, the counselor verifies or disproves inferences and hypotheses by consistently checking with a client (Rogers, 1959).

In 1975, Rogers provided a comprehensive analysis of current research on empathy and what the construct meant to him as *a way of being.* Through a reexamination and reevaluation of the topic, Rogers (1975) stated that empathy "is one of the most delicate and powerful ways we have of using ourselves" (p. 2). In a notable shift from his earlier position as "the state of empathy" (Rogers, 1959, p. 210), he now made reference to empathy as a "process." With this semantic change, Rogers attempted to offer a more precise depiction of empathy that implied a constancy of sustained engagement on the part of the practitioner (Watson, 2002).

From a research perspective, Rogers presented recent findings on the beneficial effects of the empathic process on clients in treatment and other recipients of empathy outside of therapy. Rogers also discussed the integral place of empathy in the context of the other two facilitative conditions of therapeutic change. Citing extensive research evidence, Rogers (1975) concluded that "a high degree of empathy in a relationship is possibly *the* most potent and certainly one of the most potent factors in bringing about change and learning" (p. 3). With his emphasis on attitudinal aspects of empathy, Rogers also expressed his disdain for contemporary trends in the counseling and psychotherapy community in which empathic listening was viewed operationally as a communication skill or a technique. In explicating a description of the process of empathic understanding, Rogers provided a prominent focus to the construct of experiencing as formulated by Gendlin (1961). A counselor's awareness of the implicit *felt-level experiencing* of a client at a particular moment provides a referent for enriching empathic understanding. A practitioner also encourages a client to become aware of the "psychophysiological flow" of events that occurs continuously within the individual (Rogers, 1975).

Frame of Reference and Empathy

In his most comprehensive definition of empathy, Rogers (1957) stated that a therapist attempts "to perceive the internal frame of reference of another with accuracy . . ." (p. 210). In assuming this position, Rogers set a direction that had explicit implications for the theory and practice of his theoretical orientation. Through the course of his writings, Rogers held an enduring view of the importance of a practitioner maintaining a consistent focus on the subjective perspective of a client. In 1949, Rogers stated "that it is the counselor's function to assume, in so far as he is able, the internal frame of reference of the client, to perceive the world as the client sees it, to perceive the client himself as he is seen by himself, and to lay aside all perceptions from the external frame of reference while doing so" (p. 86). Rogers felt that as a result of maintaining an emphasis on a client's frame of reference, a therapist's personal conflicts and biases would be less likely to interfere with or hinder therapeutic process. By attempting to avoid an evaluative stance, a counselor minimizes the possibility of an antitherapeutic emotional entanglement with a client.

Citing examples from an external frame of reference, Rogers (1949) depicted the counselor as functioning in the capacity of an external perceiver who is emotionally detached from the client. In a therapy session with a client, a practitioner may experience such evaluative thoughts as, "Why this indecisiveness?" "What could be the cause?" "What is meant by this focus on marriage and family?" "The crying, the 'dam,' sound as though there must be a great deal of repression" (Rogers, 1949, p. 88). In contrast, Rogers provided examples of a counselor's thoughts that successfully focus on a client's internal frame of reference in the same treatment situation: "It's really hard for you to get started." "You want marriage, but it doesn't seem to you to be much of a possibility." "You find yourself brimming over with childish feelings." "But it has been—and is—a disturbing experience for you" (Rogers, 1949, p. 88).

An evaluation of a client typically occurs when a counselor or a therapist assumes an external frame of reference with respect to the individual. In Rogers's view, a counselor who thinks in evaluative and judgmental terms begins to perceive the client as an object and this has an effect of inhibiting understanding (Rogers, 1951). Rogers held this same perspective a number of years later when he stated, "External and evaluative understanding tends to focus the client's being on himself as object or upon intellectualizations that remove him from an ongoing contact with the experiencing going on within him" (Rogers, 1966, p. 187). Colleagues and researchers who have followed Rogers have supported his views with respect to the negative effect of imposing an evaluative external frame of reference on a client. Hansen (2000) believed that in order to truly understand the experience of a client, it was important to discard preconceived psychological conceptions or frameworks. Employing a fixed frame of reference with a client, according to Kalisch (1973), restricts the possibility that a therapist will be flexible and open-minded and in tune with the immediate feelings of the individual. Boy and Pine (1982), emphatically stated, "Looking at another person according to external and objective criteria is one of the most inhibiting barriers to effective communication" (p. 135).

In a comprehensive explication of his client-centered conceptualizations and practices, Rogers (1959) presented a specific formulation of the meaning of the internal frame of reference of a person as a locus of evaluation. Rogers wrote about the construct, "This is all of the realm of experience which is available to the awareness of the individual at a given moment. It includes the full range of perceptions, meanings, and memories which are available to consciousness" (p. 210). For Rogers, a therapeutic aim for a counselor is to sustain a focus on a client's internal frame of reference or phenomenological point of view over the duration of the therapy process. When a practitioner functions from outside of this treatment stance by offering advice, interpretations, or judgments, the possibility of therapeutic gain diminishes and the potential for practitioner bias increases (Rogers, 1966).

Contrastingly, in Rogers's view, when a client focuses on his or her internal condition, the individual begins to recognize experiencing that is at variance with psychologically healthy or congruent functioning. By minimizing the employment of therapeutic techniques, Rogers also wished to give further emphasis to the key role of the facilitative conditions for promoting therapeutic progress. In one of his later writings, Rogers (1975) reaffirmed the importance of recognizing a client's subjective perspectives. He stated, "To be with another in this way means for the time being you lay aside the views and values that you hold for yourself in order to enter another's world without prejudice" (p. 4). After reviewing written and recorded counseling transcripts, Brodley (1999) observed that in Rogers's treatment approach he expressed only a small percentage of responses that were outside of a client's frame of reference. Brodley also recognized that therapists who minimize interventions from their own frame of reference tend to promote a secure and stable treatment climate. In contrast, when a therapist does represent his or her own frame of reference, the client may experience a sense of misunderstanding and nonacceptance.

Although Rogers was clear from a theoretical standpoint about the importance of a counselor or a therapist attempting to empathically function within a client's frame of reference, others have questioned the viability of this position (Kalisch, 1973; Tobin, 1991). Furthermore, researchers have also pointed out that Rogers did occasionally express interventions from his own frame of reference, particularly in the latter phase of his career in group work activity. It is also reasonable to assume that momentary fluctuations that inevitably occur in empathic understanding and other facilitative conditions need not compromise a practitioner's commitment to the core attitudes (Brodley, 1999). Strategically, a counselor can empathically follow up interventions that are outside of a client's frame of reference, such as responses to questions and requests, in order to maintain or restore client understanding.

In an observation that suggests Rogers may have experienced conflictive positions, Bozarth (1998) stated that "During much of Rogers' life there was an inner conflict between observing an individual from the outside and understanding a person from the person's frame of reference. The former view was important to him in research and the latter view in his clinical work" (p. 64). Other investigators have also recognized a contradiction between aspects of Rogers's conceptual formulations and his therapeutic practices (Elliot, Greenberg, & Lietaer, 2004; Kalisch, 1973; Tobin, 1991). Although Rogers emphasized the facilitative conditions of unconditional positive regard, congruence, and empathic understanding, he also acknowledged that a counselor should express feelings in general, including anger, boredom, and other negative emotions if they "persist" (Tobin, 1991). In this regard, Rogers (1966) stated, "If I sense that I am feeling bored by a client and if this feeling persists, I think that I owe it to him and our relationship to share my feelings with him" (p. 185). It is apparent that such feelings relate to the external frame of reference of the practitioner.

In defense of Rogers's seemingly contradictory perspective, he recognized that a therapist's attitudinal stance of congruence was fundamental to the quality of a therapeutic relationship (Rogers & Sanford, 1985). Building a relationship predicated on a lack of honesty and genuineness was dehumanizing for Rogers, and therefore he found it necessary to occasionally express responses from his subjective orientation. Rogers also stated that the feelings of a counselor toward a client needed to persist and were not merely immediate emotional reactions subject to unrestrained and impulsive verbal expression. Finally, in the latter period of Rogers's career, he became extensively involved in group work, and it is common practice for group leaders to express personal reactions to the behavior or functioning of group members in the form of feedback (Barrett-Lennard, 1998; Rogers, 1970).

In a more critical view, Wolowitz (2002) observed that some therapists may be reluctant to function outside of an empathic stance and tend to predominantly focus on a client's frame of reference for less than therapeutic reasons. By maintaining a constant and inflexible empathic role, a practitioner as a consequence rarely has to assume responsibility to respond in a more spontaneous or authentic capacity. This point is similar to the existential call for a mutual dialogue and encounter between a client and a practitioner in a therapeutic relationship (Buber, 1957, 1958; Buber & Rogers, 1969). Kahn (1985), also writing from a less favorable perspective, found Rogers's treatment approach "limited" because it largely focused on the current functioning of a client and minimized the importance of giving consideration to an individual's developmental history or overall pattern of functioning.

Rogers (1966) did, in fact, attempt to clarify the meaning of a client's inner experience in his or her immediate frame of reference. At the same time, he also went beyond responding to the obvious phenomenological functioning of a client and sought to address implicit meanings at the edge of an individual's awareness. In this regard, Rogers (1986b) stated, "I do not minimize the importance of dealing with the past as it is remembered in the present" (p. 137). Rogers's focus, however, on the immediacy of the experience of a client's functioning may be perceived as emphasizing the present, which is consistent with his preference for a minimal counselor role with respect to client history taking (Rogers, 1951, 1961). Interventions based on efforts to therapeutically function within a client's frame of reference have direct implications for a practitioner's use of treatment interactions. As an example, Rogers (1951, 1980) rejected the use of interpretation in counseling and psychotherapy primarily because he believed that the technique imposed external and evaluative perspectives on a client.

The Facilitative Conditions

Even though Rogers had made reference to various treatment elements that promote therapeutic change in the early 1940s, it was not until 1957 that he organized his various conceptualizations into what became a classic article in counseling and psychotherapy. Rogers (1957) believed that six conditions needed to exist over a period of time in order to effect constructive personality change. The first two variables—two persons in psychological contact and a client in a state of incongruence—were assumed to exist when Rogers discussed the treatment factors in subsequent writings. The essential conditions included: "The therapist is congruent or integrated in the relationship;" "the therapist experiences unconditional positive regard for the client;" and, "the therapist experiences an empathic understanding of the client's internal frame of reference and endeavors to communicate this experience to the client" (Rogers, 1957, p. 96). Rogers also included a sixth condition that included the communication of the therapist's empathic understanding and unconditional positive regard. In his subsequent writings, Rogers integrated the communication factor with empathic understanding and unconditional positive regard, and did not continue to articulate the function as a separate variable. Thus, what remained from the original six therapeutic conditions were *congruence, unconditional positive regard,* and *empathic understanding,* and they have become known as the "core" or "facilitative" conditions within a therapeutic relationship (Norcross, 2002; Patterson, 1984; Wyatt & Sanders, 2002).

In conceptualizing the facilitative conditions, Rogers evoked controversy and debate in the psychotherapeutic community over the premise that the elements were "*necessary* to initiate constructive personality change, and which, taken together, appear to be *sufficient* to inaugurate that process" (Rogers, 1957, p. 95). In a point that is often overlooked, Rogers presented the qualities as a series of hypotheses in order to extend theoretical knowledge in the field relating to psychotherapeutic change. Extensive discussion in the professional literature centered on the role of each of the attitudinal conditions in the treatment process (Patterson, 1984). What became more debatable, however, was the question of whether, taken together, the factors were *necessary and sufficient* for psychotherapeutic change. Lambert and Barley (2002) suggested that the core conditions constitute the most studied relationship factors in the theory and practice of counseling and psychotherapy. In a contemporary view of the therapeutic conditions identified by Rogers, most investigators consider the qualities important, with varying degrees of emphasis, for contributing to a positive relationship in therapy (Bachelor & Horvath, 1999). At the same time, researchers generally agree that the facilitative conditions are not sufficient in themselves for engendering personality change.

When Rogers conceptualized the facilitative conditions, he recognized that congruence, unconditional positive regard, and empathic understanding are integrally related in treatment practice (Bozarth, 1998). Each condition converges with the other attitudinal qualities within the treatment relationship and, when effectively communicated and perceived by a client, promote therapeutic movement (Rogers, 1965, 1966; Rogers & Sanford, 1985; Wyatt & Sanders, 2002). Rogers was consistent in advocating the importance of a practitioner's attempt to maintain the attitudinal conditions over the duration of the therapy, and he did offer opinion on the order of their importance in effecting positive client growth (Bozarth, 1998). Rogers also believed that therapeutic treatment is most fully effective when all three qualities are actively present to a high degree (Rogers & Sanford, 1985). In this regard, Rogers's intent was to create a nonjudgmental therapeutic climate that enables the practitioner to accurately and sensitively communicate an understanding of a client's perspectives.

Although Rogers believed that the facilitative conditions for therapy were logically intertwined, he recognized congruence as the most basic in terms of therapeutic importance (Rogers & Sanford, 1985; Van Balen, 1990). Rogers (1966) reasoned that unless a counselor or therapist attempts to be genuine and fully integrated in the treatment relationship, the other attitudinal conditions could not possibly be meaningful. Characteristic qualities of a congruent practitioner involved the individual's awareness of his or her experiencing with a client and an ability to openly and honestly express feelings and perceptions. Congruence also implies that the counselor is "real" and spontaneous in the relationship, and that there is a consistency in the individual's behavior over a period of time. Furthermore, the therapist avoids conveying a "false front" by judiciously expressing or acknowledging his or her persistent feelings toward a client. In this regard, a quest for authenticity does not mean that a therapist impulsively divulges or blurts out all reactions about a client that come to mind (Corey, 2005; Rogers & Sanford, 1985). As with other effective interventions, self-disclosures by a practitioner should be purposeful and well timed. Although congruence may be sought by a counselor in the treatment relationship, it does not mean that the individual must be genuine or authentic in all phases of his or her life (Fall, Holden, & Marquis, 2004). Finally, as with each of the other facilitative elements, the existence of congruence with respect to a therapist may be represented on a continuum instead of an absolute presence or absence of the factor (Corey, 2005).

In a counseling example of congruence, an early-adolescent client is uncharacteristically withdrawn over the last two treatment sessions. In response, the counselor discloses, "I'm trying hard to reach you, but I feel like I'm becoming even more distant from you, and I find this frustrating." By expressing this self-involving statement, the counselor openly acknowledges feelings rather than maintaining a pretense that a satisfactory level of mutual communication exists in interactions with the client. Consequently, treatment can be inhibited if a practitioner experiences persistent feelings toward a client and feigns acceptance by acting in a way that overlooks or minimizes his or her feelings (Corey, 2005). After a disclosure, the practitioner is also in a position to empathically respond to the client and address any possible misunderstanding.

To continue the example of the adolescent who is uncharacteristically withdrawn, the client reacts in a hurt and resentful tone after the practitioner acknowledges her growing frustrations: "You told me that you would ask for my permission before calling my mother, and you called her without telling me." In response, the counselor empathically relates, "You are hurt that I let you down and broke an agreement that we had between us." In these instances, a higher level of a counselors' or therapists' congruence contributes to the effectiveness of empathic understanding because the practitioner is less prone to being diverted by inner referents and defensive reactions that may interfere with open communication (Vanaerschot, 1990). Consider the breakdown in the client's perception of the counselor's congruence if the practitioner had said, "Well, there are times in my professional position when I have to take steps that are for your own good even though it may not seem that way to you right now."

Unconditional positive regard was the second condition that Rogers (1957) identified as being essential for therapeutic gain in the treatment process. In this stance, the therapist experiences and communicates a deep and sensitive caring that affirms a client's constructive potentialities and worth as a person (Rogers, 1966; Rogers & Sanford, 1985; Schmid, 2003). Rogers came to use various other terms for unconditional positive regard including *warmth, nonpossessive warmth or caring, acceptance, caring,* and *prizing.* He thought that caring needed to be uncontaminated by judgments about an individual's feelings, thoughts, or behaviors (Rogers, 1966). In this regard, a counselor or therapist demonstrates positive feelings toward a client and a warm acceptance that is relatively free of evaluation (Fall et al., 2004). The acceptance of a client does not depend on the individual's functioning in a particular way that happens to meet the conditional approval of the counselor. The nonpossessive or attitudinal response of the practitioner also affirms the autonomy of a client. Fall et al. (2004) observed that a therapeutic environment that is conducive to self-prizing and growth serves as a counterconditioning function in which a client's negative sense of self-worth is deconstructed and modified in the direction of unconditional self-regard.

In a therapy example of unconditional positive regard, Jerry, a 50-year-old client, expresses conflictive feelings because he failed to visit his elderly parent when he was on a recent business trip to the city in which she resides. Rather than visiting his mother in her apartment, Jerry decided to stay overnight in a hotel. Jerry states to the therapist, "I feel kind of guilty that I didn't drop in to see her when I was in town, but I just wasn't up to it." In response, the therapist empathetically relates, "You feel like you let your mother down. At the same time, you have also talked about being quite busy lately, and perhaps needed some time alone." The practitioner's statement reflects a nonjudgmental stance that respectfully acknowledges the client's feelings and behavior. It is also possible that a therapist might react from a position that indicates a lack of unconditional positive regard. In contrast, consider an alternative response in which the counselor says, "You're feeling some guilt about not dropping in to visit your mother, and this is fully understandable because she does live alone and is quite elderly." Although the counselor acknowledges an aspect of the client's feelings, it is done with an underlying evaluative and judgmental tone. The statement may also imply that the acceptance of the client by the counselor is contingent on a conditional way of behaving. Bozarth (1998) makes the point that unconditional positive regard is inseparable from empathic understanding and also suggests that ultimately they are the same condition.

As the third conceptualization of the facilitative conditions that promote constructive client change, empathy converges with the other attitudinal elements of congruence and unconditional positive regard in the immediacy of the therapeutic relationship (Bozarth, 1998; Raskin, 2001). An explicit assumption of the factor of unconditional positive regard of a client requires that it be integral to a practitioner's experience of empathic understanding. In this regard, there is a sensitive and acceptant understanding of a client's feelings and experiences, and the meaning that they have for the individual (Rogers & Sanford, 1985). Through a sustained process of warm acceptance, true empathy must not be compromised with evaluative or diagnostic formulations on the part of a therapist (Rogers, 1980). In Rogers's later writings, the theoretical link between empathic understanding and congruence became even stronger (Rogers, 1975, 1980; Rogers & Sanford, 1985). At this point in his evolving thinking, Rogers began to emphasize the intuitive function of the therapist. He also saw empathy as an extremely active process in terms of a "total" attunement with a client (Bozarth, 1998; Rogers & Sanford, 1985). "It is in moments when therapists experience empathy with their clients so deep as to become intuitive, a response by the whole organism, that major shifts occur" (Rogers & Sanford, 1985, p. 1374). In this late period of his conceptualizing, Rogers recognized the discrete functions of each core condition, and he was more fully aware of the interactive nature of the attitudinal qualities.

In an interesting observation, Watts (1996) and Watts and Pietrzak (2000) presented evidence suggesting that Alfred Adler may have influenced Rogers's conceptualization of the facilitative conditions (Feller & Cottone, 2003). Rogers held an internship position at the Institute of Child Guidance (now defunct) in New York City from 1927 to 1928. As an intern at the institute, Rogers stated, "I had the privilege of meeting, listening to, and observing Dr. Alfred Adler" (Ansbacher, 1990, p. 47). Adler was a visiting instructor at the institute, and Rogers related, "It took me some time to realize how much I had learned from him" (Ansbacher, 1990, p. 47). Watts (1996) felt that Adler's description of social interest in the treatment relationship had apparent commonalities with Rogers's (1957) therapeutic conditions of congruence, unconditional positive regard, and empathic understanding. In his therapy approach, Adler expressed a respect for and confidence in his clients, and he demonstrated an encouraging and empathic way of listening. Watts (1996) thought that of the three conditions of therapeutic change, empathic understanding was most directly related to the expression of social interest.

Personality Constructs and Empathy

Several prominent constructs within the person-centered approach have direct implications for empathic understanding. The actualizing tendency, the self, and congruence are basic formulations that have evolved through the writings of Rogers and his colleagues (Thorne, 2003). An awareness of each conception enhances a practitioner's ability to understand a client's behavior and employ empathy in the therapeutic process. Rogers (1961, 1975, 1980) held an optimistic view about the inherent capacity of individuals to develop their potentialities (Thorne, 2003). Through a striving for fulfillment, there is a movement toward growth and autonomy in ways that enhance the organism (Barrett-Lennard, 1993, 1998, 2003; Rogers & Sanford, 1985). This actualizing tendency is a natural process that occurs when individuals are provided supportive and nurturing environmental conditions. As persons actualize their potentialities they become less defensive, more flexible, more self-directed and able to accurately perceive reality (Nystul, 2003). In terms of empathic understanding, maintaining an assumption that individuals strive toward growth enhancement enables a counselor or a therapist to recognize and foster the actualizing tendency of clients. On the other hand, a client's lack of striving or psychological dysfunction suggests the existence of possible external forces of a pathogenic environment that restrict or impede growth and development (Ewen, 2003).

In a treatment process that manifests the facilitative conditions, a client is able to experience support and understanding in order to progress toward actualizing his or her potentialities and to gain an undistorted perception of the self. The self is a concept of utmost importance in person-centered therapy, and therapeutic progress is integrally related to constructive change in the abstraction of the self (Rogers, 1964). The concept of the self involves a set of organized perceptions about the self that is a constant referent for an individual to use in terms of a "tool" or a "map" to guide behavior (Bohart, 1991; Rogers & Sanford, 1985). Rogers (1964) often hypothesized the self as the dynamic core of the personality that includes perceived values that are attached to the self-concept. Another major personality construct, congruence, represents a state of psychological adjustment that is achieved through a compatibility between an individual's experiencing and the concept of the self. When congruent, one is less defensive, more accepting of oneself and others, more able to problem solve, and has more realistic and objective perceptions (Rogers, 1959). These qualities are consistent with an individual who is actualizing his or her potentialities in the mental health model of a fully functioning person (Rogers, 1959; Rogers & Sanford, 1985).

An experience that is not congruent with the self structure frequently is perceived as threatening and produces a defensive reaction or response. Inherent in a defensive reaction is a state reflecting tension, confusion, and anxiety. Consider the example of a young-adulthood client, Allen, who has a diagnosis of dependent personality disorder. Allen believes that he lacks the capabilities to act in more independent ways and has come to repeatedly rely on others to assist him in numerous facets of his life. On occasions when Allen finds himself in a position that requires that he take action on his own, he frequently experiences threat, and his behavior becomes even more constricted and anxiety-laden. Functioning in an autonomous way is not congruent with Allen's self or self-concept, and he resists endeavors to prompt movement in this direction. Instead, Allen evokes defensive responses that rationalize his perceived inability to act more independently. Allen expresses such statements as, "I can't possibly make this decision without first talking to a couple of my friends," "I'm not ready to go it alone, and it is unfair to ask me to do it," and "I need to wait until my father is back from California so I can talk to him." A practitioner's ability to empathically understand the threat that independent functioning evokes for individuals such as Allen will be in a more favorable position to therapeutically address incongruence in counseling and psychotherapy.

THE TREATMENT RELATIONSHIP, THERAPEUTIC INTERVENTIONS, AND EMPATHY

In person-centered therapy, the treatment relationship as a central factor is grounded in a practitioner's acceptance, genuineness, and empathic way of being. Particular therapeutic interventions provide methods for conveying the facilitative attitudes. As early as 1949, Rogers made reference to client-centered therapy involving a "set of attitudes, which is implemented by techniques and methods consistent with it" (Rogers, 1949, p. 82). A counselor or a therapist attempts to sustain an empathic understanding by focusing on the internal frame of reference of a client while processing client interventions. Empathy has often been equated with the technique of reflection in the therapy process, and this misunderstanding has restricted full consideration of the employment of other interventions that involve empathic understanding. Although Rogers cautioned against the use of interpretation, his method of sensing the implicit meanings of a client is similar to the inferential or interpretation process found in various other treatment orientations.

The Treatment Relationship and Empathy

Integral to empathic understanding is a practitioner's ability to perceive the phenomenological experience of a client and to communicate aspects of this experiencing in a therapeutic relationship that emphasizes the value and worth of the person (Bozarth, 1998; Rogers, 1961). In the treatment relationship, Rogers (1980) wrote about becoming aware of the importance of a listening stance on the part of a therapist: "First, I had learned through hard and frustrating experiences that simply to listen understandingly to a client and to attempt to convey that understanding were potent forces for individual therapeutic change" (p. 50). In a similar direction, Breggin (1997, 2002) discussed the indispensability of allowing sufficient time and patience to create a *healing presence* that is consistent with the highest ethical standards. Rather than overly focusing on symptom relief, a practitioner must be able to perceptively listen and to share the meanings of a person's experience.

In an early work on empathy, Stewart (1956) wrote poignantly about the meaning of the construct from a perspective that is harmonious with the person-centered approach:

> What matters in empathy, or knowing about empathy, is the need to understand it as a participant activity, an activity requiring a belief in persons as the ultimate term of reference, as the ultimate reality, not minds, not bodies, not concepts, but persons, actual or imagined. (p. 134)

In contemporary research, there is a consensus that the therapeutic relationship is a significant component in person-centered therapy and other types of therapy in positively influencing the outcome of treatment (Bachelor & Horvath, 1999). To this point, Moursund and Erskine (2004) wrote, "Empathic understanding and empathic responsiveness lie at the roots of the therapeutic relationship. The various skills of empathy undergird all of the major psychotherapies being practiced today" (p. 95).

Therapeutic Interventions and Empathy

As much as Rogers wished to emphasize the relationship domain in the treatment process, he also recognized the importance of the technical sphere for substantiating the effectiveness of client-centered, and later, person-centered therapy. In the early 1950s, Rogers assumed a central leadership role in a large-scale research program that empirically evaluated the outcomes and concomitants of psychotherapy (Rogers & Dymond, 1954). The project examined the function of the therapist and the process of therapy from a client-centered perspective with disturbed or maladjusted clients. A number of years later, Rogers led a research program that studied the therapeutic relationship with hospitalized individuals with a diagnosis of schizophrenia and other psychotic disorders (Rogers, Gendlin, Kiesler, & Truax, 1967). Rogers and his associates compiled extensive psychometric data in order to appraise the therapeutic effect of the facilitative conditions and related factors in promoting personality and behavior change. Generally speaking, with respect to both treatment projects, client-centered therapy was found to be less effective with clients diagnosed with schizophrenia than with individuals who were more integrated in their psychological functioning.

After Rogers (1957) postulated the necessary and sufficient conditions for therapeutic growth, major research and training programs began to prominently focus on the development of practitioner skills. From the 1960s into the 1970s and beyond, training in counseling and psychotherapy programs frequently emphasized the acquisition of therapeutic competencies through the intentional development of effective practitioner responses. These instructional endeavors focused on identifying measures to assess the quality of the facilitative variables within the treatment and other interpersonal relationships (Carkhuff, 1987; Carkhuff & Berenson, 1977; Jacobs & Williams, 1983). As an example, a training and research instrument was devised for evaluating a counselor's expression of empathic understanding on a five-point scale from a minimal to an optimal level. Training efforts were undertaken to improve a student's therapy proficiency in executing empathic responses in the direction of the highest rating. The following examples of counselor responses represent quantitative and qualitative extremes of empathic understanding. A client states, "I have so many things that I'm mixed up about. I can't even begin to get at all of it." In response, a therapist conveys a minimal level of empathic understanding, "What you need to do is to draw up a list of things that are bothering you and address each item in terms of priorities." In another response that manifests a more optimal level of empathic understanding by validating the client's experience, the practitioner relates, "It seems that there is so much that is troubling to you, and even thinking about where to begin seems overwhelming."

After observing the progression of the skill development movement with dismay, Rogers (1980) stated that a focus on a therapist's responses rather than attitudes led to "appalling consequences" and a "complete distortion of client-centered therapy" (p. 139). Rather than emphasizing the internal state of a client, communication interactions had become a training and research focus (Bozarth, 1984; Hackney, 1978). Rogers repudiated the skills-oriented approach for narrowly stressing the technical and instrumental qualities of the counselor or therapist and bypassing critical aspects of experiencing a client as a unique and valued person (Hartley, 1995; Jacobs & Williams, 1983). At the same time, however, an emphasis on conceptualizing empathic understanding and other therapeutic qualities in operational terms created evaluative tools for assessing what largely is an abstract construct (Clark, 2004a). Having access to explicit descriptions of means to process and communicate empathic understanding enables practitioners to evaluate the therapeutic effectiveness of their treatment. In contemporary research, efforts continue to be made to explicate operational processes in person-centered therapy for practice purposes while concurrently retaining essential aspects of the facilitative conditions (Bozarth, 1998; Brink & Farber, 1996; Brodley, 1999; Glauser & Bozarth, 2001; Greenberg, Rice, & Elliot, 1993).

In an effort to convey empathic understanding, the verbal reflective mode of Rogers became prominent in the counseling and psychotherapy literature and in training endeavors (Bozarth, 1984; Noonan, 1981; Tolan, 2003). With an emphasis on reflection as the primary way to demonstrate empathy, other modes of expressing empathic understanding, such as counselor self-disclosure and inferential observations, were largely ignored (Bohart & Greenberg, 1997). As empathy became equated with the technique of reflection, research investigations began to narrowly focus on the measurement of operational methods for acting empathic (Bozarth, 1984). A confusing factor that contributed to this constricted view is that reflection as a technique inherently involves the expression of empathic understanding (Bozarth, 1998). Furthermore, other modes of employing empathy in the therapeutic process are less apparent and less amenable to training. Complicating matters even more, Carkhuff (1969) distinguished between the communication of an explicit level of empathy or interchangeable empathy, and an implicit empathy level or additive empathy (Turock, 1978). A similar explicit–implicit differentiation for communicating empathy became linked to the respective terms of primary empathy and advanced empathy. In each level of empathy, reflection is primarily represented, leading to the belief that empathy equates with reflection. Although leaders in the skill development movement in counseling and psychotherapy cautioned about confusing empathy with the client-centered mode of reflection (Carkhuff & Berenson, 1977), conceptualizing empathic understanding as an attitudinal aspect of a practitioner's human functioning was becoming more remote.

Toward the end of his life, Rogers (1986a) remarked that the greatest distortion of his professional work was the misunderstanding of reflection of feeling as a therapeutic technique (Bozarth, 1998). Rogers was disturbed that reflection of feeling was being rigidly taught as a technological expression of empathic understanding, and the attitudinal conditions were being marginalized. Rogers's determination to distance himself from reflection was so strong that he proposed the alternative linguistic terms of *testing understandings* and *checking perceptions* (Rogers, 1986a). At the same time, Rogers (1986a) acknowledged that although many of his responses in treatment practice could be perceived to be "reflections of feeling," it was not his intention to merely "reflect feelings." From Rogers's perspective, the meaning of reflection was being depicted as a superficial means of merely repeating or parroting a client's verbalized expressions. In the worst-case scenarios, Rogers's reflective statements were being repeated through wooden expressions that made a parody of his approach. As an example of this constricted interaction, consider the following exchange between an early-adolescent client and a school counselor. The client states, with feelings of dejection and humiliation, "I went into the school cafeteria for the first time, and I sat down and ate all by myself. Nobody sat down beside me. I felt like I was going to cry." In response, counselor says, "Going into the school cafeteria for the first time, you ate alone because nobody joined you. You almost cried."

Although Rogers recognized distortions of his positions as they related to reflection of feeling, he also observed that the misconceptions were in a large part due to his early emphasis on a therapist's methods rather than attitudes (Glauser & Bozarth, 2001). It is likely that Rogers was referring to his extensive research projects (Rogers & Dymond, 1954; Rogers et al., 1967) in which he and his associates operationally defined a number of client-centered constructs in order to quantify psychometric findings. In separating himself from the technique of reflection, Rogers also did not wish to have person-centered therapy linked with a particular method or methods. Yet, even though Rogers expressed misgivings about the use of reflection, his orientation continues to be identified with the technique. As an example, Wolowitz (2002) expressed a critical view of Rogers's approach relating to a therapist's persistent use of reflection, and the effect this has on foreclosing the creative implementation of alternative interventions. In this regard, a therapist assumes a subordinate position that is valued only for its mirroring function to reflect a client's feelings and perceptions. Consequently, it becomes unlikely that a practitioner will act outside of the role of an empathic therapist and begin to challenge a client with differences in perspectives.

Although reflection may be dismissed as superficial or trivial, when therapists attempt to convey an accurate understanding of a client's feelings and meanings, they are engaging in an indispensable process that "runs to the heart of person-centered theory" (Wilkins, 2003, p. 108). As a fundamental empathic activity, reflection involves a primary means by which a practitioner is able to verify the inner experience of a client (Brodley, 1996). When Rogers lamented the use of reflection as a term in person-centered therapy, it was not primarily a semantic concern that he found adverse; it was more the loss of the human element that was particularly troubling to him. Rogers resisted the movement of therapy toward a mechanical and manualized treatment approach that objectifies a client.

Yet, as much as Rogers wished to focus on empathic understanding and the other facilitative conditions within the therapeutic relationship, many researchers and practitioners pursued legitimate attempts to operationally define counseling and psychotherapy practices. In another broad consideration with training implications, there have been serious attempts to distinguish how practitioners and clients relate to each other in contrast with the specific techniques a counselor employs; yet it is difficult, if not impossible, to separate the two processes. Norcross (2002) summarized it in this way: "The relationship does not exist apart from what the therapist does in terms of technique, and we cannot imagine any techniques that would not have some relational impact" (p. 8). To this extent, the treatment relationship and therapeutic techniques are complementary and inseparable.

Rather than abandon the operational formulations of reflection, it seems to be a sound therapeutic direction to integrate the technique with empathic understanding and the other attitudinal conditions. In this respect, reflection has the potential to bridge the gap between the technical stance of a practitioner and the relationship domain that is essential for therapeutic progress. To this end, in recent years, prominent scholars in counseling and psychotherapy have published works that clarify reflection as a treatment skill, while acknowledging its broader function through empathic understanding as a facilitative condition (Cormier & Nurius, 2003; Egan, 2002; Ivey & Ivey, 2003; Welfel & Patterson, 2005). More specifically, for example, Ivey and Ivey (2003) distinguished between the interventions of reflection of feeling and reflection of meaning through an extensive discussion of empathy in the treatment relationship. Egan (2002) stated, "Empathy is seen as a basic *value* that informs and drives *all* helping behavior" (p. 48). In designating the use of a new term, Egan made reference to the "sharing empathic highlights" as a communication skill involving understanding and communicating key points that a client makes.

It is apparent that there are numerous contemporary attempts to employ reflection, or a variation of the term, within the broader forces of the therapeutic relationship in ways that seem to do justice to Rogers's facilitative conditions. Research continues to expand in this area, as suggested by the following discussion of *markers of vulnerability* (Greenberg, Rice, & Elliot, 1993), which defines markers as indicating those moments when clients experience intense vulnerability. These instances present opportunities for an empathic, highly affirming response by a therapist or a counselor. In the interpersonal context of the therapeutic relationship, the practitioner may employ reflection of feeling and reflection of meaning in situations in which the client expresses intense negative emotions that seem bottomless and engulfing. Because the client fears a loss of control and potential rejection as a result of having disclosed the emotions, he or she may be reluctant to reveal threatening experiences. The sensitive practitioner assumes a full awareness of the client's hesitancy to discuss markers that may be perceived, by the client as well as the counselor, as shameful, abnormal, or frightening.

Greenberg, Rice, and Elliot (1993) presented examples of markers of vulnerability, and in one instance a client expresses overwhelming feelings of loss, bitterness, and envy. The client states, "I wanted so badly to have a child myself, and I can't [sob]. And now my sister-in-law is having one, and it's terrible that I can't feel glad for her, I even have bad feelings about the baby" (Greenberg et al., 1993, p. 272). In other marker examples, clients relate "at the end of the road" expressions of their dreaded negative feelings: "When I've been talking to friends, I don't even tell them how bad I feel. They wouldn't understand" [deadness in voice]. "I just feel so full of regret, like there are so many things I've done I deeply regret. And now all I have are the consequences." "I feel total despair, but there's no sense in talking about it—nothing is going to change" (Greenberg et al., 1993, p. 275). When a practitioner responds to such marker statements through an expression of empathic understanding inherent in a reflection, a client typically experiences the full intensity of the humanly acceptable feeling without being overwhelmed. This supportive interaction enables the individual to reduce a sense of personal isolation and fragmentation and begin again toward personal growth.

Greenberg et al. (1993, p. 278) provided a treatment example of a client expressing markers of intense vulnerability and the therapist's expression of empathic understanding through the therapeutic technique of reflection.

Client: I'm not needed anymore. I have nothing left to live for.
Therapist: Uh-huh. Just like what's the use of carrying on—I'm not needed anymore by anyone. . . .
Client: Yeah, like I'm spent, just nothing left to give [Hits bottom].
Therapist: Uh-huh, just all out of steam, just . . . no more . . . nothing left to give.
Client: Yeah. [Sighs, takes a deep breath] I have an idea for a story I want to write, and I get kind of interested, but then I'm not sure I . . . ah . . . have the energy.
Therapist: It would take a lot of energy, but it sounds like you're sort of intrigued by it [Growth-oriented reflection].
Client: Yes, I even get sort of excited.

In this example, the therapist employs reflection to enable the client to experience both the painful and potentially growth-enhancing aspects of the self.

Although many others have followed Rogers in effectively utilizing reflection in the context of a facilitative condition, Rogers was a master of the intervention. Rogers was also the first researcher to provide verbatim transcripts of his treatment through case studies and brief dialogue illustrations, and he further demonstrated his proficiency in film presentations (Raskin & Rogers, 2005; Rogers, 1942, 1951, 1961, 1980; Rogers & Dymond, 1954; Shostrum, Shostrum, & Ratner, 1977). For example, in a case study of "Mrs. Oak," Rogers (1954, 1961) frequently employed reflection to empathically respond to her often confused feelings and meanings. Mrs. Oak "was a housewife in her late thirties, who was having difficulties in marital and family relationships when she came in for therapy" (Rogers, 1961, p. 77). In her ninth session, Mrs. Oak hesitantly revealed something about herself that she had not previously told anyone. She began to disclose after a pause of several minutes duration, and her revelation represents a marker of vulnerability.

Mrs. Oak: You know this is kind of goofy, but I've never told anyone this [nervous laugh] and it'll probably do me good. For years, oh, probably from early youth, from seventeen probably on, I, I have had what I have come to call to myself, told myself were "flashes of sanity." I've never told anyone this, [another embarrassed laugh] wherein, in, really I feel sane. And, and pretty much aware of life. And always with a terrific kind of concern and sadness of how far away, how far astray that we have actually gone. It's just a feeling once in a while of finding myself a whole kind of person in a terribly chaotic kind of world.

Rogers: It's been fleeting and it's been infrequent, but there have been times when it seems the whole of you is functioning and feeling in the world, a very chaotic world to be sure. (Rogers, 1961, p. 89).

In this brief response, Rogers employs a reflection to succinctly and perceptively communicate an understanding of Mrs. Oak's private and confusing experiencing.

In a treatment example from the eighth session, Mrs. Oak expresses strong and conflicting feelings as she begins to reduce her defense reactions.

Mrs. Oak: You know over in this area of, of sexual disturbance, I have a feeling that I'm beginning to discover that it's pretty bad, pretty bad. I'm finding out that, that I'm bitter, really. Damn bitter. I—and I'm not turning it back in, into myself. . . . I think what I probably feel is a certain element of "I've been cheated." [*Her voice is very tight and her throat chokes up*]. And I've covered up very nicely, to the point of consciously not caring. But I'm, I'm sort of amazed to find that in this practice of, what shall I call it, a kind of sublimation that right under it—again words—there's a, a kind of passive force that's, it's pas- it's very passive, but at the same time, it's just kind of *murderous*.

Rogers: So there's the feeling, "I've really been cheated. I've covered that up and seem not to care and yet underneath that there's a kind of a, a latent but very much present bitterness that is very, very strong" (Rogers, 1961, p. 92).

In this exchange, Rogers captures the essence of Mrs. Oak's threatening feelings and he articulates a reflection or "testing understanding" in a first person voice, as if he were Mrs. Oak. This formulation has a potential effect of enhancing empathic understanding and concern (Brink & Farber, 1996).

In terms of another major therapeutic intervention, Rogers cautioned against the utilization of interpretations that involve going outside the frame of reference of clients in counseling and psychotherapy (Rogers,

1942, 1951, 1961, 1969; Rogers & Sanford, 1985). Early in his career Rogers (1942) wrote, "The more accurate the interpretation, the more likely it is to encounter defensive resistance. The counselor and his interpretations are something to be feared" (p. 205). In this respect, Rogers felt that imposing external and evaluative formulations on a client produces threat and defensive reactions. It was counterproductive, in Rogers's view, for a practitioner to express intellectualized propositions relating to causative explanations of a client's behavior. In functioning outside of a client's frame of reference, an interpretation has the effect of minimizing an individual's self-exploration and experiencing (Gazzola & Stalikas, 1997, 2003). Rogers also thought it was perilous for a counselor or a therapist to use empathy for the purposes of gaining information about a client in order to subsequently use it to make interpretations (Rogers & Sanford, 1985). From a person-centered perspective, a practitioner's employment of interpretations contradicts the assumption that individuals have, within themselves, the internal resources to grow; an "expert" inhibits this tendency with imposed frames of reference that are in opposition to empathic understanding (Troemel-Ploetz, 1980).

In spite of Rogers's expressed views about the negative effect of a practitioner's use of interpretations, various contemporary researchers recognize that when Rogers utilized interventions that were just outside of a client's awareness, the process appeared to constitute properties of an interpretation (Elliot, Greenberg, & Lietaer, 2004; Gazzola & Stalikas, 1997, 2003; Troemel-Ploetz, 1980). Not only did the researchers identify interpretations being used in client- and person-centered therapy, they found the interventions to be productive in promoting constructive client change. In the context of responding to criticism of his approach as superficial and focusing on the obvious subjective experiences of clients, Rogers (1966) stated, "The client-centered therapist aims to dip from the pool of implicit meanings just at the edge of a client's awareness" (p. 190). When Rogers (1957) voiced "meanings in client's experience of which the client is scarcely aware" (p. 99), it is reasonable to assume that this exchange represented an inferential response (Cormier & Nurius, 2003). At the same time, Rogers does not state that a counselor or a therapist should present a new or alternative perspective that is outside of a client's frame of reference.

Gazzola and Stalikas (1997, 2003) found that Rogers infrequently made interpretive responses, but when he did, they usually stimulated more positive or "good moments" when compared with other interventions in client-centered therapy. Brink and Farber (1996) also noted that Rogers infrequently rendered interpretations, yet, when he did, "they sound remarkably similar to those of any analytically oriented therapist" (p. 21). To conclude the case of "Mrs. Oak," Rogers (1961) appears to be using an interpretation, or at least inferential comments, as he responds to her conflictive feelings.

> **Mrs. Oak:** And then of course, I've come to—to see and to feel that over this—see, I've covered it up. [Weeps] But I've covered it up with so much *bitterness,* which in turn I had to cover up. [Weeping] *That's* what I want to get rid of! I almost don't *care* if I hurt.
>
> **Rogers** [Softly, and with an empathic tenderness toward the hurt she is experiencing]: You feel that here at the basis of it as you experience it is a feeling of real tears for yourself. But *that* you can't show, mustn't show, so that's been covered by bitterness that you don't like, that you'd like to be rid of. You almost feel you'd rather absorb the hurt than to—than to feel the bitterness. [Pause] And what you seem to be saying quite strongly is, I do *hurt,* and I've tried to cover it up. (pp. 93–94)

In support of the role of interpretations from a person-centered perspective, Troemel-Ploetz (1980) provided a group therapy example. In a group session, a participant expressing both anger and humiliation states to the other members, "That's enough, I don't want to talk about it anymore." In response, the therapist empathically says, "I feel a lot of pain when I see you try so hard and not get what you want" (Troemel-Ploetz, 1980, pp. 248–249). The client reacts positively to the therapist's inferential statement, and begins to disclose the hurt and anger that he feels when failing to be recognized by others in spite of making strong efforts. If the group therapist had remained in the client's overtly verbalized frame of reference, he would have ended the discussion based on the insistence of the individual. Instead, the practitioner empathically addressed the group member's painful feelings at an implicit level, which prompted therapeutic gain. The group treatment example suggests a deeper, indirect, and more complex level of meaning in the person-centered approach that frequently is overlooked when restricting the range of the treatment interventions to more superficial and repetitious levels of communication (Troemel-Ploetz, 1980).

Gazzola and Stalikas (1997, 2003) also acknowledged support for the use of interpretations from a Rogerian perspective when expressed in a caring manner, phrased tentatively, and tendered in reference to immediate and specific client feelings. In this sense, an interpretation is presented from a new frame of reference to a client, but the perspective resonates within the individual because it is close to his or her awareness. Investigators have also observed a trend in the later work of Rogers in which he expresses interventions, including feedback, personal self-disclosure, confrontation, and interpretations, from his own frame of reference (Elliot et al., 2004). In these instances, empathic understanding is more accurately perceived in the context of a relationship "climate" than functions that are unilaterally "provided" by the counselor. From this perspective, a practitioner's empathic understanding relates to thinking *with* rather than *for* or *about* the helpee (Brammer & MacDonald, 2003, p. 30).

Even though Rogers emphasized the importance of the facilitative conditions, it is also possible, as in the case of reflection and interpretation, to discern the operation of various therapeutic techniques in his interactions with clients. From a person-centered perspective, Rogers was consistent in the expression of empathic understanding and the other attitudinal elements, and he adapted specific interventions to the unique needs of clients in immediate contexts (Brink & Farber, 1996). In his filmed presentations and written transcripts, it is apparent that Rogers employed what has been referred to as *attending behavior* (Ivey & Ivey, 2003) or *affirming attention* (Brink & Farber, 1996). In these exchanges, Rogers typically would lean forward, direct steady eye contact toward the client, nod his head affirmatively, and verbalize a simple "M-hm, M-hm." In other instances, Rogers acknowledged a client's unstated feelings. As an example, Rogers might state, "I hear a tremor in your voice," or "There is a tear coming to your eye as you talk about this." At different times, Rogers provided a type of reassurance to a client by accepting the issue or problem and attempting to situate it in a broader context or perspective (Brink & Farber, 1996). In this regard, consider the example in the celebrated filmed case presentation with Gloria, in which she expressed a feeling of receiving insufficient support from others in her life (Shostrum, Shostrum, & Ratner, 1977). In response, Rogers stated, "I suspect none of us get it as often as we would like."

In another treatment direction, Rogers seldom asked clients a question, and when he did employ the technique, it was usually to check the accuracy of his empathic responses. Examples of questions that Rogers (1961) expresssed in the case study with Mrs. Oak include, "Does this catch it?" (p. 101); "Would this get it?" (p. 95); and, "Because that whole you does exist with all your feelings. Is that it, you're more aware of feelings?" (p. 90). In the later stage of his career, Rogers began to use self-disclosure more frequently, especially when he entered the group treatment phase of his experience. He felt that in order for a counselor to be congruent, it was necessary for him or her to express both positive and negative feelings toward a client that were "persistent" (Rogers, 1966). In these instances, Rogers attempted to distinguish between observations directed at the client or at the behavior of the individual. Rogers (1966) used an example of persistent feelings of boredom when he wrote, "I will recognize that I am expressing my own feeling of being bored and not some supposed fact about him as a boring person" (p. 185).

Other theorists beyond Rogers have considered the status of therapeutic techniques within the person-centered treatment approach (Bozarth, 1998; Brink & Farber, 1996; Brodley, 1999). A common concern associated with these interventions is the question of attempting to maintain a focus within the client's frame of reference. With respect to responding to questions or requests, Brodley (1999) thought that a sound direction for the therapist is to provide straightforward and nonevaluative responses. Once a practitioner renders a respectful statement, it is also helpful to express empathic understanding directed at the manner in which the client emotionally receives the information. At the same time, Brodley recognized some risk in providing information, particularly when it is not requested by a client. He felt that the exchange has a potential to be countertherapeutic if a client assumes that he or she must accept or follow through with the information provided or disappoint the counselor. Brodley (1999) mentioned information-based examples such as the possible use of medication or a behavioral technique for public-speaking as representative of therapist-framed responses that can produce misunderstanding within the treatment relationship. Finally, Brink and Farber (1996) believed that it is therapeutic to occasionally confront clients when they seem to be avoiding or evading a painful issue. This challenging stance would be assumed by a therapist for the purpose of enabling a client to further his or her self-understanding.

SUMMARY

More than any other individual, Carl Rogers brought prominence to the potent influence of empathy in the therapeutic process. Through the efforts of Rogers and his colleagues, empathic understanding has achieved a consensus standing as a critical change element in counseling and psychotherapy. Over a period of decades, Rogers's definitions and descriptions of empathy in treatment practice evolved and became more refined, and his writings stimulated extensive research relating to the topics. From Rogers's perspective, empathy, in addition to congruence and unconditional positive regard, constitute the facilitative qualities *necessary and sufficient* for constructive client growth in therapy. Rogers was constant in his view of recognizing the therapeutic conditions as attitudinal processes provided by a counselor or a therapist that focus on the internal frame of reference of a client. This position was largely in opposition to a popular skill-training movement in the therapeutic community that attempted to define empathic understanding and the other therapeutic elements in operational terms. In particular, the technique of reflection became equated with empathy. In response, Rogers spoke out against the contradictory position of these technologically oriented developments with respect to person-centered theory and therapy. The role and legitimacy of reflection, interpretation, and other treatment interventions are subjects of continuing debate among researchers and practitioners in person-centered therapy.

Chapter 5

Psychoanalytic Therapy and Empathy

The capacity to communicate empathically with patients is the basis of psychoanalysis and psychodynamic psychotherapies.
—Schlesinger (1981, p. 415)

When I first considered the place of empathy in psychoanalytic therapy in my early research for this text, it seemed that the yield of the construct was unlikely to produce robust findings. With its somewhat austere and intellectualized approach to treatment, the psychoanalytic tradition did not appear to be integrally related to empathic understanding. However, in contrast to these personal views, I was aware that I had for many years employed particular psychoanalytic conceptions in my treatment practice with direct links to empathy. What I had previously found was that empathic understanding played a key role in the operation of defense mechanisms and with the processing of the technique of interpretation. Attempting to empathically grasp a client's defensive reactions and convey aspects of these observations back to the client appeared to be a sound treatment direction. With interpretation, connecting a client's experiences with his or her current functioning also seemed to work most effectively in the context of an empathic disposition. In recent years, I also became familiar with self psychology and recognized the central role of empathy in this psychoanalytic approach. Thus, on further consideration, it seemed clear that I was inaccurate in my initial assumption of a minimal relationship between psychoanalytic therapy and empathy.

PSYCHOANALYTIC FIGURES AND EMPATHY

In the history of psychoanalytic therapy, the literature on empathy extends over a period of more than 100 years since Sigmund Freud first made reference to the construct in his treatise on jokes (Freud, 1905/1960). At the same time, empathy in psychoanalytic theory and practice, with notable exceptions, was generally neglected until Kohut (1959) brought prominence to its therapeutic function. Although Kohut did not believe that his self psychology approach was a radical departure from the classic psychoanalytic model, his treatment, which centered on empathy, ushered in new ways of thinking about empathic functioning (Silverstein, 1999). Beyond Freud and Kohut, Sándor Ferenczi was another leading figure in the psychoanalytic tradition who recognized the role of empathic functioning in the therapeutic relationship. Ferenczi's (1928/1955) introduction of empathy into treatment practice involved technical recommendations for the development of a more emotionally responsive climate. Various other psychoanalysts have also made contributions to the advancement of the role of empathy through specific comments on the topic.

Sigmund Freud and Empathy

Freud made infrequent, brief, but intriguing references to empathy across the vast body of his writings. Although Freud was the first psychoanalytic figure to mention empathy in his works, he did not provide a major essay relating to the topic or expand on the construct as a central instrument in analysis (Shapiro, 1981; Wolf, 1983). It is probable that Freud was influenced by the insights of Theodor Lipps, who was responsible for extending the concept of empathy from aesthetics to the psychological domain of understanding others (Pigman, 1995; Sharma, 1992). Freud's personal library, now in the Freud Museum in Hampstead, includes nine books written by Lipps in which Freud wrote margin notes (Pigman, 1995; Wolf, 1983). Freud (1905/1960) initially made reference to empathy as a term in 1905 in the final chapter of *Jokes and Their Relation to the Unconscious*. Freud refers to empathy eight times in this nonclinical volume, and in all of his publications he employs the use of empathy 20 times (Pigman, 1995). In his discussion of the nature of jokes, Freud (1905/1960) stated:

> Thus we take the producing person's psychical state into consideration, put ourselves into it and try to understand it by comparing it with our own. It

> is these processes of empathy and comparison that result in the economy in expenditure which we discharge by laughing. (p. 186)

Accordingly, to Freud, empathy involved an attempt to briefly assume another's psychic state and make personal comparisons in order to further understanding (Pigman, 1995). Freud's conception of empathy emphasizes its cognitive or intellectual aspects and tends to minimize a focus on a person's affective functioning.

In another nonclinical essay with implications for empathy, Freud (1914/1955b) wrote at length about the intent of Michelangelo when he sculptured the marble statue of Moses that was to be used as an adornment for the tomb of Pope Julius II in Rome. In this classic work of art, Moses is in a sitting posture holding the Tables of the Ten Commandments by his side. Freud painstakingly raised questions about Michelangelo's motivation in creating the statue and what he wished to convey in the piece. Freud attempted to comprehend the state of Moses, through the eyes of Michelangelo, at a critical moment in time in religious history. By attending to minute details relating to Moses's hair, fingers, eyes, beard, and posture, Freud speculated about the possible emotions and conflicts that Moses was experiencing. Michelangelo, from Freud's perspective, wished to depict Moses incurring feelings of pain mingled with contempt as he is about to rise from his chair. As Freud wrestled with the expressive meanings of Michelangelo, it is apparent that he was attempting to *feel himself into* or empathically understand the great work of art. At no point in the treatise, however, does Freud extend his observations and insights to the therapeutic domain of psychoanalytic treatment. At the same time, the essay conveys an astute capacity of Freud to empathically evaluate an artist's rendition of a compelling piece of sculpture.

One of Freud's most provocative references to empathy occurs in a chapter on identification in his work, *Group Psychology and the Analysis of the Ego* (1921/1955a). In a footnote relating to a broader discussion of identification in groups, Freud (1921/1955a) stated, "A path leads from identification by way of imitation to empathy, that is, to the comprehension of the mechanism by which we are enabled to take up any attitude at all towards another mental life" (p. 42). In a sequential process, Freud conceptualizes imitation as a precursor to empathy, whereas identification is considered as a later or subsequent event (Shapiro, 1981). In this brief passage, Freud calls attention to the fundamental importance of the relationship of empathy to the culminating state of identification that is employed by individuals in the context of group experiences (Schafer, 1959;

Shapiro, 1974). Surprisingly, however, after Freud briefly alludes to empathy, he does not expand on his thoughts about the construct. At another point in his continuing discussion on identification, Freud (1921/1955a) refers to "the process psychology calls 'empathy [Einfühlung]' and which plays the largest part in our understanding of what is inherently foreign to our ego in other people" (p. 40). In this statement it appears that Freud is suggesting that empathy enables individuals to understand what other people do not comprehend about themselves (Pigman, 1995). Yet, as in the previous reference to empathy, Freud does not develop this seemingly critical line of reasoning and instead returns to his main discussion topic of identification.

Considering Freud's awareness of the concept of empathy over a period of many years, his comments relating to the term are not extensive. At the same time, Freud introduced empathy into the psychoanalytic literature, and his observations may be considered a part of early contributions or a *thought collective* (Sharma, 1992) of various ideas relating to empathy that were subsequently developed and refined. A question does arise, however, as to why Freud did not make use of empathy to a greater degree, particularly as it relates to the therapeutic function. Agosta (1984) suggested that the popular usage of empathy in the realm of aesthetics deterred Freud from aligning his treatment approach with the construct. He may have wished to avoid an association with a nonscientific and less objective term as he was trying to establish psychoanalysis as a body of thought that could sustain scientific scrutiny (Sharma, 1992). In this regard, the orientation might have diminished its intellectual character if it were to become associated with a mystical element (Rachman, 1997). It is also possible that Freud recognized inherent difficulties in attempting to differentiate empathy from the capacity of individuals to project their own feelings to another person. Freud was aware of the hazards of both the projective and identification processes in terms of crossing psychological boundaries. Furthermore, through the conceptualization of countertransference, Freud (1910/1957) was sensitive to the potential for analysts to introduce personal conflictive issues into the therapeutic situation, and the manner in which expressions of empathy might potentially confound this occurrence.

From a broader perspective, it may also be that Freud had already established a systematic treatment modality that theoretically did not allow a central role for empathy. In 1912, Freud described the psychoanalytic technique of analysts maintaining an *evenly suspended attention* (p. 111) that facilitated conditions conducive for free association (Freud, 1912/1958; Sharma, 1992). The process of the evenly suspended attention of the analyst was accompanied by a logical scrutiny of random client material that was raised in the course of analysis. Conceptually and in practice, this therapeutic model is fundamentally different from a therapist maintaining a posture of empathic understanding (Shapiro, 1981). This assumption, however, does not mean that Freud was unempathic; it does suggest that a different conceptual mode of being with a patient was fundamental to his treatment approach.

Sándor Ferenczi and Empathy

Although Sándor Ferenczi is not widely known outside of psychoanalytic circles, his innovative treatment approach has direct implications for the integration of empathy in a therapeutic context. In particular, Ferenczi's (1928/1955, 1929/1955, 1931/1955, 1933/1955) later works focused on the empathic method in a series of significant papers (Rachman, 1997). Ferenczi was a devoted and talented supporter of the psychoanalytic movement, and he traveled with Freud on the trip to the United States in 1909 for the presentation of the notable lecture series at Clark University (Gedo, 1986; Lorand, 1966). Ferenczi made numerous contributions to the advancement of psychoanalysis through his original publications and organizational talents. As a person, Ferenczi was known for his warmth, charm, intellect, and the joyous quality of his personality that was captivating to both colleagues and patients (Jones, 1933; Lorand, 1966). In a professional capacity, Ferenczi was sought out for his abilities as a therapist in treating difficult cases and as an inspiring lecturer at psychoanalytic gatherings (Thompson, 1944). Ferenczi underwent personal analysis with Freud and was invited to accompany the Freud family on summer vacations for a number of years (Hoffman, 2003; Lorand, 1966). Yet, in spite of Ferenczi's significant contributions, when he parted from central psychoanalytic tenets in his later writings, his mental stability was called into question by major figures within the psychoanalytic community (Dupont, 1988; Thompson, 1944). These views cast serious doubt on the validity of his treatment observations and the worth of his final publications that recognized empathy as a prominent function.

After many years of attempting to work within the classic mode of psychoanalysis, it became evident to Ferenczi that he was not successful with a sizable number of challenging patients. Rather than continue to adhere to an approach that was characterized by a somewhat remote and stern quality, Ferenczi began to transform the emotional climate of his sessions into a responsive, warm, and empathic process (Hoffman, 2003; Rachman, 1988,

1989). He was particularly interested in providing technical recommendations designed to explain processes that would enable analysts to recognize the function of empathic understanding in psychoanalytic treatment. In this regard, Ferenczi (1928/1955) wrote:

> I have come to the conclusion that it is above all a question of psychological tact whether or when one should tell the patient some particular thing, when the material he has produced should be considered sufficient to draw conclusions, in what form these should be presented to the patient, how one should react to an unexpected or bewildering reaction on the patient's part, when one should keep silent and await further associations, and at what point the further maintenance of silence would result only in causing the patient useless suffering, etc. As you can see, using the word 'tact' has enabled me to reduce the uncertainty to a simple and appropriate formula. But what is 'tact'? The answer is not very difficult. It is the capacity for empathy. (p. 89)

Over the last 6 or 7 years of his life, Ferenczi devoted himself to a treatment direction that was a distinct departure from the traditional methods of psychoanalysis prevailing in the late 1920s and early 1930s (Stanton, 1991; Thompson, 1944). Ferenczi believed that an analyst should avoid assuming an authoritarian stance, and that his or her observations should be presented in a tentative way that would allow for the possibility of clinical error. In this regard, Ferenczi (1928/1955) stated:

> Nothing is more harmful to analysis than a schoolmasterish or even an authoritative attitude on the physician's part. Anything we say to the patient should be put to him in the form of a tentative suggestion and not of a confidently held opinion, not only to avoid irritating him, but because there is always a possibility that we can be mistaken." (p. 94)

It is apparent that Ferenczi's therapeutic posture was markedly different from the analytic attitudes of the period, which often produced an intimidating, exacting, and submissive atmosphere in a treatment situation (Rachman, 1988).

In many cases involving severe pathology, Ferenczi came to the conclusion that the emotionally distant and objective stance of the analyst might very well create similar conditions associated with a patient's original traumatic experiences (Balint, 1967; Rachman, 1997). For Ferenczi (1929/1955), it became a sound treatment direction to respond to patients with tact and understanding in order to avoid a repetition of regressive reactions and symptoms that are sometimes elicited by aloof authority figures. To this end, Ferenczi (1931/1955) stated, "It is important for the analysis that the analyst should be able to meet with the patient as far as possible with almost inexhaustible patience, understanding, goodwill, and kindliness" (p. 132). Through the establishment of tolerant and supportive therapeutic conditions, Ferenczi believed that patients would recognize a contrast with the vulnerabilities associated with early trauma circumstances and feel safe from an emotional reproduction of such painful situations (Ferenczi, 1931/1955). Furthermore, the development of a reservoir of sincere goodwill during analysis is important and can be called on as a resource as treatment progresses and the patient is challenged to encounter emotional conflicts.

In another innovative direction within psychoanalysis, Ferenczi described the analyst's role in oscillating between an involved and a detached therapeutic stance (Greenson, 1960). Through a process that many years later Sullivan (1953, 1954) labeled *participant observer*, Ferenczi recognized the analyst's capacity to become emotionally involved with the patient and then to oscillate to a more observational position in order to evaluate the meaning of what had been empathically understood. This approach contrasted with the classical model of treatment that advocated the evenly suspended attention (Freud, 1912/1958) of the analyst with greater emphasis on a detached observational role. With respect to the analyst's function, Ferenczi (1928/1955) stated, "One might say that his mind swings continuously between empathy, self-observation, and making judgments" (p. 96). Through this interactive process, over a sustained period, it then becomes possible for an analyst to make interpretations relating to the causation of a patient's functioning. With his focus on involved observation, Ferenczi was also alert to the meaning of the nonverbal communication of patients as expressed through body movements, postures, and gestures (Dupont, 1988; Lorand, 1966). In order to facilitate this type of observation, Ferenczi departed from the traditional use of the couch, with a patient lying down in analytic treatment, and instead began to employ a seating arrangement that allowed for face-to-face contact between the patient and analyst. Although Ferenczi emphasized an emotional involvement of the analyst in a treatment situation, he was also sensitive to being open to criticism within psychoanalysis for excessively focusing on subjective perspectives at the expense of an objective evaluation. With this concern in mind, Ferenczi (1928/1955) wrote:

> There is no doubt that many—and not only beginners, but all who have a tendency to exaggeration—will seize upon what I have said about the importance of empathy to lay the chief emphasis on their handling of patients

> on the subjective factor, i.e. on intuition and will disregard what I stated to be the all important factor, the conscious assessment of the dynamic situation. (p. 100)

As a pioneer in psychoanalysis, Ferenczi considered his contributions to be a viable means of strengthening the professional standing of the organizational cause. Yet, in reality, Ferenczi's creative directions in his later works brought him into opposition with mainstream psychoanalytic thought, and he became one of the first dissidents of the analytic movement (Hoffman, 2003). In another example of the treatment methods that set a new direction in psychoanalytic practice, Ferenczi was the first analyst to recognize *countertransference* as a potentially constructive treatment phenomenon (Gedo, 1986; Haynal, 1993; Rachman, 1988, 1997). Unlike many analysts of his time, who thought that countertransference was troublesome and had to be neutralized as fully as possible, Ferenczi (1988) felt that a practitioner's countertransferential responses could serve as a major therapeutic tool that, although difficult to manage, could be indispensable for analytic progress (Dupont, 1988). In ways similarly observed by others in the psychoanalytic movement decades later, Ferenczi believed that an analyst's willingness and capacity for evaluating countertransference reactions were fundamental qualities for engendering personal and professional growth in the practitioner (Rachman, 1989). By attempting to identify and address personal conflicts, it was possible for an analyst to reduce or remove those inner barriers that contribute to a countertransference response in interactions with a patient. In agreement with other psychoanalysts of his era, Ferenczi recognized the value of personal analysis in order for an analyst to be in a stronger position to provide sound treatment (de Forest, 1954; Ferenczi, 1928/1955). In support of this recommendation, Ferenczi (1928/1955) stated, "The processes of empathy and assessment will obviously take place, not in the unconscious, but at the preconscious level of the well-analyzed analyst's mind" (p. 100).

Ferenczi (1933/1955) also thought that it was advantageous for an analyst to acknowledge mistakes and be receptive to patient criticisms. Ferenczi (1928/1955) felt that an analyst should never be ashamed to admit mistakes, and he recognized that this *empathy rule* contrasted with "the lofty attitude to the patient adopted by the omniscient and omnipotent doctor" (p. 94). In Ferenczi's (1933/1955) view, an occasional reproach of a patient directed at the analyst, including labels such as "insensitive," "cold," "selfish," and "conceited" may contain elements of truth. By avoiding a defensive response and evaluating the perceived accuracy of particular accusations, an analyst is in a position to admit recognizable mistakes and gain the confidence of a patient. Admitting therapeutic errors may also be healing for a patient and enhance communication within the treatment relationship (de Forest, 1954; Zausner, 2003).

Even though Ferenczi believed that patients should be free to be critical, he also was aware that individuals frequently express negative reactions toward the analyst that needed to be challenged. In this regard, Ferenczi (1931/1955) said:

> Very often patients try to provoke an expression of ill-will which they imagine us to be concealing, by their bad behavior, by sarcastic or cynical remarks, by all sorts of rudeness, and even making faces. It is not satisfactory to go on playing even in these circumstances the part of the grown-up who is always indulgent and kind; it is better to admit honestly that we find the patient's behavior unpleasant, but we feel it our duty to control ourselves since we know that he is not going to the trouble of being naughty for no reason. (p. 133)

Ferenczi received harsh criticism within the psychoanalytic orientation for being indulgent with his patients, and in this statement he affirms the importance of providing direct and critical observations. At the same time, in encounters with even the most unpleasant and repulsive patients, Ferenczi (1928/1955) also believed that it is possible for an analyst to perceive and understand the individuals as persons in need of help. Ferenczi attributed the capacity of an analyst to maintain a therapeutic level of open communication and tolerance of the patient to empathic understanding. Ferenczi (1928/1955) wrote, "I must once more emphasize that here too only real empathy helps; the patient's sharp wits will easily detect any pose" (p. 95).

Although Ferenczi's involvement with empathic techniques deviated from classical psychoanalysis, it was more his dissenting views about the reality of childhood sexual trauma that alarmed and made him unacceptable to Freud and most adherents of the psychoanalytic point of view (Masson, 1984; Rachman, 1988, 1997). Through his practice with patients who had severe emotional disorders, Ferenczi came to believe that the etiology of their pathology was related to experiences of sexual abuse and trauma suffered at the hands of parental figures. This position was in opposition to Freud's (1905/1953) prevailing theory that the memories of sexual abuse of patients were fantasy-based and therefore were unreliable indicators of actual incidents. In contrast to this hypothesis, Ferenczi (1933/1955) stated, "The immediate explanation—that these are only sexual fantasies of the child, a kind of hysterical lying—is unfortunately made invalid by the number of such confessions, e.g. of assaults upon children, committed by patients actually in analysis" (p. 161). In stating that traumas were real and had taken place, Ferenczi challenged a central tenet of psychoanalysis that rested on the universality of the Oedipal complex to explain reports of childhood sexual experiences and developmental arrests (Rachman, 1989). Through experience in his treatment caseload, Ferenczi (1933/1955) felt that individuals became disturbed as a result of the reality of exploitation and abuse and not what they only imagined happened to them. Ferenczi (1933/1955) related, "These children feel physically and morally helpless, their personalities are not sufficiently consolidated in order to protest, even only in thought for the overpowering force and authority of the adult makes them dumb and can rob them of their senses" (p. 162). It was also evident to Ferenczi that patients who had endured childhood trauma needed to process and work through their history of abuse in a supportive and understanding therapeutic milieu.

Ferenczi's challenge of the universality of the theory of fantasy-based infantile sexuality and his venture into empathic technique met with strong resistance within the psychoanalytic movement. Although there was criticism of both Ferenczi's approach and the legitimacy of his ideas as precepts of psychoanalysis, most attacks were directed at allegations of his deteriorating mental health. Jones (1933), a prominent psychoanalyst who later wrote an authorized biography of Freud, stated in an obituary to Ferenczi, "Probably many have been deterred from intensively studying and pursuing the line of thought there opened up by the fact that in his still later writings Ferenczi showed unmistakable signs of mental regression in his attitude towards the fundamental problems of psycho-analysis" (pp. 465–466). With few exceptions, the psychoanalytic community uncritically accepted Jones's assertions and attributed the ideas in Ferenczi's final contributions to a disturbed mind (Dupont, 1988). Although Ferenczi wished to maintain the admiration and approval of Freud and others within the psychoanalytic movement, and the clarity and the richness of his collected and final papers are indisputable, his later works were broadly discredited on the basis of an unsubstantiated personality impairment (Loraud, 1966). Yet, after many years during which Ferenczi's works were assigned to a rather obscure place in psychoanalysis, his contributions are now being recognized for their seminal role in analytic treatment and for the advancement of empathy as a critical function in the therapeutic process (Aron & Harris, 1993; Dupont, 1988; Loraud, 1966; Rachman, 1988, 1989, 1997; Zausner, 2003).

Heinz Kohut and Empathy

Almost three decades after the publication of Ferenczi's final contributions, Heinz Kohut (1959) introduced empathy as a pivotal construct in his treatment approach. In the history of psychoanalytic therapy, Ferenczi and Kohut are the leading figures in affirming the central role of empathy. Like Ferenczi, Kohut did not consider his empathic ideas as a radical departure from the major principles of psychoanalysis (Silverstein, 1999). Kohut (1984) defined empathy as a *vicarious introspection* that enables an analyst to "think and feel oneself into the inner life of another person" (p. 82). In Kohut's (1990) view, a deeper understanding of an individual occurs through the sustained engagement of empathy and introspection. Both therapeutic processes provide essential means of acquiring a comprehensive clinical knowledge of a patient through an *experience-near* modality (Rowe & MacIsaac, 1989). In turn, the observed data is formulated in an *experience-distant* theoretical context and conveyed to a patient in the form of an interpretation. As an analytic function, according to Kohut, an interpretation contributes to a higher form of empathy based on a broader understanding of a patient. In addition to detailing the function of empathy in treatment, Kohut conceptualized empathy as a critical factor in the emotional and psychological growth of individuals. In the absence of requisite empathic understanding during infancy and childhood, a person is susceptible to the development of psychopathology (Levy, 1985). In the next chapter, Kohut's work is comprehensively reviewed as it relates to empathy.

Other Psychoanalytic Contributors and Empathy

In the period between Ferenczi's final writings in the early 1930s and the emergence of the work of Kohut in the late 1950s, some of the contributions of several other psychoanalytic figures may be characterized as having an empathic focus. In particular, Theodor Reik (1948) conceptualized identifiable phases of empathy processing in a treatment situation. Harry Stack Sullivan (1953, 1954) recognized the central role of empathy in human development and in enabling the therapist to better understand and relate to patients in therapy. Fenichel (1953), Fliess (1942), and Fromm-Reichmann (1950) were among a small number of psychoanalysts who suggested that the function of empathy held promise for advancing the therapeutic process.

Theodor Reik. In his classic text, *Listening With the Third Ear,* Reik (1948) presented four phases that depict varying levels of involvement and disengagement on the part of the analyst. Although Reik rarely made reference to empathy in this work, some researchers simply equate Reik's theoretical positions with empathy (Teich, 1992a). In particular, Teich (1992a) stated that Katz's (1963) schematization of Reik's four phases went beyond, and in some instances distorted, Reik's views. At the same time, with the important attributable cautions in mind, the schematized material has a utility for clarifying the empathic process in a treatment situation. Although the phases do not necessarily occur in this particular sequence, they include the topics of identification, incorporation, reverberation, and detachment.

As the analyst becomes emotionally engrossed in contemplating the experiences of the patient, *identification* is the most basic and distinctive quality in the process. Through a deliberate activity, the analyst temporarily loses consciousness of him- or herself, yet also retains the capability of immediately recovering his or her own sense of identity. In this regard, identification relates to the role of the practitioner in projecting him- or herself into what the patient feels. In the *incorporation* phase of empathic processing, the analyst takes in and feels the experience of the patient "as if" it were his or her own (Katz, 1963). It is possible that the introduction of the patient's state or condition may be partly foreign or alien to the consciousness of the practitioner. Consequently, in a momentary reaction, the analyst assimilates the experience of the patient in order to reduce the perceived distance between their respective perspectives. Both the identification and incorporation phases employ means of establishing emotional connections between the practitioner and the patient and opportunities for sensing the reality or the functioning of diverse individuals in a treatment situation.

In the third or *reverberation* phase of Reik's model of empathic understanding, the analyst is absorbed in the identity of the patient, but is also simultaneously aware of continuing to function as a separate personality (Katz, 1963). Through a process that is implicit and more unconscious than conscious, the practitioner senses familiar aspects of his or her experience that are similar to that of the patient. The analyst then is in a position to imagine what it would be like if he or she were in the position of the patient. This anticipatory response frequently contributes to a deeper understanding of the patient through a rapidly processed fantasy activity. With respect to the reverberation phase, Katz (1963) stated, "I personally feel that I only 'understand' if I can detect in my own mind the germ of a similar feeling as the one which I try to understand, given that a similar thing should happen to me" (p. 45). *Detachment* represents the fourth and concluding phase of Reik's schematization in which the analyst withdraws from subjective involvement and makes comparisons between the information gained relating to a patient and data available from other sources. Through a dispassionate analysis, the practitioner scrutinizes content material for pertinent insights, such as observations acquired from a patient's family, and deliberately attempts to integrate the knowledge into an intelligible pattern of a patient's state of mind (Bennett, 2001).

It may be apparent that it is difficult to describe a dynamic empathic process in terms of phases that occur through static verbal statements over a fleeting period of time (Katz, 1963). The operation of empathy is paradoxical in that the analyst is emotionally engaged with the patient, but also sufficiently disengaged in order to more objectively weigh insights gathered. At the same time, in both dimensions, the patient is consistently responded to as a person and not as an object in a climate of empathic understanding. In a treatment example relating to Reik's four phases, an adolescent named Harold describes a time that he became lost as a young child while playing in his urban neighborhood. As Harold expresses escalating feelings of tension and fright due to his inability to locate familiar surroundings, the analyst immediately identifies with Harold's situation and becomes absorbed in the narration. Through an incorporation activity, the analyst begins to feel the panic that Harold experiences, and this interaction increases her emotional connection with the patient. In a reverberation of the feelings evoked by Harold, the analyst senses what she would feel under similar circumstances. This subjective response seemed vaguely connected to situations that she experienced as a child and served to provide a means for evaluating Harold's experience. The analyst fleetingly recalled a time in which responsible adults were desperately searching for her in a park when as a child she became lost at a family gathering. As the empathic process concludes, the analyst experiences a sense of detachment and wonders why this seemingly traumatic incident was not brought up by Harold's parents in a lengthy consultation period.

Harry Stack Sullivan. With an emphasis on interpersonal aspects of human development, H. S. Sullivan recognized the importance of empathy as an early bond between mother and child (Bromberg, 1980; Sharma, 1992). In a developmental context, Sullivan viewed these emotional linkages as essential means for nurturing a child's self-esteem and for transmitting sex roles and cultural mores. From a treatment perspective, although

Sullivan rarely used the term empathy, empathic understanding is implied in various instances in his writings as an undefined interpersonal process (Bromberg, 1980; Teich, 1992a). As an example, Sullivan (1954) stated:

> Thus whenever the psychiatrist's attempt to discover what the patient is talking about leads the patient to be somewhat more clear on what he is thinking about or attempting to communicate or conceal, his grasp on life is to some extent enhanced. And no one can have grave difficulties in living if he has a very good grasp on what is happening to him. (p. 23)

From an interpersonal perspective, Sullivan (1954) believed that an individual's self-esteem is a product of "the influences of significant others upon one's feeling of well-being" (p. 101). The self-system evaluates esteem measures as they relate to such factors as respect, deference, and prestige in relationships with others. As a reaction to anxiety-provoking threat, a person typically engages *security operations* in an effort to protect one's self-esteem. With respect to self-esteem, security operations function in a protective fashion similar to Adler's safeguarding tendencies (Clark, 1999a, 2000). In a treatment situation, an interviewer attempts to empathically process a patient's security operations without increasing the intensity of the responses (Sullivan, 1953, 1954).

In a conceptualization that has implications for empathic understanding, Sullivan (1953) stated that "psychiatry is particularly the field of participant observation" (p. 3). As a *participant observer,* a practitioner assumes both the role of an emotional involvement in an interview with a patient and an emotional detachment that allows for a more objective appraisal. As an observer in a treatment alliance that emphasizes interpersonal relations, Sullivan (1953, 1954) felt that a primary instrument for patient understanding was the personality or the person of the practitioner. As an example of a participant observer stance, Sullivan (1954) described a case in working with a young-adulthood patient in therapy who expressed strong hostility toward his parents, but, at the same time, was unable to identify instances in which they were anything but kind and tolerant toward him. In a participant role, Sullivan empathized with the college-age patient as he voiced his resentment and harsh criticisms of his parents, even in the absence of identifying negative experiences in interactions with them. At one point, Sullivan (1954) assumed an observer role in his thought, "Oh yeah? It doesn't sound so to me. It doesn't make sense. Maybe you have overlooked something" (p. 22). This consideration prompted Sullivan (1954) to inquire further about the patient's relationship with his parents in which they "didn't learn how to dance, or play games, or otherwise engage in the frivolous social life of people of your age" (p. 22). A confirmation of this observation led to the recognition that the patient had not developed the social skills that would enable him to relate to other young adults, and he felt deficient in this area throughout his life. At that point, a connection was made to the patient's hostility toward his parents as it related to their neglect of the development of his interpersonal capacities that resulted in an impaired ability to relate with peers. In a participant stance, Sullivan experienced the intensity of the patient's hostility, and through an observer function was able to assume a somewhat detached perspective that enabled him to attribute a plausible degree of meaning to the patient's experience.

Fenichel, Fleiss, and Fromm-Reichmann. Various other psychoanalysts have contributed further commentary and ideas on empathy and empathic understanding in the treatment situation. In an article on the topic of identification, Otto Fenichel (1953) made reference to empathy as it relates to Freud's concept of narcissistic identification. Fenichel wrote:

> Empathy—viz., the intuitive grasp of real psychic states of another person—is closely related to such identification, but is not identical with it. If we consider that in the final analysis it is only by empathy that we know of the existence of psychic life other than our own, then that agrees well with the fact that at the bottom of every object love we find identification. (p. 104)

With a focus on the metapsychology of the analyst, Robert Fliess (1942) stated that a practitioner gains an understanding of a patient through a process he referred to as *trial identification.* Specifically, Fliess raised a question about an analyst's inherent or learned psychological aptitude that enables him or her to grasp the meaning of a patient's communications. In this regard, Fleiss (1942) stated that this metapsychological capacity depended:

> essentially on his ability to put himself in the latter's place, to step into his shoes, and to obtain in this way an inside knowledge that is almost first-hand. The common name for such a procedure is 'empathy'; and we, as a suitable term for it in our own nomenclature, should like to suggest calling it trial identification. (pp. 212–213)

Fleiss also compared a practitioner's ability to briefly and accurately interject oneself into a patient's mind to that of a tea taster who takes in a small sample only long enough to taste it.

In *Principles of Intensive Psychotherapy* (1950), Frieda Fromm-Reichmann emphasized the importance of establishing an empathic relationship with challenging patients. To this point the psychoanalyst stated, "We know now that the success or failure of psychoanalytic psychotherapy is, in addition, greatly dependent on the question of whether or not there is an empathic quality between the psychiatrist and the patient" (Fromm-Reichmann, 1950, p. 62). In Fromm-Reichmann's view, a practitioner's sensitivity is particularly important in working with individuals diagnosed with schizoid and schizophrenic disorders because they often experience threat in response to the prospect of becoming emotionally close with others. These patients are often afraid of the rebuke by a therapist that may occur after becoming involved in a caring relationship. They may also be fearful of personal reactions of hatred toward the practitioner that the rebuke will engender in them. Fromm-Reichmann also believed that it was possible to expand a practitioner's empathy toward diverse and challenging patients through professional training. Her engagement of empathic understanding was frequently evident in the context of her published case studies (Fromm-Reichmann, 1950; Szalita, 1976).

PSYCHOANALYTIC CONCEPTIONS AND EMPATHY

In the history of psychoanalytic therapy, particular conceptions have advanced treatment effectiveness and demonstrated that empathy is integral to their function in the therapeutic process. A *participant observer* stance enables a practitioner to oscillate between involvement and detachment while maintaining an empathic connection with a patient. An awareness of *countertransference* reactions alerts a therapist to recognize his or her biases and preoccupations that may restrict empathic understanding in a treatment relationship. The engagement of *defense mechanisms* by a patient indicates the presence of conflictive functioning, and an empathic climate frequently diminishes threat and promotes more open communication. The *model of a patient* pertains to the knowledge that is acquired by a therapist about an individual through sustained empathic interactions over the course of the treatment relationship. *Interpretation* is a major technique employed in psychoanalytic therapy in which a practitioner attempts to empathically clarify causal relationships in the experience of a patient.

Participant Observer

Years before Sullivan (1953, 1954) used the phrase *participant observer*, other psychoanalytic figures made reference to an oscillating function of a practitioner between the processes of introspection and observation (Greenson, 1960). Ferenczi (1928/1955) and Reik (1948) both described an empathic interaction of the analyst that rapidly shifts from an emotional involvement to a more detached objective perspective. When Freud (1912/1958) recommended that analysts assume a therapeutic stance of *evenly suspended attention*, a case can be made that he was referring to an activity that provided for a reposition in focus from a patient's communications to an analyst's internal perceptions (Greenson, 1967; Spencer & Balter, 1984). In this regard, the participant role of an analyst relates to thinking *with* the patient and the observer function pertains to thinking *about* the patient (Jaffe, 1986). An oscillation occurs between a position of an affective connection with a patient to that of assuming an intellectual evaluation of the individual's experience in a broader context (Berger, 1987; Paivio & Laurent, 2001). The observer phase also entails a critical scrutiny that presupposes a flexible ability to be able to oscillate to a participant position of emotional attunement with a patient. It is important to note that by including a practitioner's observations, the traditional scope of empathy goes beyond the subjective experience of the patient and, thus, extends the usual and more circumscribed meaning of the construct. At the same time, integrating an analyst's observations and objective data has the potential to provide a more comprehensive understanding of a patient.

In a participant response, an analyst engages the experiential reactions that resonate with aspects of the patient's internal states (Basch, 1983; Berger, 1987). In this therapeutic stance, a practitioner listens from within in order to subjectively feel in relative harmony with the patient. As an analyst oscillates to an observer function, a shift occurs that allows for an evaluation of material from external sources beyond the immediate interactions of a patient. From this perspective, an analyst listens from without in order to more objectively enhance an empathic understanding of a patient. A practitioner is able to call on psychoanalytic theory and his or her treatment experience to serve as preconceptions for organizing patient data engendered from the participant experiential mode (Josephs, 1995). As an example, the identification of a patient's employment of defense mechanisms is the result of a resonation with the analyst during the participant phase and a subsequent conceptualization of the construct while in the observer phase. In psychoanalytic practice, empathically derived observations in turn contribute to the formulation of an explanation of a patient's functioning through the intervention of an interpretation (Ornstein, 1979).

Although the participant observer interaction may be understood in terms of discrete functions, in practice the shift between each perspective merges and is accomplished without conscious intentionality. As an example of an analyst's participant observation, a young-adulthood client discusses instances of extreme neglect that she experienced in childhood when being raised by a parent with schizophrenia disorder. As the patient, Joan, relates occasions when she was left alone in a bedroom for hours at a time in soiled undergarments, the analyst experiences feelings of repulsion at the situation and hostility toward Joan's mother. Although Joan explicitly described periods when she felt abandoned and faced lengthy stretches of fear and despair, her feelings did not seem to fully resonate within the analyst. When oscillating to an observer stance, the analyst became aware that there appeared to be an incongruency between Joan's harrowing experiences and her ability to express her feelings about them. Joan talked about the most adverse conditions of neglect in emotionally muted and measured tones. The analyst conceptually recognized the possible operation of the defense mechanism of isolation in which there is a severance between cognitive and affective processes under threatening conditions. As the analyst oscillated back to a participant function, she sensed along with Joan the urgency of warding off painful feelings sufficiently to enable her to discuss a painful topic without becoming emotionally engulfed and psychologically destabilized. In conceptualizing isolation as a defense, the analyst became more empathic as a result of an increased understanding of the pattern of threat inherent in connecting emotionally with the traumatic neglect.

In the therapy example, through a combination of involvement and detachment, the analyst was able to gain access to the patient's inner state and to reach a deeper level of empathic understanding. Yet, although a shift between participant and observer functioning potentially enhances therapeutic movement, it is also possible for practitioners to overemphasize one phase or the other (Kernberg, 1979). Greenson (1960) discussed the condition of an *uncontrolled empathizer* who becomes so emotionally involved with a patient that he or she is unable to readily become detached and oscillate to a more objective stance. This situation could have occurred in the case illustration had the analyst felt such strong hostility toward Joan's mother that she maintained a prolonged degree of rebuke toward the individual. In this interaction, the analyst's affective intensity might have evoked a strong reaction from Joan, causing her to prematurely expose herself to threatening material and become emotionally overwhelmed. Greenson (1967) also recognized that impulse-ridden therapists tend to emotionally identify with a patient to the point that they mutually act out and confront potentially inflammatory issues without appropriate emotional restraint.

In contrast to an unmodulated and intrusive degree of participation on the part of an analyst, Greenson (1960) identified an *inhibited empathizer* who is fearful of becoming emotionally involved with a patient and remains largely fixed in an observer role. In assuming this treatment stance, an analyst is fearful of experiencing the affects and impulses evoked by a patient and may consequently misperceive the meaning of an individual's verbal and nonverbal communications. In a final example relating to the patient Joan, an analyst who primarily maintains an observer role may fail to perceive her lack of emotional expression and accompanying use of isolation. In this treatment circumstance, the analyst would simply continue to allow Joan to make reference to her early neglect experiences and would thus miss an opportunity to integrate an affective component into the discussion. The analyst inaccurately believes that Joan will psychologically come to terms with her personal history simply by describing particular incidents of neglect. Significantly, the practitioner lacks awareness of the relative absence of emotional expression on Joan's part. Greenson (1967) also observed that obsessional analysts typically maintain rigid control over their affective expression, and this constriction limits their ability to empathically evaluate a patient's functioning. In these instances, misdirections may occur when a practitioner is unable to attune to the feelings of a patient and verbalizes premature or poorly timed interpretations and related inferential interventions that are potentially destabilizing or traumatizing.

Countertransference

In an address at the opening of the Second Psychoanalytic Congress held in Nuremberg in 1910, Freud introduced the conceptualization of *countertransference* as an innovation in technique strongly linked to the personal functioning of the analyst. Freud (1910/1957) observed that an analyst's own complexes and internal resistance hindered the psychoanalytic process and that such obstacles needed to be done away with as quickly as possible (Feiner, 1979; Gelso & Carter, 1985). To this point, Freud (1910/1957) stated,

"We have become aware of the 'counter-transference,' which arises in him as a result of the patient's influence on his unconscious feelings, and we are most inclined to insist that he shall recognize this counter-transference in himself and overcome it" (pp. 144–145). In Freud's view, an analyst's countertransference is a reaction to the transference of a patient. Through self-analysis, Freud contended, an analyst could identify conflictive issues and resolve them to the point that they would not impede analytic progress. Freud also felt that it was imperative for an analyst to commit to a personal analysis. In this regard, Freud (1912/1958) stated, "It may be insisted, rather, that he should have undergone a psycho-analytic purification and have become aware of these complexes of his own which would be apt to interfere with his grasp of what the patient tells him" (p. 116). For several decades after Freud asserted that countertransference was a hindrance in treatment and needed to be eradicated, his position, with few exceptions, was upheld in the psychoanalytic community (Gelso & Carter, 1985; Orr, 1954). Ferenczi (1928/1955) was one of the few early psychoanalysts who recognized that countertransference potentially offered a means for an analyst to become aware of subjective biases in a way that could possibly enhance treatment communication and patient understanding.

In the 1950s, alternative perspectives began to emerge in the psychoanalytic literature that recognized the therapeutic value of processing an analyst's conflictive issues (Gelso & Hayes, 2002; Tansey & Burke, 1989). Annie Reich (1951, 1960) was a prominent figure in proposing that the effects of an analyst's unconscious needs and conflicts influenced patient understanding and constructive progress in psychoanalysis. Reich was also concerned that countertransference could interfere with an analyst's ability to empathically respond to patient material and seriously impede analytic treatment. Reich (1951) stated:

> If the analyst has some reasons of his own for being preoccupied, for being unable to associate freely, for shrinking back from certain topics, or if he is unable to identify with the patient, or has to identify to such a degree that he cannot put himself outside the patient again—to mention only a few of the possible difficulties—he will be unable to listen in this effortless way, to remember, to understand, to respond correctly. (p. 26)

Furthermore, Reich felt that an analyst must be constantly aware of his or her own countertransference and to employ self-analysis in order to cope with and manage particular preoccupations.

In other writings that are representative of the emerging views in the 1950s, Heimann (1950) contended that countertransference related to all the feelings that an analyst experiences toward a patient rather than narrowly focused reactions to the transference. She also believed that analysts should be able to effectively manage countertransference feelings without acting on them because they have received a training analysis. In a process with implications for a participant observer role, Racker (1953) argued that it is necessary for an analyst to adopt an objective perspective toward his or her own subjectivity and countertransference. Through a type of inner duality, an analyst is able to observe and analyze his or her subjective and countertransference functioning. In another direction, Spitz (1956) observed that an analyst should achieve a countertransference that is sufficiently sublimated in order to be able to briefly identify with a patient in a treatment situation. In particular, the transient identification enables the analyst to empathize with infantile aspects of a patient's behavior.

The scope of Freud's *classic* approach in defining countertransference was limited to an analyst's unconscious reactions to a patient's transference in the treatment relationship. Unfortunately, Freud made only minimal comments with respect to his thoughts on the critical topic across his vast writings. As countertransference research expanded in the 1950s and beyond, the definition of countertransference broadened considerably to include virtually all feelings and attitudes of a therapist toward a patient or a client (Peabody & Gelso, 1982). This *totalistic* position was believed to be necessarily broad and comprehensive by providing full consideration to the entirety of an analyst's emotion-related behavior when interacting with a patient (Bouchard, Normandin, & Séguin, 1995; Heimann, 1950). Critics of Freud's classic conception of countertransference contended that the approach was essentially negative, reactive, and too narrowly focused, whereas criticisms directed at the totalistic approach found it to be so broad that the conception could lead to confusion or even prove to be meaningless in a treatment situation (Bouchard et al., 1995; Gelso & Hayes, 2002). In a more recent conceptualization that has been termed a *complementary* view, the definition of countertransference involves a therapist's reactions emanating from unresolved conflicts that are largely unconscious (Gelso & Hayes, 2002). In contrast to the totalistic view, Gelso and Hayes (2002) contended that the complementary position involved inevitable conflictive feelings of a therapist that occur in treatment and is therefore more scientifically useful and clinically meaningful.

Even though there has been varying opinion relating to the meaning of countertransference, there has been a general agreement that countertransference reactions that are inappropriately managed can have harmful effects in the treatment situation (Bouchard et al., 1995). Conversely, countertransference responses that are relatively controlled and intentionally processed have the potential to promote therapeutic gain. An important distinction has also been made between the emotional reactions as they relate to a therapist's unresolved conflicts and an enactment by the therapist on the feelings in the treatment relationship (Gelso & Carter, 1985). A therapist's awareness of countertransference reactions may serve to bring to light his or her personal issues that are important for empathically understanding a patient. On the other hand, the overt behavior of the therapist or the acting out of the conflictual affect in therapy can frequently be harmful. The intensity of a therapist's countertransference feeling may vary from being highly positive to highly negative in interactions with a patient. Behavioral expressions of countertransference range from avoidance, withdrawal, and underinvolvement to overinvolvement, intrusion, and excessive control (Gelso & Hayes, 2002). Extending beyond the psychoanalytic orientation, countertransference has been theorized to exist across all treatment persuasions and is an inherent and inevitable aspect of interactions between a therapist and a patient or client (Gelso & Hayes, 2002).

In an example of countertransference in treatment, a therapist named Susan resonates with strong feelings of protectiveness toward a patient. Reflecting on this seemingly excessive emotional reaction, Susan recognizes a long-term need to shield herself from adverse reactions that relate to conditions of deprivation in her childhood. An awareness of these conflictive feelings alerts Susan to try to control her overprotective tendencies. Susan's sensitivity to her internal conflict also enhances an empathic understanding of what it is like for the patient to experience a sense of vulnerability and a protective response. In a contrasting example, another therapist named Jacob also experiences strong feelings of protectiveness toward a patient. In this instance, Jacob fails to reflect on these reactions and on the extent to which they are derived from developmental issues in his personal life. As was the case with Susan, Jacob has an unfulfilled longing to be protected and cared for that emanates from neglectful conditions in his childhood. As treatment continues, the therapist avoids discussion of topics that may be threatening or even unpleasant for the patient or for himself. Even as the patient begins to demonstrate an emotional readiness to explore more challenging material, the therapist maintains a protective and affectively constrictive treatment stance. These brief examples suggest how countertransference potentially hinders therapy progress by gratifying a therapist's needs, but also how the effective management of a practitioner's emotional reactions may promote the treatment process.

Defense Mechanisms

At the end of the 19th century, Freud conceptualized patterns of an individual's defensive responses to psychological threat, and he described the operation of six *defense mechanisms* (Freud, 1894/1962, 1896/1962). Conversion, displacement, isolation, projection, repression, and retreat or withdrawal from reality were among the defenses identified by Freud (Clark, 1998a). Freud's positions on the nature and number of defense mechanisms evolved over a period of many years after his initial theorizing about the defenses. Throughout scattered and extensive commentary on the topic, Freud made reference to as many as seventeen relatively discrete defenses. Nearly all of the defense mechanisms that Freud introduced were used interchangeably with repression, and for a lengthy period repression was synonymous with defense. In 1926, Freud reverted to his original conception and determined that the defense mechanisms should be distinguished as separate entities, and repression was acknowledged as a "special" method of defense (Freud, 1926/1959).

Freud never wrote a definitive essay on the defenses, and this endeavor was left to be completed by his daughter, Anna Freud. In her widely acclaimed volume, *The Ego and the Mechanisms of Defense* (1936/1966), she detailed 10 defense mechanisms. Since Sigmund and Anna Freud's original conceptualizations of the defenses, the number of mechanisms enumerated in the professional literature has climbed to over fifty. Fortunately however, a much smaller and more manageable number of defense mechanisms have become prominent in therapy and research. From a contemporary perspective, the following defense mechanisms are most identifiable in counseling and psychotherapy: denial, displacement, identification, isolation, projection, rationalization, reaction formation, regression, repression, and undoing (Clark, 1998a).

There have been numerous published definitions of individual defense mechanisms and the general meaning of a defense mechanism as a term in the therapeutic literature (Blum, 1982). The construct typically involves an individual subjectively distorting conflictive reactions that are emotionally intolerable (Clark, 1998a). Defense mechanisms are also generally defined as relating to a largely unconscious process on the part of an individual that engenders reactive and undifferentiated responses to threat. In a treatment situation, for example, a patient feels threatened when discussion turns to his possible abuse of alcohol. The patient becomes tense as the topic is raised by the therapist and immediately begins to minimize the extent and frequency of his drinking. The patient's perception that he may have a serious alcohol problem evokes an internal conflict, and he quite automatically reacts to the threat with an avoidance pattern. From a perspective of empathic understanding, the therapist resonates with anxious feelings emanating from the individual and also experiences a sense of the threat and destabilization incurred in the interaction. As discussion with the patient continues, the therapist hypothesizes that the person is employing the defense mechanism of denial as it relates to his behavioral functioning. From a participant observer stance, the therapist is not only able to empathically involve himself with the patient, but also has the capacity to assume a detached position that enables him to consider the possibility of a defense engagement.

In the absence of a conceptualization of a patient's defensive reaction to threat, it is possible that a therapist may respond indiscriminately and unempathically to an individual. If a practitioner prematurely challenges a patient to explore his or her defensive functioning, typically the individual either emotionally withdraws or becomes hostile. In these instances, the therapeutic relationship may be jeopardized to the extent of curtailing open communication relating to the patient's conflictive issues. To continue with the example of the patient demonstrating possible alcohol abuse, the therapist states early in treatment, "It may be best for you to honestly share with me how frequently you find yourself drinking. You will get more out of treatment if you do this." In response, the patient states in angry tone, "I am being honest, and I resent the fact that you even bring this up!" In this interaction, the therapist's ill-advised comment evokes an even further entrenchment of the patient's defensive functioning. In a contrasting example, a therapist responds to a patient's threat in the context of discussing his alcohol consumption. In this exchange, the therapist empathically comments, "Apparently it doesn't make much sense to you for us to talk about your drinking when you don't feel it is that much of a problem."

Maintaining an empathic stance, however, with respect to an individual's defensive reactions can preclude consideration of the emotional conflicts that possibly stimulate the defense mechanisms in the first place. Furthermore, if a therapist continues to express an understanding of a patient's perspectives, discussion may be restricted to his or her frame of reference, regardless of how distorted or fragmented it may be. One therapeutic direction through which these important concerns may be addressed is for the therapist to challenge a patient's defenses only after the response to threat is generally understood, and the therapeutic relationship is more fully established. In this respect, Greenson (1967) stated:

> It is better to be deceived going along with the patient's productions than to reject them prematurely as false. The ability to suspend judgment even to the point of gullibility makes it possible to empathize with the patient, which may eventually lead to an understanding of the underlying motives. (p. 381)

In this regard, a conceptual grasp of the operation of particular defense mechanisms enables a therapist to gain a deeper understanding of a patient's functioning in an immediate situation and over the course of treatment. As an example, a college-age patient expresses extremely harsh comments about the sexual promiscuity of his peers in a university setting. The urgency and intensity of the patient's moral stance prompts the therapist to suspect the engagement of reaction formation as a defense. Over a period of time, this hypothesis proves to be accurate, and as discussion evolves, the patient slowly begins to express the deep sense of shame that he experiences with respect to sexuality.

In another direction, similar to a patient or a client, a practitioner is also susceptible to the employment of various defense mechanisms. In a treatment situation, a therapist's emotional conflicts and related defensive reactions may interfere with his or her empathic functioning and ability to provide reliable patient care (Halpern, 1993). As an example, in a supervision session a therapist-in-training enthusiastically reports that she has a positive relationship with almost all of the patients in her caseload. When it is brought to the therapist's attention by her supervisor that several of the patients seem to experience strained and ambivalent interactions with her, the therapist becomes emotionally upset and largely rejects the supervisor's assertions. After a period of consultation and personal reflection, the therapist becomes aware of her conflictive needs for acceptance and approval. In this example, the therapist's engagement of denial as a defense mechanism distorted her evaluation of the patients and also precluded an open-minded consideration of the supervisor's critical feedback.

Additional instances of a therapist's defense mechanism engagement may be cited that potentially impair therapeutic treatment. For example, a therapist employs a pattern of rationalization to justify his inability to achieve a satisfactory outcome with a number of the patients in his caseload. When asked about his caseload treatment progress by a colleague, the practitioner states, "It's almost impossible to expect any positive change as long as most of them are unwilling to open up." With respect to a particular patient, the same therapist relates, "You've got to be kidding me. With her background very little can be expected out of therapy." On another occasion, the rationalizing practitioner decries, "With the high numbers in my caseload, I've just about given up trying to form a relationship with any one of them." Even though the statements of the therapist may seem plausible to the individual, his lack of awareness of a repeated use of rationalization obviates the possibility of a fair and accurate appraisal of the quality of his treatment care. It may also be apparent that the therapist's preconceived views of his patients is inconsistent with an empathic stance that could potentially promote treatment gain. One explanation of the causation of the therapist's employment of rationalization may be that he has uncertainties about his therapeutic competence. It is clear that as long as the individual is able to maintain a perception that treatment progress is subject to conditions that are beyond his control, his professional expertise is less often called into question.

With respect to particular processes, identification and projection assume central positions in a practitioner's ability to empathize with a patient. Identification enables one to emotionally put oneself in the place of the patient. Projection relates to the capacity of a therapist to project himself or herself into what the patient feels (Reik, 1948). In this sense, there is a close association between identification and projection, and Reik (1948) merges the processes in the first phase of his empathy process model. In contrast, however, to facilitative interactions in treatment, a practitioner's employment of identification and projection as defense mechanisms can distort patient understanding and undermine therapeutic progress. As with other responses to threat, when identification and projection assume defensive proportions, the therapist's conflictive issues and needs frequently become manifest in treatment interactions. In these instances, a therapist may identify with a patient to the extent that psychological boundaries become enmeshed, and the practitioner's ability to assume a more detached and objective function is compromised. With respect to projection, a practitioner attributes his or her conflictual functioning to a patient, and this exchange creates distortions in client understanding. In a treatment example involving a practitioner's employment of both identification and projection as defense mechanisms, a late-adulthood patient discusses her experiences relating to the loss of her husband 2 years ago. The therapist, who experiences emotional conflicts relating to issues of death and loss, immediately and intensely identifies with the patient. At one point the therapist begins to sob as the patient speaks about her feelings of loneliness. Although the patient has made a relatively reasonable adjustment to her husband's passing, the practitioner, projecting from his frame of reference, continues discussion of the topic for an extended period of time. Additionally, the therapist's strong emotional reaction is confusing and unsettling to the patient, and she decides not to discuss her feelings of loneliness further because it is upsetting to the therapist.

As is the case with other defense mechanisms, identification and projection represent processes that are largely unconscious, and it may be difficult for a therapist to recognize his or her own defensive responses. In a procedural direction that is similar to that employed when addressing countertransference, a practitioner is in a position to consider the influence of his or her defensive functioning in the treatment situation. Through a process of self-reflection, a therapist may begin to recognize instances that evoke strong feelings of threat with respect to particular topics or concerns in therapy. This awareness may suggest preoccupations that require personal consideration and exploration on the part of the therapist. When a practitioner's defenses are more ingrained and less accessible to conscious processing, supervision or consultation is a viable option to assist in clarifying particular defensive patterns that may result from unresolved conflicts. In more extensive instances of a therapist's defense engagement, therapy may be needed in order to work through personal issues that continue to impede an empathic understanding of patients and the provision of quality treatment. Finally, as a practitioner evaluates his or her own defense patterns, this examination may enhance the therapist's empathic capacity to understand a patient's employment of defense mechanisms.

Model of a Patient

In an innovative direction that has implications for empathy in psychoanalytic therapy, Greenson (1960, 1967) conceptualized a *model of a patient* that articulated a framework for organizing a comprehensive understanding of a patient. In working with a patient over an extended period of time, Greenson believed, a therapist builds up an internal version of the individual that is influenced and shaped by multiple sources of knowledge. Through an empathic process that enables a practitioner to identify with a patient, a conception of a working model begins to develop within the therapist. In attempting to describe what is an elusive form of understanding, Greenson (1967) cited an illustration in working with a female patient: "As I have worked with this patient over the years, I have built up a working model of the patient consisting of her appearance, her behavior, her ways of moving, her desires, feelings, defenses, values, attitudes, etc." (p. 368). In Greenson's conception, this form of knowledge provided a basic and tentative structure in which further data may be integrated in order to refine the model and enhance its accuracy. As a therapist continues to increase his or her empathic understanding and appreciation of an individual's experience, the model of a patient becomes increasingly complex (Berger, 1987).

In Greenson's (1960, 1967) view, the working model is not a replication of a patient's experience nor is it identical with the individual. Instead, the model is a modified conception that contains a therapist's expectations for the patient and an anticipation of the potentialities of the person (Bennett, 2001). In this respect, a therapist is in a position to make predictions about a patient's functioning during the course of analysis and formulate assumptions relating to the potential of the patient. Additionally, a therapist's theoretical knowledge and clinical experiencc is "lightly sketched into the model" (Greenson, 1967, p. 422). Accordingly, a therapist is able to call on his or her experience derived from patients with similar backgrounds and disorders and to utilize theoretical perspectives from psychoanalytic models and various other sources (Patton & Meara, 1992). In turn, the constellation of the observations embodied in the model of the patient are used to inform the use of interpretation and other change interventions in psychoanalytic treatment.

In a treatment situation, a therapist constructs a specific conceptual referent of a patient, and the longer that the practitioner works with the individual, the more extensive, reliable, and useful the model becomes (Buie, 1981). In conceptualizing a working model of a patient, however, Greenson (1967) was critical of therapists who ignored a need to intellectually integrate patient data that had been made available or is accessible to enhance treatment. In this regard, Greenson (1967) stated, "As a consequence there is no overall view of the patient, no reconstructions of larger segments of a patient's life, there are just a collection of insights" (p. 16). At the same time, Greenson also criticized analysts who hastily formulate patient conceptualizations based on limited and fragmented clinical data. These practitioners fail to enrich their observations by taking into consideration theoretical systems and pertinent patient data for organizing and clarifying clinical material (Schafer, 1959). More fully *knowing* the experience of a patient at a given moment depends on an apprehension of his or her personal history and future prospects in a relationship to better understand how the individual perceives reality (Bachrach, 1976; Schafer, 1959).

Over the course of the treatment process, the mental model of the patient remains open to revision and refinement as more is learned about the individual (Jenkins, 1997). In this regard, Berger (1987) discussed a case in which the therapist's model of a patient changed over a period of time. In the initial model, the patient was understood in terms of having been a victim of difficult women. This perception was largely based on the patient's developmental history with a troubled and excessively demanding mother. As a result of working through a number of the patient's issues, this original model evolved into a more complex conception that also included the patient as a victimizer with respect to his relationships with women. The revised model encompassed a broader and more accurate understanding in which the patient was perceived as having conflictive perceptions toward women in addition to experiencing material deficiencies in various aspects of his life. In this instance, the therapist transiently shares the patient's experience and then integrates these perceptions into the context of a broader, more complex, and more objective perspective of the individual (Levy, 1985).

In constructing the model of a patient, the therapist is often able to activate affective and imaginative processes that provide an empathic understanding of a patient's experiential state (Berger, 1987; Schafer, 1959). In this regard, Greenson (1967) related:

> By shifting the working model of the patient into the foreground, the rest of me was relatively de-emphasized and isolated. Only those personal experiences and reactions of mine similar to the patient's remained near the model, or might be used to fill out the model. (p. 421)

In this sense, the implicit aim of the model is to empathically enhance an understanding of the patient through the therapist's inner awareness and hypothesis testing (Schafer, 1959; Spengler, Strohmer, Dixon, & Shivy, 1995). As a practitioner becomes progressively more able to sense and evaluate a patient's experiencing through the model of the patient, the therapist is in a position to anticipate the individual's potential responses to various therapeutic interventions. In a treatment situation, this experiencing is then used as a resource and as a guide in the formulation and communication of interpretations and other insight-related activity (Bohart, 1991; Patton & Meara, 1992).

Interpretation

In psychoanalytic therapy, the function of interpretation as a treatment technique has a long and enduring history (Auld, Hyman, & Rudzinski, 2005). Over a period of time in the analytic process, a therapist draws inferences from interactions with a patient and from inner responses evoked during treatment sessions (Szalita, 1976). At an appropriate time, the practitioner is able to convey the inferential material to the patient in the form of an interpretation. In this endeavor, the therapist progresses from a mode of understanding to one of communicating what has been understood (Basch, 1983; Kohut, 1984). Empathy plays a central role in the understanding phase of an evolving inferential function by preparing the way for an interpretation. To this end, Patton and Meara (1992) cited an example of a practitioner's empathic understanding serving to calm a patient while fostering a readiness to discuss threatening material in greater depth. As the therapist articulates what is understood, and the interpretation is perceived to be reasonably accurate by the patient, a deeper level of empathic understanding may occur (Ornstein, 1979). In this regard, what is apprehended derives from an extended period of empathic immersion with a patient and is a precursor to the explanation phase that must follow in the form of an interpretation. Agosta (1984) emphasized this point when he stated, "Empathy most authentically becomes a mode of understanding as it is transformed to and communicated as an interpretation" (p. 51).

Although there are various ways an interpretation may be conveyed in psychoanalytic therapy and other theories of counseling and psychotherapy, contemporary treatment focuses on establishing causal relationships between a patient's past and current experiences or between here-and-now referents (Auld, Hyman, & Rudzinski, 2005; Clark, 1995a; Ivey, D'Andrea, Ivey, & Simek-Morgan, 2002). As an example, a patient exhibits perfectionistic tendencies to the point where they create a high level of tension in the individual's life and interfere with his ability to function on a daily basis. In treatment, the patient discusses his current situation but also describes at length and with an anxious intensity what it was like for him to grow up in a home under the supervision of stern parents with strict expectations. After expressing an empathic understanding of the patient's current situation and developmental history, the therapist begins to hypothesize about elements in the patient's life that seem to relate to his emotional disorder. In communicating the inferences in the form of an interpretation, the therapist relates, "Could it be that the high expectations that you place on yourself possibly relate to what you came to know so well as a child in your parent's home?" In this instance, the practitioner conveys an interpretation in a tentative form that is phrased as a question or a hypothesis. Psychoanalytic topics that serve as content material for interpretations include such potentially conflictive matters as transference, defense mechanisms, dreams, resistance, personality traits, physical reactions, and gestures (Auld, Hyman, & Rudzinski, 2005; Garduk & Haggard, 1972).

When criticism is directed at the employment of interpretations in psychoanalytic therapy and other psychotherapies, it is usually in the context of a therapist imposing interpretations on a patient that are insensitive or poorly timed. Mahrer, Dessaulles, Gervaize, and Nadler (1987) spoke of the exalted role of the therapist as a *grand interpreter* who assumes responsibility for patients and fosters dependent relationships. In most negative interactions involving interpretations, a practitioner lacks an empathic understanding of a patient, and this becomes evident in the delivery of an interpretation. Benedek (1953), for example, discussed the case of a young woman with artistic training and skill who happened to glance at a drawing that was made by the therapist. Reacting to the drawing, the patient expressed enthusiastic and positive comments. In response to the patient's praise, the therapist defensively and coldly replied, "This (namely her praise) is just a denial of your competition with men" (p. 204). Understandably, the patient felt belittled, hurt, and punished. The patient also began to realize that a person who could be so insensitive and lacking in understanding of her intentions simply lacked the capacity to understand her at all. Although the therapist may have been accurate at some level with his interpretation, the timing and deprecating response demonstrated a misunderstanding of the patient's desire to be taken seriously in a field in which she was competent. In this example, and others like it, a practitioner's poorly timed and intrusive interpretations may confuse and embarrass patients and create doubt about the capabilities of the practitioner (Seligman, 2004).

In a controversy that continues today, there is varying opinion with respect to the role of an interpretation and empathy in effecting change in a patient or a client (Hill, 2004; Spence, 1982). From one point of view, interpretations are recognized as curative in a psychoanalytic sense (Basch, 1983). Empathy facilitates the acquisition of knowledge inherent in an interpretation that makes the intervention appropriate and effective. Yet, it is the therapist's verbalizations that engender therapeutic change in a patient. From another perspective (Kahn, 1985), empathic understanding fosters a bond between a patient and a practitioner. In the context of an emotional attunement with a patient over a sustained period of time, it becomes possible for a therapist to express an interpretation that creates an even deeper level of empathic understanding. In this respect, empathy is viewed as being more than a vehicle that contributes to a sound interpretation, and is perceived as therapeutic in itself in the working alliance between the patient and the practitioner.

SUMMARY

Over a period of 100 years, a number of individuals have made notable contributions to advancing the place of empathy and empathic understanding in psychoanalytic therapy. Although Freud made only brief and scattered references to empathy, he was the first to use the term in psychoanalysis. His views are a part of the thought collective of various early contributors who have developed and refined ideas relating to empathy over many years. Ferenczi's innovative practices gave prominence to the practice of instituting an emotionally warm and empathic treatment relationship. Ferenczi also recognized countertransference as a potential resource for clarifying conflictive issues of the therapist, and he voiced dissenting views on the reality of childhood sexual abuse. Between the period of Ferenczi's final papers in the early 1930s and the emergence of Kohut's writing in the late 1950s, several other psychoanalytic figures provided incisive observations relating to empathy. Reik conceptualized four phases relating to empathic processing, and Sullivan described interpersonal aspects of human development and therapeutic practice that involved empathic understanding. Sullivan also introduced the term participant observer that has implications for empathy in the treatment context. Other psychoanalysts, including Fenichel, Fleiss, and Fromm-Reichman, made reference to empathy in their works.

Various psychoanalytic conceptions are prominent in their relationship to empathy. From a participant observer stance, a therapist may oscillate between an emotional involvement and a more detached response. As another central construct, countertransference may hinder or enhance an empathic understanding of patients. A practitioner's recognition of patient defense mechanisms provides a means for conceptualizing how individuals react to perceived threat involving conflictual personal issues. The model of the patient offers a framework for organizing an evolving conceptual referent for the patient. A therapist may also communicate an understanding of a patient through an interpretation in the context of a sustained level of empathic understanding.

Chapter 6

Self Psychology and Empathy

Empathy is the operation that defines the field of psychoanalysis.

—Kohut (1984, p. 174)

When I first read an introduction to the work of Heinz Kohut and his theoretical orientation of self psychology, I quickly dismissed the approach as untenable and unappealing. With such terms as *twinship, idealization, selfobject,* and *selfobject needs,* self psychology seemed burdened down with cumbersome vocabulary and conceptualizations. I maintained my negative views of this psychoanalytic therapy for some time until I happened to read an article by Ornstein (1979) on the essential place of empathy in psychoanalysis. Ornstein largely focused on Kohut's thoughts relating to empathy, and the piece prompted me to take a look at some of his original writings. From the outset, I found Kohut's (1959) article on introspection and empathy in psychoanalysis to be particularly important in breaking through resistance to the concepts of self psychology. In following up on this thought-provoking essay, I read Kohut's (1982) subsequent paper that expanded his views on the same topics in the broader context of mental health. With my enthusiasm for self psychology increasing, I decided to read the three books that Kohut (1971, 1977, 1984) wrote in his lifetime. Although I was not persuaded to accept all of Kohut's concepts and theoretical positions, I began to feel more comfortable with his ideas. Twinship, selfobject, and related terms that once seemed unwieldy to me began to make sense in the context of human development and empathic understanding. Yet, what I found most appealing in the material on self psychology were the conceptions and practices relating to empathy in the therapeutic process. In this regard, once I progressed beyond my initial cursory understanding of the approach, my own thinking was enriched with many of the innovative ideas of self psychology.

THEORETICAL PERSPECTIVES AND EMPATHY

Kohut (1977) succinctly defined empathy as a *vicarious introspection*, and he viewed the construct as a primary means for acquiring psychological information with respect to a patient that could subsequently be used to inform therapeutic interventions. In a treatment situation, Kohut also felt that empathy was value-neutral and he semantically separated the construct from such qualities as compassion, kindness, and benevolence. Extending his conceptualizations beyond the therapeutic process, Kohut gave extensive consideration to the influence of empathy in normal and psychopathological aspects of human development. Kohut formulated a theory that emphasized an individual's essential need for empathy and empathic understanding as originating in an early developmental period and continuing throughout the life span. Self psychology represents a major school of psychoanalytic thought, in addition to ego psychology, object relations, and interpersonal psychoanalysis, that has emerged from Freud's classical tradition of psychoanalysis (Fall, Holden, & Marquis, 2004).

Defining Empathy

In the history of psychoanalysis, the analyst's subjective capacity for self-analysis and self-reflection has long been referred to as the process of introspection. In 1959, Kohut theoretically melded the trained introspective skill of an analyst with the experience of a vicarious interaction with a patient. Accordingly, *vicarious introspection* became Kohut's (1959) new term for defining empathy in the context of the analytic process. In Kohut's view, vicarious introspection assumes the position as the central means for understanding a patient's subjective functioning that serves as a prerequisite for the subsequent employment of interpretations and other inferentially based interventions. In this sense, empathy specifically refers to a practitioner's ability to listen introspectively and gather data relating to the inner life of a patient (Silverstein, 1999; Wispé, 1987). Kohut continued to emphasize the traditional use of introspection in treatment, but he also viewed empathy as a definer of the field and a major tool in psychoanalysis (Kohut, 1991; Rowe & MacIsaac, 1989). In 1984, Kohut further clarified the meaning of empathy: "The best definition of empathy—the analogue to my terse scientific definition of empathy as 'vicarious introspection' . . . —is that it is the capacity to think and feel oneself into the inner life of another person" (p. 82).

In an innovative direction that relates to empathic understanding, Kohut (1984) made reference to a therapist's *experience-near* mode of observation in a treatment situation. In this theoretical capacity, a practitioner attempts as closely as possible to sense the experiencing of another person (Rowe & MacIsaac, 1989). Through a basic psychological bond, an analyst or a therapist strives to grasp the motives and intentions of a patient (Silverstein, 1999). In this respect, an experience-near function provides organized patient data obtained from an empathic listening stance. This observational material may then be processed through what Kohut described as an *experience-distant* mode that represents a therapist's theoretical conceptualizations, knowledge about human behavior, and personal values (Kohut, 1984; Ornstein, 1994). Explanatory processes integral to experience-distant perspectives are sufficiently removed from the emotionally active area of a patient's functioning and are based on a higher level of abstraction (Kohut, 1984). Although Kohut did not consider the experience-distant level to involve directly the process of empathy, what is learned about a patient through this mode of experience can ultimately produce a more comprehensive and informed quality of empathic understanding.

In a treatment example relating to the experience modalities, a therapist recently began working with a patient, Diane, who had been previously diagnosed with a borderline personality disorder. In an experience-near mode, the therapist resonates with Diane's persistent feelings of emptiness and senses both a disturbance and an unstable quality in her sense of self. The practitioner also modulates to the changeable nature of Diane's mood, which responds variously to her feelings of irritability, dysphoria, and anxiety. As Diane discusses relationships in her life, the therapist experiences the intensity of her alternating reactions to individuals and her desperate fears of abandonment. As the practitioner shifts to an experience-distant mode, she recognizes a pervasive pattern in Diane's functioning that is consistent with a borderline diagnosis. From this vantage point, the analyst is sufficiently detached emotionally to be able to detect that Diane's expression of anger is often inappropriate and her frantic efforts to avoid abandonment are marked by extremes of idealization and devaluation in her relationships with others. As treatment continues, the therapist also begins to observe an impulsive pattern of self-damaging substance abuse and sexually acting out. With perspectives from both experience modes, the practitioner is able to integrate felt-level experiencing with more analytical and abstract observations. In combination, contributions from each of the experience levels enables the therapist to gain a broader sense of empathic understanding that can be employed in subsequent therapeutic interactions with the patient.

Kohut (1971) was aware that he would be subject to criticism within psychoanalytic circles when he began to give a prominent focus toward empathy as a developmental need and as a treatment variable. Kohut considered his therapeutic approach to be within the mainstream of psychoanalytic thought and did not view his ideas on empathy as constituting a radical departure from the framework of psychoanalysis (Silverstein, 1999). In this regard, Kohut (1984) stated, "Although self psychology must not claim that it has provided psychoanalysis with a new kind of empathy, it can claim that it has supplied analysis with new theories which broaden and deepen the field of empathic perception" (p. 175). However, in order to attain a more scientific and credible standing, Kohut realized that he needed to separate empathy from associated terms, such as intuition and compassion. In terms of intuition, Kohut (1971) recognized that the function was occasionally considered to be synonymous with empathy and, therefore, viewed as a sentimental and untestable interaction. In principle, Kohut thought that intuition was not related to empathy as intuitive reactions essentially involve the rapid execution of mental activities. As an inherently value-neutral mode of observation, Kohut also recognized that empathy has the potential to be motivated by constructive or destructive aims. Even though individuals may have an innate need for empathic understanding, it is possible to sentimentalize about the process and overlook the possibility that empathy can betray a person when misused or abused (Lang, 1994; Wolf, 1988). In a treatment example, a therapist empathically recognizes that one of her patients wishes to avoid the discussion of certain unpleasant topics that are essential for her to address in treatment. Even though the therapist is aware that it is a therapeutically appropriate time to examine the sensitive issues, she decides to be "nice" to the patient and shift to less distressing concerns. In this instance, although the practitioner empathically responds to the patient, her failure to explore difficult and uncomfortable material precludes a potential opportunity for client growth and constitutes a misuse of empathy.

In a related direction, Kohut (1977) was also concerned about the possibility of confusing empathy with a treatment approach primarily designed to gratify a patient's needs. In spite of the possibility that an individual may have been developmentally deprived of his or her needs for empathic understanding, the intent of analysis should not be influenced by efforts to make up for what has been unfulfilled. This is an approach that was associated with the work of Alexander and French (1946), who sought to provide a *corrective emotional experience.* It is a program of treatment that had been largely discredited as a psychoanalytic method (Rangell, 1982). If the exclusive focus of therapeutic process centers on developing an empathic milieu, patients may feel patronized, and the inappropriate gratification of their needs might inhibit the possibility of emotionally working through the perceived deficits. Ideally, an analyst will employ a more sophisticated approach through efforts to empathically understand a patient's unfulfilled needs and by subsequently explaining the insights gained through interpretation and related inferential interventions (Rowe & MacIsaac, 1989). Although Kohut (1982) continued to emphasize the importance of interpretation in effecting patient change, he began in the latter phase of his writings to acknowledge the value of empathy in its own right as a powerful emotional bond between an analyst and a patient that in itself might be therapeutic (Gardner, 1991).

Developmental Conceptualizations and Empathy

In addition to recognizing empathy as a central variable in therapeutic treatment, Kohut formulated a theory that gave prominence to empathy as an essential factor in the promotion of human development (Fall et al., 2004). It is apparent from a related line of inquiry that self psychology has evolved in a period when research in social and developmental psychology has given increasing attention to the importance of empathy throughout the life span (Davis, 1996; Eisenberg & Strayer, 1987; Wispé, 1987). Within self psychology, early empathic interactions are viewed as having a major influence on the emotional development of individuals (Binder, 1998; Schwaber, 1981). The emphasis of self psychology on the quality of empathic responsiveness in the early years of development and throughout the life span have implications that are closely related to interpersonal, environmental, and cultural forces (Cooper, 1983; Hoffman, 2000). In particular, the functions of primary caregivers are significant in the development of the self and in engendering the capacity for bonding and social relatedness in diverse contexts (Binder, 1998). Under sustained conditions, clients who are deprived of empathically responsive interactions are susceptible to the development of psychopathology (Decety & Jackson, 2004).

Kohut employed several key constructs in the developmental conceptualizations of self psychology that emphasize empathy as an essential psychological nutrient. Kohut identified the *self* as a basic structure that represents a person's sense of continuity and cohesion (Fall et al., 2004). In an extrapolated definition, Kohut (1977) stated, "The self is a unit, cohesive in space and enduring in time, which is a center of initiative and a recipient of impressions" (p. 452). As the dynamic core of the personality, the self is subject to study and understanding as a form of organization (Goldberg, 1988; Tobin, 1991). In this respect, Kohut (1971) described how the structure of the self develops in terms of relating with others through what he referred to as a *selfobject.* Selfobjects are a class of psychological functions that have a capacity to maintain, restore, or transform the sense of self of an individual (Kahn, 1985; Stolorow, 1986).

In introducing the selfobject as a term, Kohut attempted to conceptualize experience with another as it influences the formation of the self (Rowe & MacIsaac, 1989). Through sustained interactions with primary caretakers, aspects of selfobject functions are gradually internalized into an individual's structure of the self in a process that Kohut referred to as *transmuting internalizations* (St. Clair & Wigren, 2004). A more cohesive and stable self begins to evolve through the functions provided by the selfobjects. In this regard, the selfobject involves need interactions that are provided by a person rather than being the objective person. Kohut (1984) also referred to one other term that contributes to the formation of the self. Through an *optimal frustration,* a person stops providing a selfobject need, and the developmentally capable self must then take over the function (Tobin, 1991).

Kohut (1971) used the term selfobject not only as a provider of an individual's emotional needs but also as an innate human need in itself (Fall et al., 2004). Kohut (1971, 1984) identified *empathic attunement* and *mirroring, idealization,* and *twinship* as being primary selfobject needs. The first selfobject need is for an *empathic attunement* and *mirroring* that communicates a sense of self-importance and value to an infant or child through an engaging interaction of approval and admiration. As an example of empathic attunement, an infant pokes himself on the nose with a rattle and begins to cry. In response, the baby's mother immediately begins to soothe and caress him. In an instance of empathic mirroring, a young child throws a ball for the first time, and a parent expresses joy and delight while returning the ball to the child in order for her to throw it again. According to Kohut (1977), mirroring needs include such emotional expressions as approval, support, love, and acceptance. The mirroring need is typically experienced by the person as confirmation or affirmation of his or her existence as a human being, and in the latter period of Kohut's writings, he primarily made reference to the selfobject needs for empathic attunement and mirroring under the single designation of mirroring (Goodman, 1992; Zausner, 2003). Gradually, over a period of time, a child becomes able to comfort oneself and to act independently as the self develops the inner structure to perform the functions. A healthy climate for meeting the emerging self of the child is a mature and cohesive parental self that is responsive and in tune with the varying needs of the child and its in-born potentials (Kohut, 1977; St. Clair & Wigren, 2004).

Kohut identified another innate selfobject need for *idealization* in which an individual perceives at least one person in an image of infallibility and omnipotence (Fall et al., 2004; Kohut, 1977). The child can look up to the provider of the selfobject need of idealization in terms of merging and affecting contact with a presence that is larger and more powerful than itself (Tobin, 1991). As an example of idealization, a young child, who has only recently begun to take steps, is walking slowly with her mother when she falls down and bumps her knee. The child cries softly as her mother picks her up. After holding her closely for a few minutes, the mother puts her down, and they both hold hands in continuing their walk together. *Twinship* is the final selfobject need that conveys an essential similarity or a likeness with another person. In a need that emerges at approximately 18 months, a child derives a sense of belonging and competence in the fulfillment of this need (Fall et al., 2004). An example of twinship occurs when a young child sweeps the floor or rakes leaves alongside a parent. Selfobjects and selfobject needs evolve as a person develops across the life span. From caretakers in infancy, selfobjects typically extend to teachers and peers in childhood and adolescence and to a spouse and work supervisors in adulthood (Fall et al., 2004). Selfobjects may also include a group or an abstract ideal that serves to support the cohesion of the self (Leider, 1996). This may, for example, include political or religious groups or ethical and moral systems. In this respect, Kohut (1971) believed that individuals have lifelong needs for the functions that selfobjects provide (Rowe & MacIsaac, 1989). As an example, in late adulthood, a spouse provides a selfobject need for the mirroring of comfort and love to a partner who suffers with a chronic illness. Kohut also thought that once a cohesive and mature self is formed, it tends to be resilient. According to Kohut (1984):

> A healthy self, is a structure that—except perhaps as an outcome of the most severe forms of traumatization such as prolonged confinement in concentration camps and other protracted dehumanizing experiences—is not prone to become fragmented, weakened, or disharmonious during maturity, at least not severely and/or for long periods. (p. 70)

Psychopathology and Empathy

In Kohut's (1977) view, the foremost contributor to the emergence of psychopathology is the failure of primary caretakers to empathically understand the child during early periods of development (Fall et al., 2004; Kohut & Wolf, 1978). In such instances, a young child may endure indifferent, neglectful, or abusive relationships with caregivers. In the absence of continuing expressions of empathy, there is little opportunity to meet his or her selfobject needs. A weakened or damaged self becomes evident when chronic patterns of empathic failures occur. In addition, developmentally earlier and more extensive negative experiences contribute to more severe emotional disorders. By largely attributing the origins of psychopathology to dysfunctional early life experiences, Kohut's theoretical position was consistent with a central tenet within the psychoanalytic tradition (Rowe & MacIsaac, 1989). At the same time, in his later works, Kohut deviated from the classical orientation by minimizing the importance of the libidinal or aggressive drives as an internal source of motivation and potential disturbance. Instead, Kohut believed that even the most disturbed behavior represented an attempt by an individual to maintain and preserve the vulnerable structure of the self (Kohut & Wolf, 1978; Tobin, 1991). In this respect, Kohut recognized the function of the defenses as a means to protect the cohesiveness of the self when subject to threat.

In his analytic practice and theorizing, Kohut was particularly concerned with the more severe disturbances of the self that included the primary disorders of narcissistic, borderline, and psychotic functioning (Fall et al., 2004). Across his writings, Kohut emphasized the dynamics and treatment of narcissism, and he considered the condition to represent a much higher percentage of the patient population in comparison to other mental health professionals. Kohut believed that the relative degree of an individual's psychopathology depended on the developmental timing and extent of empathic failure. In this regard, psychosis is considered a result of early and extensive caregiver deficiencies in providing empathic understanding to a young child. Borderline disorders characterize a population with a somewhat lesser pattern of empathic caregiver failure relative to the psychoses. With narcissistic conditions and with the neuroses, the provision of empathy is less inconsistent than with the developmental experiences of individuals diagnosed with a borderline disorder. With each type of disorder, Kohut thought that the early structuralization of the self was incomplete, and its development was relative to the intensity or severity of the disorder. In instances of traumatic selfobject failure, the individual loses any faith in the particular source of the selfobject functions and typically resorts to defensive processes in order to protect the vulnerable self from perceived threat and exposure to overwhelming negative emotions (Tobin, 1991).

Kohut recognized that a young child's developing self is heavily influenced by the interplay of the innate capacities of the individual and the qualitative responses of selfobjects (Kohut & Wolf, 1978). The potentialities of a child may be encouraged or met with indifference or even hostility on the part of the primary caretaker. In the case of the primary disorders, the subjective experience of an excessive frustration of requisite selfobject needs, or empathic failures, may contribute to a fragmentation of the self and disordered functioning (Segal, 1981; Stolorow, 1986). Although it is a pattern of faulty empathic interactions that relate to psychopathology, an illustration may help clarify a type of dysfunctional caretaker response. In the example, a 3-year-old boy puts on and takes off a baseball cap in front of his father, who is sitting in a chair in the living room. In accomplishing the routine three or four times, the boy is exuberant as he smiles broadly. The father observes his son, nods, and returns to reading the newspaper. The child moves closer to his father and pushes his leg while putting on and taking off the hat. The father, appearing indifferent to his son's behavior and showing little emotion, gets out of his chair and goes to the kitchen to get a drink of water. In this instance, the child's selfobject need for mirroring is not met, and the potential for the provision of twinship in the mutual use of the cap does not occur. In Kohut's view, such examples of empathic failure over a sustained period of time are associated with the development of varying disorders of the self.

In another departure from the classical psychoanalytic approach, Kohut, rather than viewing defenses as sources of resistance that needed to be eliminated, believed that a patient employs a pattern of defenses in order to protect a precarious and vulnerable self from perceived threat (Kohut, 1977; Rowe & MacIsaac, 1989). Kohut felt that the defensive structure of a patient primarily functions to mask signal defects in the self and to prevent a dreaded exposure to rebuff and ridicule (Kohut, 1977; Kohut & Wolf, 1978). Because the defenses also involve attempts to maintain a sense of self-equilibrium and self-cohesion, Kohut observed that patients frequently experience a therapist's attempt to remove the defenses as humiliating assaults on their self structure (Silverstein, 1999). In these instances, empathic failures that patients experienced in early development may be replicated, and therefore, once again, their selfobject needs are not met. In an example of a patient employing a defense, again consider Diane, who was previously mentioned as having a diagnosis of borderline personality disorder. As treatment continued with Diane, she frequently belittled the therapist by questioning her competencies and pointing out limitations in her professional background. In these instances, Diane seemed relieved, as she was able to identify with the practitioner's perceived sense of inadequacy and self-contempt prompted by her verbal attacks. In recognizing the possible engagement of projective identification (Clark, 1995c) as a defense, the therapist was able to avoid succumbing to either an emotional withdrawal or a verbal retaliation against the emotionally abusive patient. From Diane's perspective, the defense serves to prevent the exposure of her central defect of feelings of emptiness and a sense of being seriously damaged. If the practitioner is able to therapeutically progress through the treatment process, it may be possible at a subsequent point to clarify the protective function of Diane's defense functioning as it pertains to her perception of a deeply flawed and loathsome self.

Negative evaluations of the theoretical positions of self psychology largely focus on what is perceived as overemphasis on the role of empathy as an influence on development and as a means of understanding patients. In Wallerstein's (1983) view, Kohut and his followers, functioning within the realm of self psychology, maintained an excessive and one-dimensional stance on the determining effect of caregiver empathy on the developmental capacities of an individual. In this regard, disturbances in development are largely attributed to the single etiological factor of defective maternal or paternal empathy. According to Wallerstein (1983), explaining extremely complex issues through a single determining factor oversimplifies the nature of human development and psychopathology. Furthermore, by minimizing the function of drives and other innate forces involving internal conflict, Kohut is viewed as elevating nurturing functions to a predominant developmental role that is deterministic. In another criticism, Levy (1985) felt that Kohut's conceptualization of faulty empathy, as it relates to the emergence of psychopathology, does not capture the complexity and variety of specific interactions that occur between a child and a caregiver except in a broad and general way. Gill (1994) also thought that there is a major risk of assuming that a patient's perceptions will essentially be accepted as objective data while minimizing a therapist's perspective of psychic reality. Finally, in an attack on a central construct of self psychology, the self or the self-state was seen as a rather vague and limited concept on which to define a comprehensive psychology (Blum, 1982; Treurniet, 1980). Making a similar point, Segal (1981) stated, with respect to Kohut's conceptions, "It is not his view of the self or its development that is the problem, but the need to set it up as a separate kingdom (p. 470)."

EMPATHY IN THE TREATMENT PROCESS AND EMPATHY AND THERAPEUTIC INTERVENTIONS

In self psychology, empathy constitutes a mode of gathering psychological data relating to a patient in a treatment situation (Goldberg, 1980). Through an experience-near level of participation, an analyst or a therapist is able to acquire information that relates to the structure and functioning of the self. In this understanding phase of treatment, a therapist employs an observational stance involving the processes of introspection and empathy. On assuming an experience-distant vantage point, a practitioner is in a position to organize abstract and theoretical perspectives derived from a prolonged empathic immersion with an individual in a treatment situation. As a therapist formulates the coherent meaning of a patient's experience, the understandings are then used as a guide for communicating interpretations and related inferential techniques. In this explanation phase of treatment, a practitioner expresses tentative ways of conceptualizing a patient's subjective experiencing that broadens and deepens empathic understanding. In a contrasting perspective, a major criticism of self psychology is that the approach distorts the meaning of empathy when the construct is used as an intentional means of acquiring information relating to an individual's functioning. Another critical perspective relates to the potential for error and biases when a practitioner employs an introspective or subjective process during efforts to understand an individual.

Empathy in the Treatment Process

Kohut believed that only through an empathic immersion in the experience of a patient was it possible to acquire the in-depth psychological data needed to develop a penetrating understanding of an individual (Rowe & MacIsaac, 1989). At the same time, Kohut felt that it was essential for a therapist to assume a perspective beyond an understanding level in order to be able to conceptualize what is empathically understood. From an explanatory perspective, a practitioner is in a position to shift to a more objective stance in order to organize coherent patient understandings. With respect to the two-phase levels, Kohut (1971) stated:

> The scientific psychologist in general, and the psychoanalyst in particular, not only must have free access to empathic understanding; they must also be able to relinquish the empathic attitude. If they cannot be empathic, they cannot observe and collect the data which they need; if they cannot step beyond empathy, they cannot set up hypotheses and theories, and thus, ultimately, cannot achieve explanations. (p. 303)

In this regard, Kohut (1971) restricted empathy as a mode of observation or a scientific tool for psychological data gathering. In his view, however, empathic understanding does not by itself provide an explanation with respect to a patient's functioning. Only through the scrutiny and ordering of observations is it possible for a practitioner to provide meanings with the potential to reach deeper levels of empathy.

Understanding Phase of Treatment. As a mode of observation, Kohut's experience-near level of therapeutic processing relates to his abstract definition of empathy as a vicarious introspection (MacIsaac, 1997). By introspectively attempting to understand one's experience-near interactions, it becomes possible for a therapist to vicariously relate to the diverse backgrounds of patients. Although a practitioner's experiences may be attenuated in comparison to those of a patient, an awareness of such personal occurrences of rejection, fear, or humiliation is often sufficient in order to empathize with an individual's relatively more intense or severe situations. Through a vicarious introspection, an understanding of an individual's feeling states is possible because, to varying degrees, there is a universal sharing of fundamental human emotions (Ornstein, 1994). A practitioner need not experience the actual occurrence of an event that parallels that of a patient. What is necessary, however, is for a therapist to attempt to resonate with immediate feelings and images evoked by a patient's communicated states (Goodman, 1992; Katz, 1963; Wallace, 1985). As a result of reflection on what is vicariously experienced, a practitioner is able to anticipate what it is like for a patient to face a current reality in the context of a particular environment and personal history. Kohut also believed that it is possible for practitioners to broaden their capacity for empathy through participating in professional development endeavors (Rowe & MacIsaac, 1989). In this regard, with a touch of humor, Kohut (1984) stated, "Empathy is not God's gift bestowed only on an elect few. For the average individual, training and learning make the difference, rather than the fact of endowment" (p. 83).

Although the engagement of experience-near interactions frequently enhances the understanding of individuals, Kohut (1971, 1984) recognized that there are challenges for the reliable employment of empathy in a treatment situation. In particular, Kohut felt that it may be difficult for the therapist to formulate psychoanalytic perspectives of the early experiences of patients. In this regard, Kohut (1971) stated:

> The reliability of our empathy, a major instrument of psychoanalytic observation, declines the more dissimilar the observed is to the observer, and the early stages of mental development are thus, in particular, a challenge to our ability to empathize with ourselves, i.e., with our own past mental organizations. (p. 37)

In this sense, Kohut recognizes that there are limits to the full realization of empathic understanding as they relate to the background and psychological development of a patient and a therapist. Accordingly, in these instances, an awareness of dissimilarities may be instructive in order to alert the therapist to recognize differences rather than assume that the respective experiences are comparable. This may, in turn, prompt the practitioner to extend the exploration of experiences relating to the patient's condition in order to enhance empathic understanding.

In an illustration that relates to the difficulty of attaining empathic understanding in particular instances, a 30-year-old patient, Peter, with a diagnosis of narcissistic personality disorder, described his personal experiences relating to the divorce of his parents when he was a child. According to Peter, several days before his father moved out of the family home, Peter's mother told him that his father was leaving for good. Peter felt confused and frightened, but could recall no instance when he was comforted by his parents. What Peter primarily recollected was the crushing loss of his father's daily presence. As a child, Peter looked up to his father as a source of strength and approval. He recalled particular instances when his father appeared to be an all powerful and knowledgeable figure. When Peter's father abruptly left his family and did not return to visit for an extended period of time, Peter experienced feelings of abandonment and an engulfment of fear and isolation. As an idealized selfobject, the loss of Peter's father exposed him to a traumatization that he was able to emotionally evoke in his current experiencing. As Peter began working through his selfobject loss, the practitioner felt emotionally connected to Peter at an experience-near level. At the same time, never having experienced the depth of abandonment and profound despair that Peter had incurred, the practitioner at times was forced to intellectually evoke an intensity level in order to grasp the impact and implications of what he was hearing. As the therapist spent more time empathically listening to Peter, he experienced fewer occasions where he was less able to emotionally relate to Peter's developmental experiences.

Kohut also acknowledged that the varying backgrounds and the extent of patient pathology affected the reliability of the experience-near mode of gathering psychological data and the duration of the understanding phase of treatment. In this regard, Kohut (1984) felt that with certain severely traumatized individuals, the understanding phase must be extended to a very lengthy period of time. Kohut reasoned that until the point is reached where the therapist is able to genuinely feel what a patient is experiencing, any type of interpretation or inferential explanation is largely futile and lacks a true sense of empathic understanding. Furthermore, if a patient with a primary structural defect of the self enters psychoanalytic treatment, the individual reactivates the same selfobject needs that had been neglected or rejected through faulty interactions with selfobjects in his or her early life (Kohut & Wolf, 1978). The processing of the selfobject needs can be emotionally intense and require a lengthy period of affective expression and empathic understanding in order to arrive at a level where the patient is able to cognitively process the material. Kohut concluded that patients often employ a defensive structure with the prevailing purpose of covering over the primary defect of the self, which may involve such feelings as a deep sense of worthlessness, shame, or rejection (Kohut, 1977). As a long-term secondary structure, a patient's defenses can be firmly established and require an extended interval of empathic processing in order to lessen their emotional intensity.

As another means of empathically understanding patients, Kohut (1977, 1984) recognized the importance of transference from a self psychology frame of reference. Since Freud (1912/1958) initially clarified the construct, transference has held a central position in psychoanalytic thought and practice (Orr, 1954). Traditionally, transference has been viewed as a displacement of feelings and attitudes from significant persons, such as parents, siblings, or others in the earlier life of the patient, onto the therapist (Cormier & Nurius, 2003). Transferential reactions are largely unconscious and typically produce distorted perceptions of the therapist that are positive or negative. From Kohut's perspective, the empathic presence of the therapist tends to reactivate a pattern of unmet selfobject needs that surface from a patient's developmental history. Kohut (1984) stated that a patient's defect in the self engenders and maintains an individual's *selfobject transference.*

Kohut (1971) described two main types of selfobject transferences. In a *mirror transference,* a patient attempts to evoke a confirming reaction from a therapist by presenting his or her aspirations or accomplishments as products worthy of admiration (Rothstein, 1980). In the event that a practitioner demonstrates a lack of attention or interest in such exhibitionistic or grandiose portrayals, a patient typically becomes anxious or hostile. Mirror transferences have been further subdivided into related processes called merger and alter-ego or twinship (Goldberg, 1978). With respect to an *idealizing transference,* a patient manifests a wish or a desire for the therapist to be a powerful or highly capable figure (Kohut, 1971). In this respect, the idealizing transference relates to the idealized parent image (Goldberg, 1978). As a patient begins to achieve a union with the potency and calm functions of a practitioner, the patient experiences associated reactions that assuage self structure deficits. In the event that the patient is deprived of the idealized analyst, due to such situations as a slight tardiness, weekend absences, or changes in treatment schedules, the individual may begin to feel powerless, worthless, and lethargic (Kohut, 1971).

In order to clarify the transference process, it may be helpful to return to the previous example of Peter, who was diagnosed with a narcissistic personality disorder. Peter maintained selfobject needs that related to his defective and weakened sense of self. In order to meet his selfobject needs in treatment, Peter merged with the therapist's capacities of strength and calmness through an idealizing transference (Kohut & Wolf, 1978). As a behavioral manifestation of the idealizing selfobject need, Peter frequently expressed statements about the exceptional work of the therapist, and how much he admired his capabilities. Through the treatment process, the working through of the transference enables patients to pursue selfobject needs relating to defects in the self. In the case of Peter, the therapist can empathize with deficits that he experiences with respect to feelings of power and competency and begin to examine the unmet needs rooted in a developmental context.

When a patient mobilizes a selfobject transference, a therapist or analyst may momentarily react defensively due to a situational condition of stress. Under related conditions, it is also possible that a therapist may engage in a countertransference response that represents ingrained vulnerabilities that are conceptually related to a patient's transference patterns (Kohut, 1971). By taking into consideration the selfobject configurations delineated by Kohut, a practitioner is in a position to utilize a framework for recognizing and managing common countertransference phenomena (Rothstein, 1980). In this regard, it is possible for a practitioner to manifest a countertransference reaction in response to each of the self object transferences, in particular mirroring and idealization (Goldberg, 1978). In the absence of a conceptual understanding of the countertransference, a therapist may respond in a manner that lacks empathic understanding and is therapeutically detrimental. As an example, in response to a mirror transference, a therapist may experience sustained periods of boredom, withdrawal, or irritation that have been stimulated by a patient's grandiose fantasies and exhibitionistic displays (Goldberg, 1978; Leider, 1996). A practitioner's countertransference reaction may also involve chronic feelings of diminishment and negligibility that are prompted by a patient's grandiosity. If a therapist were to act on these particular reactions, it would likely impair the effectiveness of treatment.

In response to the other basic selfobject transference, a patient's idealization may prompt a therapist to experience countertransference reactions of sustained feelings of embarrassment and self-denigration (Goldberg, 1978; Kohut, 1971). It is also possible that a patient's idealizing transference may prompt a therapist to engage in a pattern of exhibitionistic displays as a result of an excessive stimulation of his or her own grandiose fantasies (Leider, 1996; Wolf, 1988). When a patient's direct expression of admiration stimulates an uncomfortable arousal of the therapist's grandiosity, the practitioner may quickly dismiss or deny his or her importance (Goldberg, 1978). An unwarranted rejection of a patient's idealization, according to Kohut (1977), may be blunt or subtle. As an example, a therapist forthrightly states, "I simply do not measure up to the type of person that you see me as." In a more subtle tone, the practitioner says, "I could only hope to be the kind of person that you see me as." In another direction, a therapist may limit an emotional reaction to a patient's idealization through a premature interpretation (Kohut, 1977). In this regard, a therapist's interpretive response may point out idealized figures in a patient's past or suggest possible underlying feelings of hostility relating to the idealization. Finally, in Kohut's (1977) view, a practitioner may reject or dismiss a patient's idealization with an overobjective comment or through a humorous and kindly reaction. For instance, a practitioner relates, "There is simply no way that your observations would stand up to scientific scrutiny," or through a humorous and kindly reaction of self-deprecation, "I do not wear my Superman cape nearly as much as you think."

In order to respond effectively to a patient's mobilization of an idealizing transference, Kohut (1971) believed that the only correct response was to accept the admiration. In this respect, a practitioner does not reject or discredit a patient's selfobject transference due to countertransference reactions experienced by the therapist but instead directly acknowledges the observations. As an example, a patient comments, "You are so calm and understanding and this is a great help to me." In response, a practitioner may say something like, "Whatever I am able to offer seems particularly important to you at this point" or "As I try to listen and help make sense of things, this seems to be quite important to you." Kohut (1977) also felt that even though a patient may feel meager and insignificant as revealed in an idealizing transference, it is therapeutically beneficial to avoid emphasizing the individual's assets by comparison to the therapist. Instead, the practitioner allows the selfobject transference to germinate by accepting or acknowledging the admiration. As is the case with other traditional views of countertransference in psychoanalytic therapy, Kohut (1971, 1977) recognized the importance of the practitioner engaging in periods of self-analysis and related considerations in order to understand and successfully manage the reactions. For instance, a therapist would need to examine possible fears of merging with a client in response to a mirroring transference or the possibility of being overstimulated by his or her grandiose exhibitionistic tendencies in response to an idealizing transference (Goldberg, 1978). An increasing understanding of such blind spots will enable a practitioner to avoid therapeutic pitfalls and promote empathic understanding through the treatment process.

Prior to completing a discussion of the understanding phase of treatment, it is important to consider criticisms of self psychology that relate to the primacy of empathy within the orientation. Wallerstein (1983) pointed out that empathically derived knowledge has the potential to be inaccurate and unreliable. In his view, it is possible that grievous errors may be made on the part of the therapist who believes that he or she grasps aspects of a patient's functioning when, in fact, the understandings may reflect features of the practitioner's personality, background, or personal convictions. From another critical perspective, Teich (1992b) felt that the phenomenological and functional nature of Kohut's work focused exclusively on the individual and did not give consideration to broader social and political forces. In Teich's opinion, cultural influences that affect an individual's development and current functioning are largely overlooked in providing a context to the structure of the self and selfobject needs (White & Weiner, 1986). In a final negative observation that strikes at a central tenet of Kohut's theorizing, Schmid (2001) thought that it was a mistake to believe that empathy involves an intentional process of acquiring data that may be used to assess or judge a patient. In Schmid's view, an information-gathering activity in what Kohut calls empathy is an aspect of cognitive social perspective pursuits. In this respect, an evaluative function conflicts with empathy, which by definition is unintentional.

Kohut (1977) was aware of particular criticisms directed toward his ideas, and he acknowledged that some viewed his emphasis on empathy in self psychology as a "quasi-religious or mystical approach" (p. 304). In response to such negative opinion, Kohut (1977) stated:

> I can well understand these objections. I know, in particular—to address myself first to the misgivings aroused by my emphasis on empathy—that some of my colleagues will say that by assigning a position of basic importance to empathy I am just trying to bring about what others have tried to bring about before me: the replacement of the staunch acceptance of the cold facts of reality by a regressive, sentimental flight toward illusions. (p. 304)

Although Kohut had been a central figure within the psychoanalytic movement for most of his professional life, there were questions raised, after he gave prominence to empathy in treatment, that his approach no longer represented analysis (Rothstein, 1980). Instead, the self psychology of Kohut and his followers was deemed to be a type of corrective emotional experience (Alexander & French, 1946) or of a psychotherapy (Rothstein, 1980). It is clear that this criticism was the strongest of all because it cast self psychology out of the psychoanalytic orientation and linked it with forms of treatment that were considered to lack sufficient breadth and depth.

Explanation Phase of Treatment. Although self psychology and the work of Kohut have been cited for supporting a dogmatic use of empathy in the treatment approach, Kohut (1971, 1977, 1984, 1990) clearly recognized that other processes beyond empathy were necessary in order to organize and give meaning to empathically derived patient information (Wolowitz, 2002). In the explanation phase of treatment, a therapist steps outside of an empathic stance in order to therapeutically participate in a more expansive and evaluative way. In this regard, Kohut (1977) stated:

> Among the sciences that inquire into the nature of man, psychoanalysis, I believe, is the only one that, in its essential activities, combines empathy, employed with scientific rigor in order to gather the data of human experience, with experience-near and experience-distant theorizing, employed with equal scientific rigor in order to fit the observed data into a context of broader meaning and significance. It is the only one among the sciences of man that explains what it has first understood. (pp. 302–303)

Kohut (1971) believed that an analyst must be able to relinquish the empathic attitude in order to employ various theories and establish hypotheses integral to explanations. In this sense, an analyst or a therapist reconstructs what is empathically understood from a patient's experience into a higher order abstract framework in an experience-distant manner (Silverstein, 1999). From this vantage point, a therapist organizes an overview of a patient's functioning that calls on a wide range of factors beyond those derived from vicarious introspection (Poland, 1984).

Although Kohut (1984) believed that it was essential for experience-near and experience-distant levels to be separated conceptually, he also recognized that a reciprocal relationship existed between both perspectives. In terms of an experience-near mode, a therapist grasps a patient's functioning in an immediate moment and at a particular stage in the individual's development. In turn, employing an experience-distant modality enables the therapist to evaluate normal–abnormal dimensions of the individual's condition based on developmental theory. In Kohut's (1984) view, observations of patterns of patient functioning also influence the theoretical positions that a therapist ultimately adopts. In this respect, as a practitioner gains experience in empathically understanding patients and groups of patients, he or she formulates particular theoretical assumptions. Conversely, as the therapist conceptualizes patient functioning through higher levels of abstraction, these perspectives inform a variety of experience-near activities and attitudes. Kohut (1990) also made the point that, although the experience-distant theorizing can be general and abstract, he felt that it should never become mechanistic on the part of the therapist. With respect to this point, Kohut (1990) stated:

> Cognitive processes that lead to empathic understanding and cognitive processes that lead to theoretical explanation must be activated and put to use, and there must be cooperation between them—abstract reasoning, basing itself on the results of empathic observation, guiding empathic observation and being guided by it—in order to achieve optimal scientific results. (p. 97)

From a broader perspective, Kohut (1971) examined carefully the relationship between empathy involving data collection and the more abstract activity pertaining to the explanation phase of treatment. Kohut recognized the interplay between the functions in which each perspective augments and enriches the other. In contrast, both processes have limitations that become apparent when consideration is given to each on an individual basis as they relate to therapeutic progress and patient growth. In this regard, Kohut (1971) stated:

> Even clinical work would lead only to ephemeral results if it did not include increasing comprehension (i.e., insight) which goes beyond empathy. And

> theoretical work which lacks continuous contact with the material that can be observed only with the aid of empathy would soon become sterile and empty, tend toward preoccupation with the niceties of psychological mechanisms and structures, and lose touch with the breadth and depth of human experience on which ultimately all of psychoanalysis must be based. (pp. 303–304)

It is clear that in this statement Kohut recognizes the importance of a practitioner's ability to step back from the more experiential functions involving empathy and attempt to process what is understood in a more analytical and objective way. At the same time, Kohut emphasizes that a therapist must also remain in contact with what has been derived empathically when considering the meaning of the material.

In order to illustrate the relationship between phases of treatment, it may be helpful to return to a previous patient example. Peter, who was diagnosed with narcissistic personality disorder, has been in weekly therapy sessions for almost 3 months. At this point, treatment has entered the explanation phase as the therapist organizes theoretical perspectives derived from experience-near interactions. During the course of the practitioner's employment of a self-psychology orientation, various conceptualizations relate to experience-distant abstract formulations. As the therapist reflects on Peter's grandiose sense of self-importance that is evident from his exaggerated declarations of success and achievement, he recalls from the understanding phase of treatment Peter's early-life empathic failures relating to perceptions of parental neglect. In particular, Peter's selfobject need for idealization and related traumatization comes to the therapist's mind. Conceptually, the practitioner associates Peter's experiencing of rejection and abandonment with a primary defect in the self and unveils Peter's attempts to defensively mask his defects through an excessive quest for admiration and a sense of entitlement. The therapist also assumes that Peter's primary self structure reflects a sense of fragmentation, emptiness, and narcissistic rage (Segal, 1981), and the secondary defensive structure protects the cohesiveness of the vulnerable self from threat. In this example, in the explanation phase, the practitioner calls on self psychology theory to provide a meaningful framework to the observations of the understanding phase of therapy.

As may be evident in the case illustration, when the therapist conceptualized Peter's early development in terms of unmet selfobject needs, this formulation provided a viable framework for grasping the meaning of his past and current functioning. In this regard, although Kohut (1971) thought that the explanatory phase involved processes that were distinct from empathy, experience-distant theoretical perspectives ultimately produce a deeper and more comprehensive understanding of a patient. As Kohut (1971) noted, after a gathering of patient data in the understanding phase of treatment, it is necessary that it be followed by a scrutiny and an ordering of the observations in order to provide an explanation of what has been understood. As a practitioner calls on clinical experience and self psychology theory, or conceptualizations from other orientations, his or her explanatory power and empathic understanding is increased (Wolf, 1983). It may also be assumed that the accuracy or reliability of a therapist's perceptions are enhanced when material is drawn from multiple perspectives. Kohut (1990) seemed to have these considerations in mind when he stated, "I do not claim that in our science all new insights must necessarily be achieved with the aid of, or even on the basis of, empathic observation" (p. 89). Although the explanation phase of treatment emphasizes experience-distant formulations, Kohut apparently did not intend to suggest that a therapist assume an emotionally remote posture with a patient (Silverstein, 1999). Instead, Kohut (1984) hypothesized that as a practitioner explains the meaning of a patient's functioning, empathy continues as a central aspect of treatment. In this regard, Kohut (1984) stated, "I will stress first of all that the explanatory phase—or, as it might well be more accurate to put it, the explanatory aspect of the analyst's interventions—is also based on empathy" (p. 184).

Finally, in Kohut's conceptualization of the understanding and explanation phases of treatment, it may appear that there is a discrete difference between the therapeutic periods in which they are always separated. Kohut, however, made reference to the treatment phases as general designations and realized that the experience-near and experience-distant modes mutually influence each other in a therapeutic situation. On this same topic, Kohut (1990) wrote:

> The analyst may well give himself over temporarily to a full empathic absorption in the mental state of his analysis and without yet losing the capacity to return to a subsequent cool scrutiny of the experience which he had thus allowed to resonate in him. The essential difference lies not in the empathic or introspective step of data collection but in the subsequent working over of the material. (p. 87)

Treurniet (1980) provided an even more explicit description by stating, "This process is 'transitional' in the sense that being in one state we are never out of touch with the other. There is a rhythmical balance between observing and experiencing, between detachment and union" (p. 327). In this sense, Treurniet thought that the subjective understanding stance of the therapist or analyst is integral with the more explanatory function.

Structural Change in Treatment. Through the therapeutic processing of selfobject transferences, self psychology treatment focuses on uncovering defects in a patient's self and the development of compensatory self structures (Rowe & MacIsaac, 1989). In the pursuit of analytic cure, there is an emphasis on strengthening the compensatory area of the self that was insufficiently established in early life (Kohut, 1984). Self psychology provides a theoretical perspective that enables a therapist to conceptualize the meaning of a patient's selfobject needs as they become recognizable in the understanding phase of treatment (Gardner, 1991). In working through the selfobject needs, the therapist has a central direction or treatment goal in mind directed toward strengthening the structure of the self. From a self psychology perspective, a patient's symptomatic functioning is viewed as a manifestation of unmet selfobject needs and defensive attempts to cover over defects in the self. Through an empathic treatment process, as a patient begins to appreciate the legitimacy of his or her selfobject needs, affects and cognitions that had been previously warded off through defensive functioning begin to emerge (Gardner, 1991; Ornstein, 1984). This transitory increase in self-cohesion reduces the imperative to protect the self from threat as treatment enters the explanation phase. In this period, through interpretations and related modes of intervention, the meaning of a patient's functioning is explored in the context of deeper levels of pathology (Ornstein, 1984).

In order to clarify self structure change, a return to the case illustration with Peter may be helpful. As Peter explores his early history of neglect and sense of abandonment, he begins to express deep feelings of hurt and anger. The therapist empathically mirrors Peter's affective experiencing for an extended period. During this time, Peter's defensive structure begins to lessen in terms of intensity, he becomes less guarded and closed in his communications, and his preoccupation with a relentless quest for admiration and entitlement diminishes somewhat. In a destabilizing direction, Peter also experiences both a sense of fragmentation and feelings of depletion relating to self functioning. As treatment continues through intensive discussion, Peter becomes aware of his unmet needs for idealization and mirroring through selfobject transferences. In one instance, the therapist commented to Peter about how hard it must have been for him to have such sad feelings built up inside of himself for so many years, and how lonely he must have felt for such a long period of time. This interpretation contributed to Peter's emotional connection to long-term unfulfilled self-object needs and the related engagement of defensive structures. Through the course of treatment, Peter's compensatory structures slowly develop as primary defects in the self are uncovered and processed. In particular, Peter's ability to experience anger and threat no longer automatically triggers grandiose narcissistic reactions. This change signifies the acquisition of a compensatory structure involving increased emotion regulation that was previously unavailable (Goldberg, 1988; Ornstein, 1994).

As depicted in this case, Peter experiences the therapist as providing selfobject functions and this enables him to safely express feelings and perceptions that had previously been a threat to his self structure. As Peter became more aware of the legitimacy of his selfobject needs, his sense of self-cohesion began to evolve. The central factor in this process was the therapist's ability to absorb and empathically understand Peter's selfobject needs through a selfobject transference. This was particularly apparent when the practitioner made an interpretation relating to the difficulties and isolation that Peter seemed to experience over a long period of time. As Peter's defensive structure began to diminish, it also became possible for him to develop a compensatory structure involving the regulation of his affective and cognitive functioning. In this regard, self psychology emphasizes the identification and working through of patient deficiencies as a therapeutic model. In the understanding phase of treatment, there is an emphasis on the need to clarify the nature of a patient's deficits in an empathic context. Although Kohut recognized this period as only preliminary to the more significant explanatory phase of treatment as it relates to patient growth, in his final writings he began to emphasize the therapeutic importance of empathy in its own right.

Interpretation in the Treatment Process

As discussed in the previous chapter, interpretation is the most prominent therapeutic intervention in psychoanalytic therapy (Clark, 1995a; Garduk & Haggard, 1972; Ornstein & Ornstein, 1980). In contrast, however, to the classical approach, which emphasizes the resolution of internal conflict, self psychology focuses on working through deficits in the self structure. In this respect, rather than attempting to explain conflictual relationships from a conflict model perspective, self psychology utilizes interpretations to explain deficits in a patient's developmental experiences (Ornstein & Ornstein, 1980). After a period of data gathering by means of a process that employs empathy as a scientific tool, the second phase of self psychology treatment focuses on explaining the meaning of a patient's experience through the use of interpretations (Rowe & MacIsaac, 1989). Over the course of treatment, an empathic understanding of the patient prepares the way for interpretations that ultimately broaden and deepen the empathic grasp of the individual (Kahn, 1985; Patton & Meara, 1992).

Although Kohut (1971) recognized the role of interpretations in advancing a therapist's empathic understanding of patients to a more mature level, he also believed that the conceptual formulations of the intervention should not involve empathy. Instead, Kohut felt that a practitioner must relinquish an empathic attitude in order to be able to assume the more objective and detached stance needed to evaluate the meaning of empathically derived data. Furthermore, Kohut (1991) asserted that treatment cure involves the employment of interpretations and not the therapist's empathic understanding of a patient. In discussing a statement that he made in *How Does Analysis Cure?* (1984), Kohut (1991) wrote:

> I submit that the most important point that I made was that analysis cures by giving explanations — interventions on the level of interpretation; not by 'understanding,' not by repeating and confirming what the patient feels and says, that's only the first step; but then [the analyst has] to move on and give an interpretation. (p. 532)

Through this assertion, Kohut disassociates his work from a type of corrective emotional experience (Alexander & French, 1946), while linking self psychology with a well-established intervention in psychoanalytic therapy (Rothstein, 1980). Kohut's position is also theoretically opposed to that of client-centered therapy, which recognized the therapeutic contribution of empathic understanding for effecting client personality change (Rogers, 1957, 1959).

It was also Kohut's belief that the extent of a therapist's theoretical knowledge of psychological dynamics is directly related to the accuracy of employed interpretations. In turn, more accurate or deeply accurate interpretations provide "proof" to the patient that the practitioner empathically understands his or her experiencing from a broader perspective. In Kohut's view, self psychology offers the most conceptually sound principles on which to understand a patient's developmental history and current functioning. By drawing from self psychology conceptions in the understanding phase of treatment, it becomes possible to formulate interpretations in the explanation period of therapy (Kohut, 1977). Kohut felt that as therapy progresses from the understanding phase of treatment to the explanation phase, the qualitative aspects of empathy also change. In this regard, Kohut (1991) stated:

> I believe that the move from understanding to explaining, from confirming that the analyst knows what the patient feels and thinks and imagines (that he's in tune with his inner life), and the next step of giving interpretations is a move from a lower form of empathy to a higher form of empathy. (p. 532)

Reflecting on hypothetical treatment episodes with implications for the therapeutic use of interpretations, Kohut (1984) presented two markedly different thinking processes and possible treatment approaches. In the first account, Kohut contemplates reacting to the patient in a manner that challenges the perceived reality of the patient. Kohut (1984) wrote:

> If a patient tells me how hurt he was because I was a minute late or because I did not respond to his prideful story of a success, should I tell him that his responses are unrealistic? Should I tell him that his perception of reality is distorted and that he is confusing me with his father or mother? (p. 176)

In contrast to these considerations, Kohut, in the second account, described his reactions as they reflect interpretive thought from a self psychology orientation. Kohut (1984) continued:

> Or should I rather say to him that we are all sensitive to the actions of people around us who have come to be as important to us as our parents were to us long ago and that, in view of his mother's unpredictability and his father's disinterest in him, his perception of the significance of my actions and omissions has been understandably heightened and his reactions to them intensified? (p. 176)

In this scenario, Kohut's responses connect to a deeper understanding of the patient's developmental history and the manner in which it relates to the demanding nature of the individual's immediate reactions. By expressing a contextural grasp of the patient's unmet selfobject needs in the past, the patient's narcissistic functioning becomes more comprehensible and a potential topic for therapeutic discussion.

With respect to Kohut's thoughts from the first depiction, it is possible that if he responded disapprovingly to the demands of the patient, this encounter may have reactivated conditions from the individual's childhood when he felt enfeebled and unimportant. In response, the patient may have possibly engaged a narcissistic defense in order to protect his vulnerable and defective self from threat. With a heightened emotional reaction, it is also likely that interpretations that suggest that the patient confuses the past with the present, or that he fails to distinguish between the therapist and the parent, would not reach the level of cognitive processing needed to more openly consider the inferences. It is also probable that if such disapproving interpretations were considered by the patient, he would reject them as intellectualized excuses offered by the therapist for being late. In this context, the following comments from a psychoanalyst from an earlier period seem apt: "The therapist thus creates an opening for the fullest possible use of all the equipment of the good psychoanalyst: technical skill, empathy, and the ability to interpret accurately the message of the unconscious" (de Forest, 1954, pp. 15–16).

From a less favorable perspective, the employment of interpretations by therapists was subject to criticism long before Kohut recognized their importance as a central intervention in self psychology treatment. Within the therapeutic enterprise, therapists who employ interpretations have been viewed as being judgmental, given to forming evaluations outside of a patient's frame of reference, and subsequently undermining the treatment relationship by objectifying the patient or the client (Schmid, 2001). Psychoanalytic practitioners in particular have been accused of providing interpretations from an "omniscient and pseudo objective vantage point" (Gedo, 1986, p. 130). In contrast to the issuance of emotionally detached and imperious interpretive comments, Kohut formulated and expressed interpretations in a manner that demonstrated a sensitivity to empathic understanding. In this regard, Kohut (1991) stated:

> Interpretations are not intellectual constructions. If they are, they won't work; [they might work] accidentally, but not in principle. A good analyst reconstructs the childhood past in the dynamics of the current transference with warmth, with understanding for the intensity of the feelings, and with the fine understanding of the various secondary conflicts that intervene as far as the expression of these [childhood wishes and needs] are concerned. (pp. 532–533)

It is evident in this statement that Kohut recognized that any interpretation must be supported by a thorough understanding of a patient's development and of the manner in which it possibly influences the individual's current experiencing involving intense feelings and a defensive posture.

In the process of rendering interpretations, it is possible or even inevitable that a therapist will in some instances express inaccurate inferential statements that conflict with a patient's point of view. From a self psychology perspective, misinterpretations constitute a subjective experience of an empathic failure and may evoke similar reactions in a patient as are associated with a painful lack of understanding that occurred in the individual's past. As a consequence, when an interpretation does not match a patient's functioning, it is typically resisted or rejected. It then becomes necessary for a practitioner to empathically respond to a patient in order to restore a sense of being understood. As the therapist repairs the misunderstanding engendered by the interpretation, the patient experiences an empathic response that typically may not have been available to the individual in the period of his or her early development. This interaction also promotes movement toward self cohesion and reduces the operation of defense engagement (Ornstein, 1984). Although there may be some advantage to an occasional misinterpretation, Kohut did not advocate that a therapist or an analyst strategically employ inaccurate interpretations in order to promote patient development (Kohut & Wolf, 1978). What he did seem to emphasize was the need for a practitioner to attune to the ways in which a patient experiences an interpretation in order to continue to extend the breadth and depth of a patient's empathic understanding.

In a treatment example involving a therapist's employment of an interpretation, a patient, Sarah, is expressing long-held perceptions of a sense of insignificance and unimportance in her relationships with other people. In this context, Sarah recalls an occasion as a young child when she was in the living room with her parents and an older sister. Sarah was sitting at a desk and had just written several letters of the alphabet for the first time and was excited about her accomplishment. At that point, she could remember looking at her mother and father across the room and holding on to the piece of paper on which she had written the letters. Sarah said that her parents did not seem to notice her and did not react to her writing. As a response, the therapist decides to express an interpretation. "Sarah, it seems that once again that you feel overlooked because your mother and father did not respond to something that was quite important to you." In reaction to this inferential statement, Sarah replies, "No. It wasn't all that way. I need to really see what happened. They didn't say anything, but I also can't remember showing them the paper either. Why should they say anything?" In response, the practitioner relates, "It seems like you don't wish to overstate the lack of involvement of your parents because you did not appear to make an effort to ask for or to seek out their attention. Is this closer to your memory of what happened?" In this interaction, the therapist repairs what was initially misconstrued in the rendering of the interpretation and thus restores a level of empathic understanding.

After a practitioner expresses an interpretation to a patient, and the individual feels understood through the exchange, it is necessary to reflect on the implications of the communication. In the context of empathic understanding, it becomes possible for the patient to engage in a more open consideration and scrutiny of the interpretation that is relatively free of a defensive reaction (Goldberg, 1988). These therapeutic conditions seem to exist in the treatment example with Sarah as she voiced a desire to explore her functioning in a way that would enable her to reach a more accurate level of understanding. She was not satisfied with the therapist's initial interpretation that portrayed her as a victim of seemingly uncaring and uninvolved parents. Instead, Sarah sought to evaluate her more passive role in which she failed to seek out the attention of her parents. As the interpretive process continues, it becomes possible for a patient to explain her functioning in a more controlled and purposive way than had previously been the case (Goldberg, 1988). In terms of patient change in the treatment process, Kohut (1977) stated, "It is not the interpretation that cures the patient" (p. 31). By this, Kohut meant that it is the subsequent working through of interpretive material in analysis that leads to structural change. In the treatment illustration with Sarah, as she extensively examines passive levels of engagement from an earlier period in her life, it becomes possible for her to recognize a similar pattern existing in her current experience. In this respect, there is a gradual change in a patient's functioning from a less fragmented to a more integrated structure of the self.

In a final observation relating to interpretation and to self psychology in general, it may appear that Kohut places all or a large part of the blame of a patient's psychopathology on empathic failings of his or her parents. In terms of an interpretation, a practitioner often explains or infers a relationship between a selfobject's lack of empathic understanding in a patient's childhood and the individual's current disturbance or emotional deficits. As Kohut (1984) was willing to listen to patients for extended periods make accusations against their parents without contradicting them, he raised the question whether he might be a "credulous victim of those of my patients who do not want to shoulder the responsibility for their symptoms, actions, and attitudes but waste their time accusing others, including and par excellence their parents?" Kohut (1984) responded in the negative to this self-questioning, which suggests that he allowed patients to avoid responsibility for their actions by unfairly targeting parents for their inadequacies in a distant past. Kohut (1984) specifically stated:

> First and most important: the self psychologically informed psychoanalyst blames no one, neither the patient nor his parents. He identifies causal sequences; he shows the patient that his feelings and reactions are explained

> by his experiences in early life, and he points out that, ultimately, his parents are not to blame since they were what they were because of the backgrounds that determined their own personalities. (p. 25)

Kohut (1984) also observed that, through the analytic process, patients come to an understanding of perceived distortions they may have held with respect to their parents and also begin to recognize how the intensity of their demands may have been provocative in past situations and continue to elicit misperceptions in current experiences.

Over a large part of his professional career, Kohut advanced the position that the sole function of empathy was to serve as a data-gathering tool to set up the curative engagement of interpretations in the treatment process. In a major shift in his view toward the end of his life, Kohut began to acknowledge that the presence of empathy might have a "therapeutic effect" in its own right (Kohut, 1991). Although Kohut had been "curiously doubtful" about the possibility that empathy could engender positive patient change, he reluctantly came to accept this proposition (Warner, 1996). In October, 1981, Kohut made his last public address at the Fifth Conference on Self Psychology in Berkeley, California. He died a few days after the conference. In his talk at the conference, Kohut (1991) reflected on a new direction relating to empathy:

> Empathy serves also, and this is now the most difficult part—namely, that despite all that I have said, empathy per se, is a therapeutic action in the broadest sense, a beneficial action in the broadest sense of the word. That seems to contradict everything I have said so far, and I wish I could just simply bypass it. But, since it is true, and I know it is true, and I've evidence for its being true, I must mention it. (p. 530)

In part, Kohut's hesitancy to recognize the therapeutic value of empathy proceeded from the fact that he had to make a major conceptual shift that varied sharply from numerous statements that he had previously made with respect to the process. At the same time, Kohut was willing to assume the risk of being criticized for changing his mind on long-held perspectives involving a pivotal topic in self psychology.

When Kohut raised the possibility that an empathic understanding of a patient's functioning in the treatment process constitutes a therapeutic action, he started a controversy that continues to the present time in self psychology. Among many in the orientation, there is a continuing belief that interpretation is the essential mechanism that effects change in a patient's self structure, and the interpretive process is buttressed by empathically derived information (Leider, 1996). In the view of others holding a self psychology perspective, there is an emphasis given to an empathic milieu as a curative factor, and explanations provided through interpretations are equally or even less prominent in influencing patient change. In this regard, self psychology began to be compared with the person-centered approach of Carl Rogers as it relates to recognizing empathy as having a capacity to effect curative change on its own (Kahn, 1985; Tobin, 1991). However, even taking into consideration Kohut's final thoughts on attesting to the therapeutic potential of empathic understanding, he did not envision standing empathy alone as curative and instead continued to recognize the importance of interpretation in transforming a patient's self structure (Leider, 1996).

SUMMARY

Self psychology has had a considerable influence within psychoanalysis and psychoanalytic therapy (Wispé, 1987), and has assumed a position of emerging interest as a psychotherapy. As the originator of self psychology, Heinz Kohut conceptualized an integrated approach that recognized empathy as a central factor in normal development, psychopathology, and the therapeutic process (Gardner, 1991). Kohut provided a definition of empathy as a vicarious introspection and recognized the conception as an essential means for understanding a patient in a treatment situation. From a developmental perspective in self psychology, Kohut identified several key constructs including the self, selfobject, and the multiple selfobject needs for mirroring, idealization, and twinship. Each of the needs are influential in the development of the self or the dynamic core of the personality. With respect to the analytic process, Kohut identified the treatment phases of understanding and explanation. In the understanding phase, a practitioner empathically relates with a patient through an experience-near modality. In the explanation phase, the therapist conceptually evaluates the data derived from the initial period of analysis and employs abstract and theoretical conceptions through an experience-distant perspective. In turn, the insights serve to inform the communication of interpretations. Criticisms of self psychology focus on what is viewed as an overemphasis on empathy as a determining influence in human development and as a pervasive variable in the treatment experience.

In the analytic process of self psychology, patients tend to evoke a pattern of defenses in order to protect the vulnerable and defective self from exposure and scrutiny. During an extended period of empathic immersion, a practitioner attempts to promote the development of patient compensatory structures through a selfobject transference. As treatment progresses, there is a working through of the defenses and deficits in the self structure. In the context of empathic understanding, the therapist participates in explaining the meaning of the patient's experience. Countertransference provides diagnostic information in treatment interactions, and a therapist must be alert to the possibility of mishandling selfobject transferences due to unresolved personal issues. For most of Kohut's professional career, he asserted that working through the interpretive process leads to patient cure. In contrast to this position, in the final years of his life, Kohut began to acknowledge the beneficial and curative effect of empathy in its own right beyond serving as a requisite condition for interpretations.

PART III

Empathy: A Multiple Perspective Approach in Counseling and Psychotherapy

Chapter 7

Multiple Ways of Knowing and Empathy

Indeed, empathic understanding requires a multi-dimensional perspective of human interaction.
—Ham (1989, p. 37)

Some years ago, I was conducting research for a book on early recollections in counseling and psychotherapy and had reached an impasse at a critical point in my investigation. At the time, I was attempting to formulate an interpretive approach to early memories as a projective technique that would extend beyond my subjective evaluation. I was aware that empathy was fundamental in my understanding of a client's first remembrances, but I was not sure how to broaden the conceptual scope of the construct. Fortunately, I remembered reading a somewhat obscure work by Carl Rogers that might be of assistance to me in this regard.

In a book chapter entitled, *Toward a Science of the Person,* Rogers (1964) wrote about *three ways of knowing* and the function of empathy within each frame of reference. In reading the essay once again, I realized that Rogers's conceptualization, with some important modifications, provided me with a framework for employing empathy from a broader perspective. Rogers, writing from a client-centered orientation, emphasized an interpersonal or phenomenological way of knowing as a way to empathically understand a client. Rogers also addressed subjective and objective ways of knowing, but he did not specify or endorse the role of these processes in the context of therapeutic treatment. It occurred to me that in interpreting early recollections, it is possible to utilize empathy from each of the three ways of knowing and not limit the assessment process to an interpersonal knowledge perspective. At that point I felt tentative in holding this view because to have conceptual differences with Rogers on the topic of empathy was a humbling experience.

After my research and writing on early recollections, it seemed that empathy was fundamental to accurately interpreting the projective technique. At that point I decided to conduct a comprehensive review of the literature on empathy in a treatment context in order to further increase my knowledge with respect to the construct. In my initial estimate, I thought that perhaps 30 to 40 articles and book chapters would sufficiently "cover" the topic on available materials. It did not take me long to surpass that number, and I began to accumulate hundreds of published sources relating to empathy in the therapeutic process. As I took notes on the vast amount of research data, it became evident that a viable framework was needed in order to coherently organize these extensive findings. Once again, as I had for early recollections, I recognized that Rogers's formulation of three ways of knowing had the potential for conceptualizing empathy in a treatment situation. In this context, the three ways of knowing took the form of a multiple perspective structure for comprehensively employing empathy and empathic understanding in counseling and psychotherapy.

THREE WAYS OF KNOWING AND EMPATHY

In 1964, Carl Rogers delineated an incisive framework for employing empathy from a threefold perspective: subjective, interpersonal, and objective. From a subjective modality, an individual directs a capacity for empathic attunement toward oneself. In an interpersonal mode, empathic understanding of the individual focuses on grasping the phenomenological experience or the frame of reference of another person. From an objective stance, an individual's empathy centers on external sources in the form of reputable reference groups. Rogers (1964) recognized the use of empathy through three ways of knowing as a tentative means for checking the accuracy of hypotheses. Rogers observed that there was a relationship among the ways of knowing, but he also acknowledged that each channel has a distinctive application as a means for understanding. In order to effectively use the avenues of knowing, Rogers felt that it was necessary to be aware of the specific function of each of the perspectives. In this regard, individual modalities potentially provide a balance and deter other knowledge sources from creating distortions or biases. Rogers also believed that errors occur when confusion exists with respect to which way of knowing is being used, or when investigators equate knowledge obtained from the three modes. More often, when multiple ways of knowing are judiciously interwoven, it becomes possible to generate perspectives that are broad and inclusive.

With respect to a *subjective way of knowing,* Rogers (1964) observed that a person is able to direct his or her capacity for empathy to his or her own frame of reference. Through a sensitive attunement to immediate conditions, an individual evaluates personal reactions that are fundamental to everyday life. By developing inner hypotheses, it is possible to validate experiences through external cues and stimuli in clarifying subjective responses. Rogers cited common examples, such as a taste reaction to a new dish, assessing one's feeling toward another individual, or experiencing a range of emotions. Although Rogers emphasized the importance of formulating creative hypotheses and pursuing unformulated directions, he also recognized that a subjective way of knowing was largely ignored in American science and psychology. Interestingly, Rogers did not suggest applications of the subjective avenue of knowledge to the treatment relationship. Apparently it was not Rogers's intention, at this point in his thinking, to use a subjective way of knowing as a resource for empathically understanding another person.

In terms of an *interpersonal way of knowing,* Rogers (1964) recognized that the direction of empathy is toward another individual as a means of understanding his or her phenomenological experiencing. This view is consistent with a practitioner's attempt to grasp the private world of meanings of a client and is a recurring theme in Rogers's writings (1951, 1957, 1961, 1964, 1975, 1980). In these instances, the counselor or the therapist focuses on a client's frame of reference while restraining one's own subjective views or values. Rogers (1964) also thought that a practitioner could empathize with a client by securing observations from significant others, such as family members or teachers, who know the person. According to Rogers, such information is helpful for confirming or disconfirming hypotheses that are developed in the treatment situation. In emphasizing an interpersonal way of knowing, a practitioner cultivates an emotionally safe climate in order to empathically understand a client's experiencing.

From the perspective of an *objective way of knowing,* Rogers (1964) suggested that it is possible to direct one's empathic understanding toward groups who represent an external frame of reference. The consensus of judgments of members of a reference group form the basis for the collective understanding of their experiences or perceptions. Reference groups that are comprised of individuals from broad and diverse backgrounds enhance the accuracy and reliability of an objective way of knowing. Rogers thought that an individual may make empathic inferences relating to the reactions of a trusted reference group who are usually a group of colleagues. At the same time, the objective observations of the qualified colleagues represent mutually understood and agreed upon individual subjective perceptions. Rogers noted that the status of an objective way of knowing was highly regarded in science and technology. Similar to a subjective way of knowing, Rogers did not acknowledge or suggest that the objective observations available from reference groups serve a function in empathically understanding a client in a treatment relationship.

MULTIPLE PERSPECTIVES OF EMPATHY: AN INTEGRAL MODEL

As a logical extension of Rogers's framework for ways of knowing, it seems safe to assume that it is possible to direct empathy toward an individual or a client through each of the three knowledge modalities. This conceptual change contrasts with Rogers's view in which the interpersonal way of knowing is the sole channel where the direction of empathy is toward the other person. In Rogers's conception, the subjective mode of empathy is turned inward toward the knower, and with objective knowing, the focus of empathy involves a reference group. Utilizing a different conceptual framework, empathy is directed toward the client from multiple vantage points in order to build a more comprehensive understanding of the individual. Diverse and potentially enlightening sources of knowledge become available when the direction of empathy extends beyond the interpersonal way of knowing. In this respect, it is possible to refer to a new term, *integral empathy,* which includes essential elements of empathic understanding.

From a subjective or *reciprocal* perspective, the counselor or therapist senses client meanings in a bodily felt way. Momentarily identifying with the individual, a practitioner imagines what it is like to be the client. From an interpersonal stance, the counselor or therapist attempts to understand the client's frame of reference. By empathizing with a person's phenomenological experience, therapeutic understanding is advanced through a *relational* exchange. A third way of empathic knowing involves an objective or *referential* perspective. Knowledge of a client is enhanced from sources such as direct observation in a cultural context and standardized assessment procedures. Integral empathy is operational in each of the ways of knowing as understandings are directed toward the client from a more expansive and comprehensive perspective.

Assumptions of Multiple Perspectives of Empathy

The accuracy and utility of a multiperspective empathy approach in counseling and psychotherapy rests on several assumptions. It is possible to consider the function of each way of knowing on a separate basis and also evaluate the application of knowledge sources in combination. As a potential means of empathic understanding, considerations of the manifold perspectives are appropriately discussed in the context of the treatment relationship. In evaluating the following assumptions, it may be evident that the viewpoints relate to a broad and encompassing conception of empathy. In this regard, the section concludes with a definition of empathy that recognizes the place of multiple perspectives as an integral quality.

Each of the three ways of knowing is a viable source of empathic understanding within theoretical orientations. This assumption is debatable because various theories of counseling and psychotherapy stress particular knowledge channels while minimizing or ignoring other perspectives. As an example, self psychology generally focuses on a practitioner's subjective (experience-near) empathic response and utilizes empathy in objective (experience-distant) formulations. In contrast, person-centered and feminist therapy emphasize empathically understanding a client from an interpersonal perspective. Yet, although there are variations in how empathy is aligned with respect to avenues of knowledge among the psychotherapies, this does not necessarily diminish the potential value of each of the ways of knowing. What it does suggest, however, is that there are qualitative differences in how empathy and empathic understanding are conceptually understood and processed, depending on particular theoretical persuasions. As the function of empathy becomes explicit within each treatment approach, the viability of and therapeutic utility of the three ways of knowing, as they relate to empathic understanding, should become clearer.

Focusing on a way of knowing provides a complementary perspective as it relates to other modalities. As a counselor or a therapist gives consideration to a specific knowledge channel, certain conceptualizations may be pertinent and may contribute to empathic understanding from other modalities. Countertransference is an example that emerges from a subjective way of knowing that transpires within a counselor's personal experiencing. The use of a countertransference framework from an objective or conceptual perspective assists a practitioner in understanding and managing personal biases and preoccupations that often emerge in a treatment situation. In another example, from an objective way of knowing, a therapist's conceptualization of a client's defense mechanisms or safeguarding tendencies provides a means for understanding how the individual responds to threat from an interpersonal knowledge perspective. Across diverse theories of counseling and psychotherapy, various other constructs and abstractions serve to inform or enlighten other knowledge modalities.

Particular constructs only have meaning as they relate to a connection between or among the modes of knowing. There are instances in which a therapeutic conception has explanatory power solely as it relates to specific perspectives. As an example, a practitioner's role as a participant observer only makes sense as it is understood in conjunction with subjective and objective vantage points. As a therapist oscillates between the modalities, the operation is definable and subject to a relative degree of control. Independent positions as a participant or as an observer lose some of their capacity to provide empathic understanding when not used in combination. In other instances, a conceptualization is more robust and purposeful when it is engaged in combination with all three knowledge sources. For example, the model of a patient or a client draws from multiple perspectives in order to formulate a comprehensive understanding of an individual.

There are constraints and limitations relating to any single way of knowing. It becomes possible to identify inherent weaknesses with respect to a knowledge channel when it is used exclusively or inflexibly within the treatment process. It is quite conceivable that a counselor or a therapist may repeatedly employ a knowledge perspective that limits the engagement of alternative positions. In this respect, there is a tenuousness of a single knowledge channel that may constrict a practitioner's range of functioning (Peloquin, 1995). As an example, for most of his career, Rogers asserted that it is therapeutic for a practitioner to maintain a focus on a client's frame of reference. Although this attitudinal position engenders an empathic climate within the treatment relationship from a person-centered perspective, it also presents problems when a counselor chooses to express views from his or her own subjective frame of reference. Rogers (1961, 1970, 1980) was well aware of this constriction or contradiction in the treatment process. He addressed the issue by stating that it is most important that a counselor or a therapist be congruent or "real" in the relationship and, when feelings persist, to speak from one's own frame of reference. Rogers (1964) recognized limitations in other theoretical orientations when they primarily rely on a single way of knowing. In this regard, he thought that behavioral therapy focused excessively on an objective stance and existential therapy largely relied on a subjective way of knowing.

It is inevitable that a practitioner will assume multiple perspectives in a treatment situation. Even though a therapist may have a preference for engaging a specific way of knowing at a particular time, there is typically a vacillation that spontaneously occurs among the perspectives. Reactions and responses continually surface from each of the knowledge channels into the consciousness of the counselor or the therapist. For example, a practitioner is listening to a client and attempting to understand the individual's internal frame of reference in an interpersonal context. As the counselor relates to the client from an interpersonal stance, thoughts and impressions come into awareness from the other ways of knowing. From a subjective knowledge source, the practitioner internally reacts: "She is fragile." "I'm feeling somewhat distant from her." and "She reminds me of someone out of the 19th century." In terms of an objective perspective, the counselor experiences more abstract and theoretical thinking: "Could she be schizophrenic?" "Denial seems to be operating as a defense." and "I need to know more about her family background." Although such cognitive reactions might appear to be intrusive, they frequently yield material for treatment considerations. It is also possible that a pattern of reactions, particularly from a subjective way of knowing, may represent a practitioner's biases and preoccupations and need to be appropriately addressed.

Recognizing multiple perspectives enables a practitioner to unite theoretical positions that initially appear incompatible. Various theoretical conceptions relate to particular ways of knowing and it is possible to integrate the formulations by appreciating and acknowledging differences in the modalities. As an example, within the tradition of Individual Psychology there is an emphasis on empathically understanding the uniqueness and indivisibility of the client (Oberst & Stewart, 2003). At the same time, the treatment orientation employs various constructs, such as the lifestyle and safeguarding tendencies, encompassing typologies that relate to an objective way of knowing. By acknowledging that the unique perspectives of clients and the various typologies involve different ways of knowing, it becomes possible to reconcile theoretical differences. In another example, counselors and therapists may view humanistic approaches to treatment as largely incompatible with the use of diagnostic systems, such as the *Diagnostic and Statistical Manual of Mental Disorders*–IV (American Psychiatric Association, 2000), that represent an objective or referential knowledge source. From a humanistic perspective that primarily emphasizes subjective and interpersonal ways of knowing, the use of a manual for categorizing clients for treatment purposes seems unacceptable in the light of values that stress the importance of relating to persons in nonevaluative terms (Hansen, 2003). Yet, in this instance, a case can be made that each way of knowing is legitimate when viewed as having different knowledge bases. By integrating the theoretically disparate views, it may be possible to advance client progress and empathic understanding while respecting the value and contribution of each frame of reference.

Integrating perspectives from each of the ways of knowing enhances the possibility of determining a more accurate and comprehensive degree of empathic understanding. The utilization of multiple knowledge sources potentially increases the reliability of a therapist's empathic understanding of a client. In this regard, the engagement or pursuit of empathy involves a hermeneutic method for classifying misunderstandings (Agosta, 1984; Keil, 1997). In its application to the treatment situation, hermeneutic processing relates to making numerous efforts to empathically understand a client from different trajectories, and each attempt provides an opportunity for a deepening of appreciation and awareness. The model of a patient or a client is an example of empathic understanding that relates to the hermeneutic process. Through a practitioner's empathic immersion with a client over an extended period of time, the model becomes progressively more accurate and refined through the use of a cross-check or corrective procedure involving multiple ways of knowing (Edwards, Dattilio, & Bromley, 2004).

A conception of empathy that has treatment utility should be sufficiently broad to include multiple ways of knowing. With this assumption in mind, the following definition of empathy would seem both useful and workable: *attunement with the feelings and meanings of an individual's experience from an immediate or extended perspective.* This definition implies an active engagement in attempting to grasp the essential components of a person's functioning. In this respect, it is consistent with current directions in counseling and psychotherapy (Ivey & Ivey, 2003), while acknowledging the essence of Rogers's (1957, 1959) classic definitions. In contrast, however, with a traditional view of empathy that primarily emphasizes the current experiencing of an individual, this conception also suggests an extended dimension. In order to encompass multiple ways of knowing, it is necessary to broaden a focus of empathy to include perspectives beyond one's immediate situation. In this respect, an extended quality allows for a more comprehensive understanding of a person developed over a period of time. By assuming a vantage point relating to the aggregate experience of an individual, it becomes possible to understand intelligible and overall patterns of his or her functioning.

Further Considerations Relating to the Assumptions of Multiple Perspectives of Empathy

Although each mode of knowing may be understood independently, in treatment practice there is a blending or a weaving together of the perspectives. In this regard, through a contextual process, an understanding of a client becomes more comprehensive and refined. Rogers (1964) pointed out that it is helpful to consider differences in the ways of knowing as diverse methods by which to tentatively check hypotheses. This view is also pertinent within the therapeutic process for each knowledge channel because it enables the practitioner to confirm or disconfirm hypotheses through a combination of the threefold perspectives. As with any evolving point of view, the multiple stances are open to refinement and revision in a treatment situation. Although multiple-track formulations of empathy may appear to be somewhat difficult to process in practice and in training, it is possible that the framework lends a clarity to therapeutic interactions. In this regard, a broader conception of empathy and empathic understanding gives rise to the question of training in counseling and psychotherapy; this topic is addressed in the latter part of the chapter.

SUBJECTIVE, INTERPERSONAL, AND OBJECTIVE PERSPECTIVES AND EMPATHIC UNDERSTANDING

As a *reciprocal* process, subjective empathy enables a counselor or a therapist to be aware of his or her own inner functioning and sensibilities in response to the experience of a client. As a form of personal knowing, a practitioner momentarily identifies with a client in a bodily felt way. Through interactions that resonate in the counselor, he or she evokes intuitive responses and hunches. A therapist is also in a position to imagine what it would be like to be the client, even for a fleeting period of time. Through these subjective reactions, a practitioner must be alert to the potential for engaging personal biases and preoccupations that may undermine the treatment relationship. In terms of another form of knowing, interpersonal empathy involves the *relational* experience between a client and a counselor or a therapist. Focusing on a client's own frame of reference, there is an emphasis on grasping both immediate and extended perspectives of the individual. Verbal and nonverbal components of a client's communication provide the counselor with a potential means to better understand the phenomenological experience of the person. Through an emphasis on the supportive qualities of the therapeutic relationship, a practitioner attempts to convey an empathic understanding of a client by means of a mutual exchange of interactions. This verbalized process enables the therapist to check the accuracy of his or her perspectives and to stay close to the emotional experiencing of a client. Expressions of the client are limited to the subjective views of the individual in this mode of knowing, and consequently there is the possibility for a personal distortion of perspectives. It is also common for conditions in the therapeutic situation to evoke reactions of threat on the part of the client.

In terms of a *referential* perspective, objective empathy relies on trustworthy sources in order to develop a broad platform for empathically understanding a client. Based on an external frame of reference, a counselor or a therapist evaluates information and conceptualizations by "stepping back" from the immediate experience of a client. In a search for patterns and meanings, a practitioner considers wide-ranging reference material that may possibly contribute to a more accurate and comprehensive perspective of an individual. In this regard, a counselor is in a position to derive data from various reputable resources, such as standardized assessments, constructs relating to theoretical orientations, and diagnostic systems. This referential information may then be organized with data from the other ways of knowing in order to formulate a coherent framework relating to a client's functioning. It is possible that this conceptualization may take the form of the model of a patient or client that becomes increasingly complex and precise over time. Considering that an objective mode of knowing is based on higher levels of abstraction and inference, a therapist must use caution in order to avoid arbitrarily fitting clients into predetermined categories or classification schemes. In this regard, it is necessary for a practitioner to conceptualize data as it is experientially grounded in the other modes of knowing in order to achieve the goal of empathically understanding a client.

Subjective Empathy

In attempting to grasp a sense of what it is like for a counselor or a therapist to empathically understand a client from a subjective perspective, it may be helpful to elucidate four reciprocal processes. *Identification* involves a practitioner's partial and transitory assumption of a client's experiencing as if it were his or her own. Through the process of deliberate identification, a practitioner may then employ his or her *imagination* in order to momentarily grasp what it is like to be the client. Another contributing factor to an enhancement of subjective empathy is the counselor's *intuition*, which has the potential to rapidly generate hunches and images relating to a client's overall functioning and environmental influences. A final reciprocal process is a therapist's capacity to resonate with visceral sensations in interactions with a client through a *felt-level experiencing*. Although it is possible to describe relatively discrete processes involving subjective empathy, in practice the conceptions do overlap or intermingle in a treatment situation.

Through a subjective avenue of knowing, a practitioner responds from his or her own frame of reference in interactions with a client (Keefe, 1976). This response, however, increases the possibility for distorting client perspectives. Consequently, a counselor or a therapist needs to be vigilant with respect to the possible emergence of personal biases and prejudices. The therapist is also able to utilize interpersonal and objective knowledge sources in order to empathically understand a client with an increased level of accuracy. Although subjectivity is intrinsic to the human condition, it is necessary to verify findings from the modality in order to minimize or limit erroneous perspectives (Post & Miller, 1984). This endeavor, to some extent, reduces the concerns of theorists and practitioners who perceive the place of subjectivity in a treatment situation as "biased or swayed by personal feelings" (Goldberg, 1983, p. 157). From a different perspective, Stewart (1956) thought that the perceived "danger" of being subjective was excessively stated, and that subjectivity served an essential function in human relations. In this regard, Stewart (1956) stated, "We can only be 'objective' if we first know the extent to which we are necessarily subjective, no matter what" (p. 3).

Identification. As a counselor or a therapist empathizes with a client, there is often a sense of feeling akin to the individual as a result of having been through similar experiences (Stewart, 1956). There may not be an exact match or the emotional intensity of the experience may vary in terms of degree, but there is sufficient commonality to evoke a level of identification. As an example, in a treatment situation, a 10-year-old client describes his reactions of fear and vulnerability when bullied by several classmates in a school setting. Although the counselor may not personally have experienced bullying in school, he is able to relate to the child's situation when he recalled a period of time as an adolescent when he was physically threatened by a neighborhood gang. In this context, through a deliberate activity, the practitioner identifies with the client for a moment. It is essential that any identification be transitory because the therapist must be in a position to objectively evaluate what has been experienced in the subjective interaction when thinking about the client (Arlow, 1979). Fleiss (1942) referred to empathy in this context as a *trial identification.* If a practitioner is not able to rapidly shift out of the identification phase, he or she may remain psychologically merged with the client and respond in less than therapeutic ways. For instance, in returning to the bullying example, the counselor, experiencing unresolved issues of aggression emanating from his adolescent episodes of threat, may suggest that the young client fight back and stand up to his tormentors.

Another condition that promotes empathic understanding, and signifies a sound treatment direction, exists whenever the shared activity between a client and a therapist constitutes an incomplete or a partial identification involving a specific memory or fantasy (Arlow, 1979). As Rogers (1957, 1959) and Reik (1948) pointed out, there is an "as if" quality to empathy that recognizes the psychological boundaries between a client and a practitioner. Reik (1948) compared the identification experience to tasting food: "What really happens in the conjecture phase is that we get just a taste of the menu, no more, just enough so that our tongue and palate recognize the food" (p. 466). Vanaerschot (1990) observed that a practitioner empathizes incorrectly if he or she does not feel an emotional distance to some degree with a client. In this respect, it is antitherapeutic when a counselor or a therapist experiences a full or total identification with a client. Weigert (1962) portrayed an extreme of possible contagion and psychopathology resulting from indiscriminating empathy on the part of a therapist. Weigert (1962) stated, "Over-identification with the patient, sharing his defense, his likes and dislikes, his rationalizations, the therapist might enter into a conspiracy with him against the world, at worst into a *folie à deux* that would not alter the patient's self alienation" (p. 154).

In the event that a practitioner becomes mired in an identification with a patient, the treatment process typically reaches an impasse (Ehmann, 1971). There is a confirmation of a client's point of view, but discussion often does not extend beyond the confines of a mutual sharing of perspectives. Importantly, identification also entails an affective dimension involving a common emotional interaction. As a worst case example, in working with a client diagnosed with an affective disorder, a practitioner becomes depressed and is not able to broaden exchanges beyond the despairing focus of the client. It is evident in such interactions that there is a lack of a complementary sense of separateness with regard to a dysphoric mood, and the identification has become inflexible (Beres & Arlow, 1974). A sound therapeutic direction for a practitioner, after momentarily identifying with a client, is to attempt to minimize further activation of the emotional state.

Specifically, in these instances, it may be helpful for a therapist to shift to an objective way of knowing in order to gain an alternative and perhaps more balanced perspective.

It is also conceivable for a counselor or a therapist to experience difficulties identifying with a client, even on a momentary or partial basis (Shapiro, 1974). The life experiences and perceptions of the client and practitioner may be dissimilar to the point that there is a paucity of understanding and reciprocity of feelings on the part of the therapist. It may be difficult, for example, for a counselor to identify with sexually abused clients without having been similarly victimized. At the same time, although the counselor may not have experienced a history of sexual trauma, the individual likely has encountered attenuated fears and distress in life that allow for a partial identification with the victimized persons. In instances of this order when identification seems inhibited or blocked, a practitioner needs to consider the possible engagement of a defense on his or her part that has been evoked in the course of interactions with a client. Another situational possibility is that the therapist may experience difficulty identifying with a client from a different culture to the extent that cultural barriers need to be explored in order to enhance empathic understanding (Ibrahim, 1985, 1991; Sciarra, 1999). Finally, a practitioner may maintain an outlook on life that restricts the possibility of identifying with certain clients due to a convictional bias (Clark, 2002b). As an example, a therapist holds a core conviction that events in life are manageable with a reasonable degree of effort and deliberation. As a result, the therapist has some difficulty identifying with clients who experience patterns of anxiety and a lack of perceived control in their lives.

Imagination. Another aspect of subjective empathy arises when the practitioner finds it possible to actively imagine the experiencing of a client in order to infer what it is like to be the client (Watson, Goldman, & Vanaerschot, 1998). The imaginable capacity of a therapist implies an exploratory and creative quality of entering a client's experience as a function of empathy that is often overlooked in the counseling and psychotherapy literature (Margulies, 1984, 1989). The act of imagination is closely related to identification in that the counselor can imagine the occurrence of similar activity in his or her own life, even for a fleeting period of time (Reik, 1948; Stern, 1988; Stewart, 1956). In these instances, a practitioner vicariously experiences the internal state of a client on a transitory basis (Agosta, 1984). It is possible for a practitioner to evoke images and emotional reactions that serve to enhance an empathic understanding of a client.

As an example involving an imaginary process, I recall working with "Ruth," who was 15 years old at the time. Early in our treatment sessions, Ruth related with embarrassment that she had nobody that she could call a friend and described her sadness in staying at home on weekend nights over a lengthy period of time. She recalled staring at the telephone and wishing that it would ring so that someone would invite her to go out. Ruth would usually watch television with her mother and then go quietly to her room to listen to records or sometimes spend time with her doll collection. As Ruth described these ordinary, yet sorrowful episodes, her solitary image was vivid as a product of my imagination. I pictured her combing her dolls' hair and changing their clothes, much as I had witnessed my own daughters do many times. For Ruth, though, there was a deep sense of anguish and social rejection that accompanied her actions as she tried to occupy herself.

Although particular states or situations of a client involve an immediate imaginal reaction of a therapist, there are also broader contexts in an individual's life that call for an extended sense of imagination. In such instances, a practitioner attempts to imagine what it would be like to grow up in a particular environment and to deal with the current reality that accompanies one's personal history (Parker, 1955; Wallace, 1985). As an example, a young-adult client named Andrew, who has a history of neglect and abuse in his childhood, is in treatment with a counselor. Andrew experiences a pattern of serious difficulties in forming intimate and caring relationships with others. The counselor empathically listens to Andrew narrate events in his current life while maintaining an extended empathic stance toward his developmental background. As Andrew relates immediate instances of interpersonal failure, the counselor imagines what it is like to endure similar episodes of feeling empty and damaged over a period of many years. With an imaginable attunement to the present and long-term experiencing of the client, the counselor consolidates a deeper and richer level of empathic understanding.

It also becomes a therapeutic endeavor for a counselor or a therapist to imagine what it is like to be a client when the individual's life functioning or perceptions are remote from or foreign to the practitioner. For example, a client diagnosed with a schizophrenia disorder experiences hallucinations in which he feels that his body is shrinking and being infiltrated by gamma rays. It is obvious that this image can only be imagined in the mind of a practitioner. It is also possible that some client perceptions are corporally distant from a therapist's condition and may only be grasped through a searching and imaginative act. The following examples seem pertinent: as a male, the experience of being pregnant; what it feels like for a thin person to "be fat"; and assuming the state of advanced aging for a young individual.

There are also numerous cultural experiences in which an imaginary posture of a practitioner potentially contributes to empathic understanding. Consider the following examples, which represent distinctly different experiences when compared with the background of a particular counselor or a therapist: what it is like to be desperately poor; to be a person of color in an intolerant environment; and to have a disability impairing mobility or a chronic illness. Finally, as a representation of a universal experience, dreams also call on a counselor's imaginable capacity in order to emotionally connect with a client in a treatment situation. For example, a client reports a dream in which he is running down the street being chased by 800-pound baby birds wearing baseball caps. It is obvious that it would not be possible to conceive this visual image without engaging one's imagination. In keeping with this line of reasoning, Santayana (1905/1935) wrote, "The human mind is nobody's mind in particular, and the science of it is necessarily imaginative" (p. 134).

Intuition. In terms of subjective empathy, a practitioner's intuitive reactions in a treatment situation represent another reciprocal process. Although interest in applying intuition in treatment practice is growing, attempts to explain its basic nature and function are in an early stage of development (Rea, 2001). As a counselor or a therapist responds to a client, intuition involves a rapid, tacit, immediate, and tentative means of apprehension. The intuitive act also implies a capacity to recognize overall patterns in a holistic context without a conscious or deliberate use of reasoning (Eisengart & Faiver, 1996). In this regard, a counselor evokes hunches, images, and flashes of insight when intuitively interacting with a client that can provide an empathic understanding that is both enlightening and qualitatively different from intentional observation processes (Beech & Brazier, 1996; Bohart, 1999; Goodyear, 1979; Petitmengin-Peugeot, 1999). Although intuition can be disparaged and linked to a mystical operation, it is a form of knowing that is constantly used in the context of everyday life and has a therapeutic potential in counseling and psychotherapy when its strengths and limitations are recognized (Gladwell, 2005; Goodyear, 1979; Rea, 2001).

In a therapeutic context, a practitioner may utilize intuition when there is a limited amount of time available to make clinical decisions. Intuitive judgments typically range from routine decision making in a treatment situation to more consequential matters. As an example, after an initial meeting with a student named Barry, a school counselor must decide whether to schedule a follow-up meeting with the adolescent. Although there was nothing that particularly stood out in the counselor's mind after talking with the client, she was left with the vague notion that there was something troubling Barry and therefore decides to arrange for another session. In another situation, a therapist, in working with a client who recently began treatment, considers asking a question that might evoke threat but also has a therapeutic potential. With respect to a different circumstance involving crisis intervention, a practitioner is on the telephone with a client who is threatening to commit suicide. The therapist is trying to decide whether to continue talking at length with the client or acknowledge that hospitalization is required and terminate the discussion in order to arrange for immediate transportation. In each of these examples, the practitioners must draw on their intuition in an attempt to make a relatively sound decision. It may also be evident that professional decision making under time constraints cannot be separated from the experience and knowledge of a counselor or a therapist, which are integral to intuitive action.

Although applications of intuition under time constraints potentially contribute to an empathic understanding of clients, it is also possible that a practitioner's intuitive insights can serve as a foundation for extended observations and evaluations (Beech & Brazier, 1996). In this regard, Stewart (1956) held the view that knowledge of persons is grounded in intuition, and that logical and scientific reasoning is based on intuitive activity. At the same time, intuition, involving hunches and illumination, provides a different form of data in comparison to inferential and abstract formulations (Goodyear, 1979). It becomes possible for a practitioner to expand on intuitive findings by applying objective realms of knowledge, such as clinical data, categories of psychopathology, and theoretical aspects of human development (Eisengart & Faiver, 1996).

As an example relating to intuition, in the previous illustration the school counselor had a hunch that Barry seemed troubled and decided to ask him to return for a follow-up counseling session. After a lengthy discussion in this meeting, Barry admitted to having suicidal thoughts, and the counselor's vague hint was confirmed. Although the counselor continued to call on her intuitive capacity, she utilized all of her knowledge channels in the mode of crisis intervention. For instance, from an interpersonal perspective, the practitioner empathically grasped a sense of hopelessness in interactions with Barry. In the context of an objective modality, the counselor systematically assessed potential suicide indicators as she continued her discussion with Barry. Finally, toward the end of the session, the counselor, in an intuitive action informed by other perspectives, decided that the student's suicidal ideation was sufficiently serious to require an immediate referral for a coordinated health service intervention.

Felt-Level Experiencing. In a function relating to intuition, felt-level experiencing involves a practitioner's bodily resonance in response to interactions with a client in a treatment situation (Gendlin, 1961, 1962, 1978, 1998; Sawyier, 1975; Vanaerschot, 1997). In a somatic, felt, inward sense, a counselor or a therapist "feels" the experiencing of a client on a fleeting basis. In this regard, Barrett-Lennard (1981, 1998) identified empathic resonance as a stage of empathic understanding that is integral to a felt-level experience as a therapist emotionally responds to a client. In the context of everyday life, Rogers (1964) made reference to "the flow of feelings in me" in which it becomes possible to form inner hypotheses. In a treatment example of felt-level experiencing, a therapist is working with an early-adulthood client diagnosed with anorexia bulimia. As the client describes frequent episodes of binging food relating to the eating disorder, the therapist vaguely senses an undesirable fullness in her stomach and "fatness" in the middle of her body. In other instances when the client depicts herself purging, the practitioner experiences an upheaval in her stomach and a slight gagging reaction. Although these sensibilities are only minimally intense and momentary, they seem physically felt to the therapist and are simultaneous with a visual image of the client's actions.

In this regard, felt-level experiencing extends beyond a cognitive and affective resonance into a somatic or physical realm (Cooper, 2001; Corcoran, 1981; Gendlin, 1961, 1962, 1978, 1998). In these instances, there is a corporeal reaction, such as a pang in the stomach or tenseness in the chest, that is not necessarily emotional in nature (Cooper, 2001). The felt sensation is usually experienced inwardly through the middle of the body in the viscera, the abdomen, the chest, the solar plexus, or the throat (Gendlin, 1998). In an embodied way, a counselor or a therapist attempts to empathically understand a client through an attunement to one's own somatic reactions in a treatment situation. As a practitioner allows his or her body to resonate in response to a client, it becomes possible to gain an enhanced sense of the totality of the individual's experiencing. In this respect, there is a broader conception of the meaning of a client's experience because the therapist engages at a visceral level of human functioning. In these encounters, the practitioner is also in a position to grasp a deeper meaning of experience that may be less familiar to the client.

As an example, a middle-adult client named Tom anxiously announces to a counselor that he expects to lose his job in a firm where he has worked for a number of years. As Tom articulates his concerns about finances and difficulties in finding another position, the practitioner resonates with mild feelings of apprehension but also experiences a decreasing level of physical tension in his chest and abdomen. After a period of listening to Tom, the counselor states, "Tom, although you have been talking about your worries over the loss of your job, it seems like I'm also picking up a sense of relief from you." In response to this confrontation, Tom pauses briefly and relates, "You know, I do feel relief at the same time. Over the last few years I've come to hate my job but have been afraid to leave it."

As a therapist attempts to allow his or her implicit bodily reactions to resonate with a client, it is possible that physical stress and tension may interfere with felt-level experiencing (Cooper, 2001). In this regard, if a practitioner is tense or rigid in certain regions of his or her body, the functions may be less accessible to synchronization with the felt sense of a client. As an example, a counselor typically sits in his chair for several treatment sessions in a row without taking a break to stretch or move about. Even though the counselor's back and limbs become tense and somewhat sore, he believes that time demands preclude any change in his routine. Another limiting factor is that a therapist may not allow for sufficient time in a session to permit a client's somatic experiencing to naturally reverberate on a felt level. Instead, a practitioner may quickly or exclusively attend to a verbal communication exchange that restricts a grasp of a client's embodied whole (Cooper, 2001). For instance, in an initial session, a client relates that she feels depressed. Rather than reflect her feelings for a period of time, the therapist immediately begins to ask a series of questions with a cognitive focus. This interaction does not allow for the therapist to more fully "know" the client on a somatic and affective level. As an alternative approach, if the practitioner took the opportunity to attune herself to the client's felt dimension of experience, subsequent questions might be even more pertinent and meaningful.

Subjective Bias and Empathy. Among the ways of knowing, subjective empathy requires more ethical controls and a heightened personal awareness due to the potential for bias and judgment error involving a practitioner's internal frame of reference (Katz, 1963). While employing a subjective modality, it is possible for a counselor or a therapist to become excessively involved and overidentify with a client. In other instances, as a counselor attempts to imagine what it is like to be the client, this process may go beyond a fleeting experience and assume a merging quality (Stern, 1988). As a result of an excessive identification and a strong imaginable activity, a counselor could intrude on a client's sense of autonomy and personal responsibility. In another undesirable direction, in engaging an intuitive response, a therapist may attend solely to factors that substantiate initial impressions in the form of confirmatory bias (Haverkamp, 1993). Similarly, with felt-level experiencing, a practitioner is susceptible to uncritically accepting "gut feelings" to the exclusion of alternative hypotheses. It is also a possibility that a therapist may engage a convictional bias by overemphasizing his or her personal belief system when empathically relating to a client (Clark, 2002b). Finally, the capacity for empathic understanding can be inhibited by unresolved conflicts and personal problems being experienced by the practitioner (Epp, 2002). At times, these issues take the form of a countertransference reaction or a defense mechanism engagement on the part of a counselor or the therapist.

Interpersonal Empathy

Representing an intermediate position between subjective and objective modes, interpersonal empathy relates to an understanding of the phenomenological experiencing of a client (Rogers, 1964). Within a relational field, a counselor or a therapist attempts to communicate a degree of empathic understanding to a client. Interactions on a verbal and nonverbal level provide a basis for formulating hypotheses with respect to the client's functioning. It then becomes possible for a practitioner to discern the accuracy of his or her inferences through various therapeutic interventions. An empathic understanding of a client potentially involves observations relating to immediate or extended points of reference. In this regard, a therapist may address a client's momentary experience in a defined context or consider perspectives that embrace a broader conception of the person over a longer term. A practitioner is also in a position to gain an empathic understanding of a client through discussions with significant persons in the client's life. Because interpersonal empathy focuses on a client's frame of reference, the modality is subject to the limitations and distortions inherent in the person's own perspectives. In these instances, a practitioner may call on subjective or objective empathic stances in order to provide corrective and possibly more balanced points of view.

Internal Frame of Reference. A primary function of a counselor or a therapist is to attempt to perceive the internal frame of reference of a client and then try to convey aspects of this understanding to the client (Rogers, 1951, 1957, 1961, 1964, 1975). The therapist listens empathically to a client in order to enhance the individual's experience of being heard and understood (Myers, 2000). In this regard, the treatment process emphasizes an endeavor to grasp the phenomenological perspectives of a client in an interpersonal context. The direction of empathy is toward the client as the practitioner strives to maintain a therapeutic focus on the perceptual field of the individual. To the extent possible, a therapist attempts to attune to a client's subjective perspectives while deemphasizing external ways of knowing. As an example, a 10-year-old client, Diane, is quietly sobbing as she discloses to a counselor that her best friend is moving with her family to a distant state. The practitioner acknowledges Diane's experiencing by reflecting her sorrowful feelings and a deep sense of loss. Even when Diane makes such statements as, "I will never have another friend as nice as her in my whole life," the counselor defers from providing an alternative viewpoint and instead, allows Diane to more fully express her grief, with the belief that this experience is transitory and therapeutic. As Diane emotionally works through her strong feelings, the practitioner subsequently assumes a more advantageous position to engender other, more hopeful perspectives that involve subjective or objective ways of knowing.

Divergent Models of Empathy in Treatment. The most prominent model of empathy in counseling and psychotherapy involves an experiential endeavor on the part of a therapist to grasp the subjective experience of a client (Bohart & Rosenbaum, 1995). The development of a relationship and the employment of empathic understanding have the potential to foster therapeutic gain. In this respect, there is a central focus in therapy on a human engagement, and the relationship itself is a primary source of client growth. In a contrasting model of empathy in the therapy process, empathic understanding of a client at an interpersonal level assists in establishing rapport and contributes to data gathering with respect to the individual (Bohart & Rosenbaum, 1995). In turn, the information about a client can subsequently be used as an integral part of therapeutic interventions. In this sense, empathic understanding is an observational tool of a practitioner, and therapeutic change largely occurs through interpretations and related insight-oriented interventions. Although the empathy models may appear to be incompatible, it is possible to integrate the processes when applying multiple perspectives of knowing. In this regard, empathic understanding can serve to enhance the counseling relationship and potentially engender therapeutic change in conjunction with other treatment factors. This occurs within the interpersonal realm by focusing on a client's internal frame of reference. At the same time, as a practitioner gathers data about a client, it is possible to conceptualize the material through an objective knowledge channel. Subsequently, the information may contribute to more informed interventions on the part of a practitioner that advance the empathic understanding of a client.

In a treatment example that attempts to integrate experiential and observational modes of empathy, a young-adult client is in therapy for alcohol dependence. A college sophomore, Greg has been missing classes and is incomplete on numerous course assignments. On several occasions he has broken university policies regarding the use of alcohol and is required to meet with a college counselor as a term of his academic probation. Greg recognizes that he has problems with alcohol and openly acknowledges an inability to control his drinking. Early in treatment Greg states, "It seems like everything that I have worked for I'm throwing out the window for no good reason." In response, the counselor empathically relates, "It is painful for you to see so much that is important to you threatened by your drinking." In numerous interactions of a similar type, the client and the practitioner focus on immediate and experiential aspects of Greg's functioning. Through this period, Greg and the counselor form an alliance and an open level of communication. As treatment continues, the counselor accrues an empathic understanding of Greg over a longer term through numerous exchanges in therapy and the assessment material. From an observational stance, the counselor begins to use the acquired data relating to Greg in order to contribute to the formulation of more challenging interventions that are largely external to Greg's subjective perceptions. At one point, for example, the practitioner confronts Greg in a supportive tone, "You are saying that you're making an effort to control your drinking, but you also just mentioned that you stopped by the bar on your way home from class last night."

Immediate and Extended Empathic Perspectives. In conceptualizing empathy, it is possible to identify momentary or sustained experiences in the life of an individual (Goldberg, 1999). In this regard, a practitioner is in a position to both apprehend what is occurring on an immediate basis with a client and to grasp a contextual understanding of a client's functioning over the long term. Without losing track of a client's *here and now* experiencing, a counselor or a therapist may attune to a general sense of how the individual experiences life (Berger, 1984, 1987; Bohart, 1991). In this respect, there is a distinction between empathically understanding a client's momentary state of mind and formulating a representation of the individual's whole experience as a person (Meissner, 1996; Poland, 1984). As an example, a middle-adult client expresses a sense of disillusionment with his work situation. The client, Michael, relates, "When I'm at work I see other people taking it easy all the time, and there I am never letting up. It makes me wonder if I'm some kind of fool for constantly working." From an immediate perspective, the therapist empathically states, "You feel resentful that your coworkers take advantage of a situation while you do nothing but work. What sense does this make?" This intervention seems to capture Michael's immediate reaction to what he perceives as an injust situation.

In a more expansive direction, it is possible for a counselor or therapist to assume an extended empathy disposition that represents a broader perspective beyond a given moment. In this regard, the practitioner continues, "Michael, you feel resentful toward your coworkers, but you also feel strongly that it is important for you to be productive and not waste time." This understanding of a client relates to the conception of a model of a patient or a client that is provisionally developed over the course of treatment (Greenson, 1960, 1967). An extended perspective of empathy may also involve a hermeneutic activity by returning again and again to an object of inquiry that provides a broader context for any particular client experience (Packer, 1985; Woolfolk, 1998). In Michael's case, the practitioner has heard him state on numerous occasions the importance of accomplishing tasks and making a sustained effort. For Michael, this value orientation is progressively evident throughout his developmental history, and personal productivity represents a core conviction in his life. Unless the therapist empathically grasps Michael's more comprehensive perspective, she may assume that his disillusionment with work merely represents a desire to scale back his degree of labor.

Communication Considerations and Empathic Understanding. In the interpersonal experience, a practitioner attempts to verify or disconfirm inferences and hypotheses by empathically checking apprehensions with a client (Rogers, 1959). It is necessary for a counselor to express or demonstrate understanding in order to make visible the explicit and implicit meanings of a client. What is understood by a therapist is based not only on a client's qualitative statements, but also on his or her gestures, movements, postures, and related nonverbal expressions (Haase & Tepper, 1972; Schmid, 2001). As an example, Ellen, an early-adulthood client diagnosed with a dependent personality disorder, anxiously states to the therapist, "Do you think that I'm making the right decision? I really need your opinion." The therapist, while observing the client's hands shaking, responds, "It is such a scary thing to think about acting on your own." Immediately, Ellen, in an elevated voice says, "It is. There are just so many things that can go wrong. Maybe I shouldn't take the job. I really need your advice." The practitioner replies to Ellen as he listens to her anguished pleas, "You are so concerned about making the wrong choice, and you want me or someone else to reassure you." As evident by the interactions between the client and the practitioner, there is an emphasis on verbalized communications and the responsive use of reflection on the part of the therapist.

Since the late 1960s, there has been a focus on developing explicit communication skills in training programs for counselors and psychotherapists. These endeavors primarily emphasize methods for enhancing a therapist's level of expertise in interpersonal exchanges with a client. Rogers (1975) found this direction in training particularly disturbing because it diminished the central attitudinal role of a practitioner while featuring technological or technique-oriented interactions. At the same time, conceptualizing empathy in observable interpersonal functions has provided skill development opportunities for students and practitioners that would not otherwise be available. As an attitudinal element, empathic understanding can be abstract, and it becomes necessary to use specific strategies to clarify communication exchanges. Although training and educational programs have emphasized the development of interpersonal skills in treatment situations, there have been limited efforts to advance the subjective and objective avenues of knowledge as they relate to empathic understanding. By broadening the conceptualization of empathy to include multiple perspectives, there is a potential for expanding beyond an interpersonal focus for skill development.

Further Means of Empathic Understanding. It is also possible to empathize with a client by employing information obtained from interpersonal sources beyond the client (Rogers, 1964). Observations secured from significant others, such as a parent, teacher, or a spouse, provide potential avenues for enhancing the empathic understanding of a client. Projective techniques, such as the Rorschach, the Thematic Apperception Test, and human figure drawings, constitute another resource for extending an empathic grasp of a client's functioning (Garb, Wood, Lilienfeld, & Nezworski, 2002). The interpersonal exchange that takes place during the administration of projectives in itself provides an opportunity to observe a client as the individual responds to various stimuli and tasks. From a multicultural perspective, the interpersonal relationship allows the therapist to assess how a particular client perceives or relates to cultural issues and topics from the individual's own frame of reference (Alexson, 2005; Jenkins, 1997; Sciarra, 1999). As an example, from an objective knowledge channel, there is an assumption that Mexican American families place a substantial emphasis on interpersonal relations in comparison with the family relationships typical of the dominant culture (Alexson, 2005). In working with a Mexican American client and lacking a more extensive evaluation of how the individual perceives his or her family relationships, it is possible that a counselor could take it for granted that the client is person-oriented and has strong feelings with respect to the importance of family.

Interpersonal Bias and Empathy. Rogers (1951, 1961) recognized that when a counselor's external evaluations are almost nonexistent, there is little possibility for his or her personal biases to become manifest. Maintaining a focus on a client's frame of reference has the advantage of minimizing the introduction of a therapist's potentially distorted perspectives that may compromise the empathic understanding of a client. From a conceptual framework that employs multiple ways of knowing with respect to empathy, Rogers's cautions are even more pertinent and require a practitioner to be alert to the potential for biases. Although a broader conception of empathy may enhance the understanding of clients, the consideration of avenues of knowing outside of a client's frame of reference presents more complex formulations that increase the possibility for formulating inaccurate hypotheses. At the same time, if multiple empathic perspectives are central to gaining a more comprehensive understanding of a client, it is essential to establish sound approaches for limiting practitioner biases when entering an individual's frame of reference from subjective or objective stances.

From an interpersonal perspective, an inherent limitation and potential source of bias is always present given the reality that a practitioner cannot directly know a client's inner experiencing, and any knowledge source is always a deduction (Vanaerschot, 1997). In this regard, observations from significant others pertaining to a client may involve an inadvertent distortion due to the difficulty in being objective within personal relationships (Welfel & Patterson, 2005). A practitioner should also be aware that when using projective techniques with a client, the psychometric properties of the instruments may be marginal (Clark, 1995d). Furthermore, in a treatment situation, clients may express incomplete or incorrect verbalizations, or they may not be successful in articulating an accurate portrayal of their personal condition or state of mind. In these frequent instances, it is possible for a therapist to judiciously draw from subjective or objective avenues of knowledge in order to empathically augment client perspectives as a type of corrective procedure. In a treatment example, a client with a diagnosis of acute stress disorder experiences difficultly explaining a persistent dreamlike state that is most uncomfortable. "I can't really explain it. It's like I'm outside of my own body. It's scary." The counselor is familiar with symptoms of depersonalization from an objective referentional source (*DSM–IV–TR*) and employs this understanding when responding to the client. "This is frightening for you. You seem to have a sense that you are detached from your body as if you were an outside observer." As the client goes on to further explain his depersonalization, the counselor is able to engage her own subjective reactions that resonate with the client's experience. In particular, the practitioner's felt experiencing enables her to empathically understand the client from a broader perspective. In the treatment example, if the client's condition had been identified as a fantasy experience by the counselor and perceived as unrelated to the individual's acute stress disorder, it would represent a form of bias or practitioner error.

Objective Empathy

A primary assumption when employing an objective way of knowing is that a practitioner utilizes theoretically informed observational data in the service of enhancing an empathic understanding of a client. It is possible for a counselor or a therapist to appraise information from referential sources that are external to a frame of reference of a client. In turn, the awareness serves to inform and enrich the applications of empathy in a treatment situation. Theoretical and conceptual observations of a counselor have a potential to expand a client's perceptions in a way that enables the individual to experience a deeper and more comprehensive sense of empathic understanding.

Conceptual sources are diverse and relate in part to the theoretical orientation of a practitioner. A therapist, for instance, may utilize a framework of defense mechanisms in order to conceptualize various ways that clients react to avoid personal threat and reduce conflictual issues. In a treatment example, relating to defense mechanisms, Willie, an early-adulthood client, repeatedly expresses somewhat plausible explanations to justify his less than responsible behavior and objectionable activities. The therapist hypothesizes the operation of rationalization as a defense and attempts to empathically and nonjudgmentally respond to Willie. Even though it appears that Willie distorts perceptions of situations in order to avoid a critical scrutiny of his actions, the practitioner recognizes that it is a therapeutically sound direction to avoid challenging or confronting Willie's specious defense engagement early in treatment. As a particular defense, the therapist is aware that Willie's use of rationalization constitutes a long-term pattern of functioning and is not merely an impulsive form of excuse making.

A practitioner's employment of objective empathy generally reflects the individual's theoretical orientation in terms of practical application and the recognition of a broad conception of the construct. Self psychology is a clear example of a theoretical approach that conceptualizes the use of objective empathy in an experience-distant formulation. In other instances, particular constructs can only be fully made operational from a multiple perspective context of empathy that includes an objective component. Theoretical conceptions, such as the model of a patient or a client, defense mechanisms, safeguarding tendencies, and countertransference represent these processes. Self-report inventories, diagnostic systems (*DSM–IV–TR*), and multicultural research data constitute other objective sources that may be integrated with subjective and interpersonal perspectives in order to enhance an empathic understanding of a client. Finally, from an objective empathy stance, it is also possible for a counselor to directly observe a client in selected contexts outside of the treatment situation.

Theoretical Orientations. As discussed in chapter 3, contemporary theories of counseling and psychotherapy place varying degrees of emphasis on empathy and empathic understanding. With some orientations, empathy receives a prominent focus in practice and in the professional literature, whereas with other treatment approaches the construct is less significant. Among the psychotherapies, when objective empathy is utilized, it typically provides a moderating and corrective influence with respect to a client's subjective perspectives. For instance, with cognitive therapy it is possible for a counselor or a therapist to begin to accept the accuracy of a client's negative and self-defeating perceptions in the absence of an alternative objective view. In another direction, a therapist may articulate an objective observation that enhances a client's empathic understanding. In a treatment example, in solution-focused brief therapy, a client expresses anxiety over performing a particular activity, and the counselor points out to the client that he had successfully managed to cope with a similar experience in the past. With some other theoretical orientations, the employment of objective empathy enables a practitioner to conceptualize a client's experience in a comprehensive way. In this regard, Gestalt therapy attempts to perceive a client from a holistic perspective that includes an objective focus, and Individual Psychology employs the construct of the lifestyle in order to enhance empathic understanding from multiple perspectives.

Nomothetic Approaches. Various resources are available to a practitioner that communicate meaningful and general distributions of variables among people. It is possible for a counselor or a therapist to utilize these nomothetic approaches in a way that enhances the idiographic understanding of an individual client (Aiken, 2003). Self-report personality inventories represent one nomothetic method that may be employed to expand peculiar understandings of a client in such frames of reference as depression, anxiety, and self-esteem. As an example, an early-adulthood client named Donna received a relatively high score on the *Beck Depression Inventory–2* (Aiken, 2003). The therapist utilizes the data from the inventory along with other objective sources of information in order to begin to formulate a broader understanding of her functioning. In particular, the relatively high depression score on the inventory alerts the therapist to the possibility that Donna is experiencing a mood disorder that requires further investigation.

Another example of an externally situated knowledge source is the *DSM–IV–TR,* which organizes descriptions of mental disorders that align with the psychotherapeutic communities best practice standards of peer review and peer acceptance (Duffy, Gillig, Tureen, & Ybarra, 2002). The *DSM–IV–TR* manual also provides a coordinated endeavor of reputable professionals interacting in a common language and forming a consensual agreement with respect to psychopathology. From a treatment perspective, Keil (1997) pointed out that knowledge relating to the effects that particular disorders have on behavior and experiencing can assist a practitioner in understanding his or her own reactions in a treatment situation. In turn, a therapist's personal response can serve as a diagnostic criteria that may assist in the recognition and understanding of pathological functions relating to an individual client. As an example, continuing the illustration with Donna, the therapist, from an objective perspective, is aware of the symptoms of a major mood episode from the *DSM–IV–TR.* As the practitioner interacts with Donna, he resonates with fleeting subjective reactions of a depressed mood, loss of energy and desire, and feelings of worthlessness. This transitory experiencing of the practitioner informs his recognition of various symptoms as they relate to a mood episode. In this regard, the nomothetic rules of psychological functioning available in the *DSM–IV–TR* serve to enhance empathic understanding and are not an end in themselves to categorize clients (Hansen, 2000).

With respect to another nomothetic approach, multicultural considerations have been a focus of a vast amount of contemporary research in counseling and psychotherapy (Ibrahim, 1991; Ivey, D'Andrea, Ivey, & Simek-Morgan, 2002; Sciarra, 1999). A wide range of diverse groups have been investigated in order to enhance the cultural competencies of practitioners (Pedersen, Draguns, Lonner, & Trimble, 2002). Although the nomothetic or objective perspectives provide an understanding of the general ways individuals perceive experiences within cultural groups, it is also necessary to empathically understand how particular individuals encounter or respond to cultural forces in their lives. In this regard, it is possible that a client may accept or engage a cultural way of being as a member of a group. At the same time, it is also conceivable that an individual may resist or reject cultural associations. To continue with the treatment example with Donna, who is a Native American, the therapist is aware that many Native Americans maintain a collective orientation toward the importance of their family or their tribe. With this objective research finding in mind, the therapist is in a position to appraise Donna's idiosyncratic perceptions as they relate to her cultural background, as she has rejected many of the traditions and customs of her tribal nation and has alienated herself from her family. This knowledge can then be integrated with other objective observations concerning Donna that will serve to achieve a more comprehensive level of empathic understanding.

Behavioral Observations. From an objective empathy perspective, it is possible for a practitioner to observe a client in selected contexts outside of the treatment experience. Observations of a client can be structured to occur within interpersonal situations with or without the direct knowledge of the individual (Murphy & Dillon, 2003). In a school situation, for example, a student may be observed in a classroom, on the playground, or in the cafeteria during lunch. In a specific instance, a classroom teacher refers a 9-year-old student, Aaron, to the school psychologist because he is frequently teased or socially rejected by his classmates. The psychologist decides to observe Aaron on the playground and subsequently sees him spend most of his time isolating himself from the other children. When the teacher encourages him to participate in a game, Aaron stands off to the side rather than join in the activity. The psychologist is able to integrate inferences from various observations in order to enhance an empathic understanding of Aaron in subsequent counseling sessions. Finally, Barrett-Lennard (1981) made the point that it is not essential for someone to actually be present in order to empathically understand an individual. It is possible to develop empathy with a person as a result of a sound or video recording or possibly from a written paper, an artistic work, or some other expressive production.

Objective Bias and Empathy. Although objective data largely derives from reputable reference groups, there is a potential for bias and error with respect to empathic understanding. Despite the fact that various theoretical orientations and abstract conceptions involve well-established treatment modalities, there is no single approach that reaches a consensus level among all of the traditions (Fall et al., 2004; Sharf, 2004). Even though self-report inventories generally detail acceptable psychometric qualities, there is a substantial degree of distortion among clients when responding to the assessment devices (Shedler, Mayman, & Manis, 1993). In another direction, the *DSM–IV–TR* classification system is generally endorsed among practitioners, yet the manual is also criticized for its relative lack of attention to cultural forces and developmental considerations (Ivey & Ivey, 1998). It is also apparent with the behavioral observations of a client that there are inherent limits in a therapist's objectivity that create room for appraisal error. As with the other modes of empathic knowing, it is necessary for a practitioner to be tentative with objective perspectives and to take into account other knowledge channels in order to minimize judgment errors.

EDUCATION AND TRAINING IMPLICATIONS OF MULTIPLE PERSPECTIVES OF EMPATHY

A primary assumption when employing multiple ways of knowing is that the conception of empathy is broadly construed. An awareness of the use of empathy involving distinct knowledge channels enables a practitioner to understand a client from an immediate or extended perspective. When empathy is conceptualized from three ways of knowing, it creates a direction for viable educational and training endeavors relating to counseling and psychotherapy. A purposeful training goal for practitioners is to be able to effectively utilize multiple perspectives to enhance empathic understanding of clients. A familiarity with particular dimensions of subjective, interpersonal, and objective empathy has a potential to provide counselors and therapists with an understanding of the capacities and limitations of each perspective. In this regard, a sound educational and training focus would require emphasis on processes in which practitioners are able to use specific ways of knowing in isolation or in combination. At the same time, a therapist would become informed about and aware of the potential for biases and judgment errors in each of the modalities and clarify means to minimize these limitations (Duan, Rose, & Kraatz, 2002).

From a subjective empathy perspective, it is possible to enhance the expertise of practitioners in using identification, imagination, intuition, and felt-level experiencing. In this training direction, Goodyear (1979) suggested that there are three basic steps for expanding a therapist's effective use of intuition. The steps involve a quieting of the mind through a type of meditation, focusing attention, and assuming a receptive attitude. Rea (2001) and Schuster (1979) also observed that a quieting of the mind is essential for a practitioner to be able to accurately perceive and process clinical data and to become aware of internal nuances. Although Gendlin (1961, 1962, 1998) primarily focused on expanding a client's felt-level experiencing, he also presented observations and guidelines that provide assistance in increasing an awareness of a therapist's felt bodily sensations.

In terms of interpersonal empathy, there have been numerous efforts to develop communication and empathic skills of students and practitioners since the 1960s. One possible limitation of these endeavors is that they have primarily focused on interpersonal skill development without sufficiently integrating subjective and objective perspectives. Expanding instructional pursuits toward a multidimensional conception of empathy perspectives would more likely capture the scope and breadth of the treatment encounter. With respect to an objective empathy, it is necessary for practitioners to recognize that referential sources offer a potential for enhancing empathic understanding and are not an inhibiting influence. In this regard, various theoretical orientations and conceptions present intelligible frameworks for apprehending the functioning of a client. Particular nomothetic approaches and strategic observations of a client represent other avenues for integrating empathic perspectives in the treatment process.

In another training direction, in order to enhance the empathic understanding of others, it is essential that a counselor or a therapist engage in self-care practices (Trusty, Ng, & Watts, 2005). When a practitioner repeatedly neglects his or her emotional and physical needs, it becomes difficult to be empathically present for others (Abend, 1986; Baker, 2003). As a counselor experiences an emotional depletion due to work overload or other excessive professional or personal demands, even the most dedicated empathic listener begins to falter. It becomes necessary for a practitioner to replenish and nourish him- or herself through a variety of self-care pursuits (Baker, 2003). These may take the form of walking, hiking, gardening, meditation, or other diversionary activities that provide an avenue for self-expression and growth. In other instances, a therapist's lack of self-understanding and self-appreciation can diminish his or her ability to provide a deep understanding and appreciation of others (Epp, 2002). The struggle to maintain an appreciation and acceptance of oneself includes an ability to withhold blame, even an ennobling self-blame (Epp, 2002). As a counselor or a therapist pursues a quest for self-understanding, including coming to terms with his or her own imperfections and contradictions, it becomes increasingly possible to empathize with others.

SUMMARY

A practitioner's utilization of a multiple perspective conception of empathy provides a framework for understanding clients from a broad vantage point. Through an extension of Rogers's (1964) formulation, three ways of empathic knowing involve subjective, interpersonal, and objective frames of reference. In each of the ways of knowing, the focus of empathy is on the client and serves as a means of attuning to the experience of the individual. Specific assumptions can contribute to clarifying an application of the threefold viewpoints in a treatment situation. In this regard, the multiple ways of knowing provide complementary and corrective avenues for empathically understanding a client. From a subjective empathy perspective, reciprocal processes enable a counselor or a therapist to empathically interact with a client. Through a transitory and partial response, a practitioner is able to identify with a particular client. In an exploratory and creative way, a therapist may actively imagine what it is like to be a client. Calling on a rapid and illuminating reaction, a counselor is in a position to employ intuitive responses. A therapist is also able to engender felt-level experiencing by allowing one's body to resonate with a client's experience for a momentary period of time. When utilizing subjective empathy in addition to each of the ways of knowing, a practitioner must be alert to the potential for biases and judgment errors.

An interpersonal empathy focus enables a therapist to acknowledge the phenomenological experience of a client through a communication endeavor. It is possible for a practitioner to perceive a client in an immediate context or to construct a general sense of the individual's functioning from an extended perspective. Through a relational channel, a practitioner communicates understandings to a client, and the assumptions are checked with the individual. Observations of significant others, projective techniques, and multicultural considerations provide selected processes for enhancing the empathic understanding of a client. A therapist may also utilize referentional sources of various types from an objective empathy perspective. Abstract formulations involving theoretical orientations and constructs furnish ways to coherently organize client observations. Various resources available to a counselor, including self-report inventories, diagnostic systems, and multicultural data, contribute to a more comprehensive grasp of a client's functioning. Finally, each of the empathy perspectives present potential training implications for students and practitioners in counseling and psychotherapy.

Chapter 8

Therapeutic Techniques and Empathy in Counseling and Psychotherapy

Could a greater miracle take place than for us to look through each other's eyes for an instant?
—Thoreau (1854/1968, p. 11)

When I first began introducing a range of treatment interventions to graduate counseling students, it seemed clear to me that empathy was integral to the technique of reflection. What was confusing to me at that time, however, was how empathy and empathic understanding related to all the other therapeutic procedures. In some cases, such as with self-disclosure and the use of projective instruments, it seemed that empathy was a prominent component. Yet, in other instances, with more challenging techniques, such as confrontation and cognitive restructuring, empathic understanding did not appear to be particularly relevant. Even though I valued empathy as a treatment focus, I found that my instruction relating to the construct was inconsistent in its application. After a period of time, however, I realized that empathy has a clear and definable role when a practitioner makes observations that are outside of a client's frame of reference. In these instances, it is possible for a therapist to express an empathic understanding with respect to how the client reacts to the intervention. Even if an individual rejects or refutes a counselor's interventions, it is a sound strategy to empathically acknowledge this position. In this way, a practitioner maintains a disposition toward empathy with the knowledge that at certain times he or she may choose to operate outside of an empathic stance.

THERAPEUTIC TECHNIQUES IN COUNSELING AND PSYCHOTHERAPY

Although research evidence indicates that specific interventions only contribute a modest percentage to the advancement of treatment outcome, there is a significant value in developing the technical skills of a counselor or a therapist (Goodheart, 2004). In conjunction with the various personal attributes of a practitioner, such as flexibility, honesty, and confidence, particular techniques enhance the working alliance in the therapy process (Ackerman & Hilsenroth, 2003). With respect to empathy, it is often difficult to separate the construct from its property as a skill dimension and its more personal quality as an attribute of a practitioner. When a counselor, for example, expresses a reflection to a client, this interaction demonstrates a technical level of proficiency, but it also conveys such personal qualities as interest and respect.

In another direction, with a contemporary emphasis on evidence-based practice in psychotherapy, it is advantageous for a therapist to be explicit in the utilization of meaningful techniques and practice guidelines (Goodheart, 2004; Messer, 2004; Norcross, 2002). In particular, an understanding of a practitioner's interventions and a client's responses in the therapeutic process contributes to an explanation of how positive change occurs in treatment (Edwards, Dattilio, & Bromley, 2004). Finally, in counselor education, there is a contemporary and expanding interest in skill-based training that provides a framework for the acquisition and self-appraisal of therapy skills (Little, Packman, Smaby, & Maddux, 2005). In these program initiatives, practitioners-in-training receive systematic training in therapeutic techniques that are linked to specific stages in the treatment process.

With a current interest in skill training in counseling and psychotherapy programs, it is important to recognize the innovative contributions of such individuals as Ivey and Ivey (2003) and Egan (2002), who provided an impetus to the development of intentional or deliberate interventions in treatment over a number of years. With respect to earlier researchers, although Carkhuff and his associates were maligned for their efforts to clarify the communication functions of counselors and therapists, they did establish procedures to make the work of a practitioner more explicit (Carkhuff, 1987; Carkhuff & Berenson, 1977). In a relatively recent development in the field, there is receptivity toward integrating the treatment alliance with the task intentions of a practitioner across diverse therapeutic approaches (Ivey, D'Andrea, Ivey, & Simek-Morgan, 2002; Kelly, 1997). This trend, however, contrasts with another direction involving the use of empirically supported treatments and training manuals that have been criticized for overemphasizing technical procedures and for failing to devote sufficient attention to therapeutic relationships (Lambert & Barley, 2002).

With this background in mind, it is important to consider empathy and empathic understanding as they manifest within therapeutic interventions in the context of the treatment relationship. A three-stage framework provides a structure for introducing specific techniques across the treatment process as they relate to empathy. In the initial or relationship stage of counseling and psychotherapy, an emphasis is given to understanding a client's experience and establishing a working alliance. In the second or integration stage, the focus of treatment is toward clarifying conflictual aspects of a client's experiencing in order to attain a more coherent and integrated level of functioning. In the third or accomplishment stage, therapeutic efforts emphasize promoting adaptive client actions and a consolidation of treatment gains.

THE RELATIONSHIP STAGE, TECHNIQUES, AND EMPATHY

The establishment of a working alliance in which a client gains a sense of trust and understanding is a fundamental process goal in many current approaches to counseling and psychotherapy (Moursund & Erskine, 2004). Efforts to engender open communication and supportive conditions often find expression through a practitioner's techniques and strategies. There is a range of interventions in treatment that are frequently used by counselors and therapists in order to enhance the therapeutic relationship and to promote client development. At the same time, client resistance often occurs in this period as individuals evoke defensive and evasive behavioral patterns. During this initial phase, empathic understanding is central to reducing the perception of psychological threat while, at the same time, advancing the treatment relationship. Empathy is integral to a number of the techniques that a counselor employs, and it is possible to clarify the role of the construct within each intervention. Among the various approaches, reflection may be the most intrinsic to the expression of empathy. Assessment, practitioner self-disclosure, questions, and the use of touch are other selected interventions that potentially communicate a therapist's empathic understanding. Although the procedures are prominent in the initial stage, they also have a treatment utility throughout the treatment process.

Reflection

As a therapeutic technique that was introduced by Rogers (1986a), reflection functions to empathically acknowledge the explicit and implicit feelings and meanings of a client (Ivey & Ivey, 2003). Rogers was critical of linking person-centered therapy with reflection because, in his view, this gave excessive focus to technological aspects of treatment. Yet, at the same time, reflection as a term and as a treatment intervention is widely recognized among practitioners and in the professional literature (Ackerman & Hilsenroth, 2003; Cormier & Hackney, 2005; Hill, 2004; Ivey & Ivey, 2003; Moursund & Erskine, 2004; Young, 2005). Through a reflection, a counselor or a therapist is able to capture the inner experience of a client and convey this understanding back to the individual from an immediate or extended perspective (Brodley, 1996; Cochran & Cochran, 2006). From a less favorable perspective, empathy has frequently been equated with the technique of reflection, and this has created confusion and misunderstandings. Reflection has also been criticized as a circular and superficial technique that merely parrots content that a client has expressed.

Over a period of time, a consistent use of reflection by a counselor or a therapist contributes to a client's working through of emotionally laden issues. As a practitioner attempts to grasp the feelings and meanings of a client, there is frequently a change in the intensity of affective expression and perspectives of the individual in a therapeutic direction (Rogers, 1975). In the following treatment example, a college senior, Tonya, has recently experienced the break-up of a long-term relationship with Larry. The selected dialogue is taken from sessions with a college counselor over a period of 6 weeks.

(Session One)

Tonya: I thought that we were going to spend the rest of our lives together. Larry was so special to me, then it all ended.

Counselor: You cared about him so much and together you had so many plans. He's gone and it hurts deeply.

Tonya: I have such a huge void in my life. I know that I will never find someone like him again. It's so painful.

Counselor: Somehow you feel that things will never be as good for you without Larry, and this leaves you with deep sadness.

(Session Three)

Tonya: When I bumped into Larry last week he acted like he didn't even know me. We had two wonderful years together, and I thought that it would be forever. It sickens me that it meant nothing to him.

Counselor: You feel betrayed. You gave so much of yourself to the relationship that you thought was going to be for a lifetime. Now it seems to you that Larry's commitment was not that important to him.

Tonya: It's so confusing. I feel so angry and then all of a sudden sad. It's all too much.

Counselor: It seems so mixed up; you have so many different feelings. Even trying to make sense of it all seems overwhelming.

(Session Six)

Tonya: I can't stay hurt forever. I tried to make things right for us, and it didn't happen.

Counselor: You feel that you gave your best effort to make the relationship work, but now you sense that you must move on. It seems possible at this point to think about the future without Larry.

Tonya: Larry is not the only guy in the world that would be good for me. I'm a survivor, and I know that I'll be all right.

Counselor: It seems that you now feel confident about being able to meet someone else who will care about you. In some ways you believe you are a stronger person after going through all of this.

From a subjective empathy perspective, the counselor immediately identified with Tonya and her experience of hurt and rejection. In college the counselor had broken up with a boyfriend, but it was her decision to end the relationship. The counselor was also able to imagine what it would be like to be Tonya and have long-term dreams vanquished. As Tonya discussed the incident when Larry acted as if he did not know her, the counselor visualized the scene and momentarily felt angry. Through initial interactions with Tonya, the counselor intuitively sensed that she was able to therapeutically express her feelings, as painful as they seemed to be. At various points, the counselor experienced felt-level responses as Tonya talked. This occurred when Tonya stated that she was a "survivor," and the counselor felt a momentary surge of warmth in her chest and face.

In terms of interpersonal empathy, the counselor reflected Tonya's feelings as she worked through a range of emotions from anguish to disgust and resentment, and eventually to relief and a relative degree of equilibrium.

With respect to objective empathy, in the second treatment session, Tonya completed a self-report depression inventory and a projective assessment. The material suggested that Tonya's outlook on life had an inner-directed quality, and her depression inventory was in the high normal range. In the third session, when Tonya expressed hostility toward Larry, the counselor reflected her feelings of betrayal with a fair degree of certainty that she had the capacity to emotionally manage her reactions. In the sixth session, the counselor had formulated a general sense of Tonya's functioning in terms of a model of a client, and her reflection reference to being a "stronger person" drew from this extended empathic perspective. The counselor's last statement is a future-oriented response that emphasizes Tonya's sense of control and efficacy (Bohart, Magallanes, Guzman, Smiljanich, Aguallo, & Humphrey, 1993).

Assessment

Although standardized and projective assessments are not typically associated with empathically understanding a client, the appraisal methods potentially offer insights for grasping what it is like to be the individual from a broader perspective (Cates, 1999). From an objective empathy stance, standardized self-reporting inventories provide data that reflect responses of a client in comparison to specific reference groups. A range of mental health factors, such as depression, anxiety, substance abuse, eating disorders, and marital satisfaction may be evaluated with respect to a particular individual (Aiken, 2003). As an example, in completing the *Beck Anxiety Inventory,* a client's score is found to be of moderate anxiety with a high elevation in a panic category. In turn, this information contributes to a more comprehensive understanding of the client in the treatment process. A counselor or a therapist may also use the standard-scale scores from general-purpose measures, such as the *Minnesota Multiphasic Personality Inventory–2* and the *Millon Clinical Multiaxial Inventory–III* (Aiken, 2003), to gain further insight into a client's functioning from an objective empathy perspective. In the appraisal endeavor, there is a focus on combining or integrating data from multiple assessment instruments in order to clarify client knowledge that may otherwise be vague or incomplete (Cates, 1999; Watkins, 2000).

Projective techniques are another assessment direction that a practitioner may consider in order to enhance the empathic understanding of a client (Garb et al., 2002). There is a range of projective devices, such as the Rorschach, the Thematic Apperception Test, human figure drawings, and sentence completion methods, that engage a client in relatively non-threatening and ambiguous tasks. Reservations, however, continue to exist about the use of projective techniques that generally focus on marginal psychometric properties and lack objective scoring procedures (Clark, 1995d). Although these are legitimate issues, they are of less concern if the projective devices are viewed as informal, hypotheses-generating tools in a treatment situation.

As an example of a projective technique, counselors and therapists may select sentence completion protocols that are available from several published sources or find it appropriate to design and construct formats that are pertinent to specific populations (Holaday, Smith, & Sherry, 2000). In a continuation of the case illustration involving Tonya, she finished a 25-item sentence completion task in her second therapy session. Tonya's responses suggested that, although she was struggling with a personal crisis in her life, her general level of psychological functioning seemed relatively normal. With respect to herself, Tonya responded, "I feel . . . so hurt and sad," "I regret . . . only a few things," and "I need . . . to make sense out of all of this." In response to sentence stems relating to others, Tonya wrote, "Other people . . . are generally good," "My father . . . is a caring man," and "Other students . . . are fun to be around." Tonya's general evaluation of events is detectable as she stated, "I am best when . . . I'm around other people," "The happiest time . . . was with Larry," and "College . . . is a wonderful experience."

Early Recollections is another projective device that, although less well-known, provides an unintrusive and participatory appraisal of a client's personality functioning (Clark, 1994a, 1995d, 1995e, 2001, 2002b; Mosak, 1958). Eliciting a small number of first memories, perhaps three, involves a client in an intrinsically interesting and engrossing task. Early recollections, as an assessment tool, was first introduced by Adler (1937). The literature on early memories extends for over 100 years and includes theoretical perspectives, taxonomic considerations, personality dimensions, and diagnostic impressions (Clark, 2002b). From a diagnostic vantage point, early recollections research has focused on most major clinical and personality disorders in the *DSM–IV–TR*. Various scoring and interpretation systems have been proposed, and a contextural approach enables a practitioner to evaluate first memories from multiple ways of knowing (Clark, 2002b). From a contextural perspective, an early recollection of Tonya's from the continuing case illustration contributes to an overview of the procedure. "I was going to go outside to play in the snow with my younger sister. Ellen couldn't get her boots on by herself and I helped her with them. She looked so happy when I got the boots on her." Tonya added that she could see the blue sky through the kitchen window. In response to a question about the most vivid part of the memory, Tonya replied, "Seeing my sister's excited face when she stood up with her boots on." At this point, Tonya felt "very happy."

In evaluating the early recollection from a subjective perspective, the counselor visually imagined the scene with Tonya and Ellen in their kitchen. Through a transitory identification with Tonya as she helped her sister, the counselor intuitively sensed that Tonya is a kind person. When Tonya said that she felt "very happy" in seeing her sister's excited face, the counselor experienced a mild uplifting sensation in her chest. From an interpersonal perspective, themes and details in a client's early recollections also contribute to an empathic understanding of the client. In the context of a unique belief system, a person maintains enduring convictions about the self, others, and events. With respect to Tonya's early recollection, she thematically perceives herself as significant and competent, and other persons as worthy; she construes events as constructive and gratifying. Tonya's visual channel is her most prominent sensory experience; color stands out in her memory and possibly suggests an artistic inclination or appreciation (Clark, 2004b). The location of the memory is in the home, and it is a positive association in terms of an experience of place. The only object, beyond the blue sky, that is notable in the remembrance is Ellen's boots. These seem important only to the extent that they provide a vehicle for Tonya for service. From an objective perspective, early recollection inferences draw on the extensive literature on taxonomic, personality, and diagnostic topics (Clark, 2002b). Tonya's early recollection seems to relate to characteristics of security, optimism as an explanatory style, and social interest. All of these considerations are viewed by the counselor as hypotheses. They must be integrated with Tonya's other two early recollections and additional assessment information in developing an evolving sense of empathic understanding (Finn & Tonsager, 1997).

Self-Disclosure

A counselor or a therapist may potentially convey empathic understanding to a client through a judicious disclosure of personal experiences and perspectives. Self-disclosure by a practitioner has been found to demonstrate an empathic attunement and involvement in the treatment situation (Goldstein, 1997; Hill & Knox, 2002). In this regard, a client may perceive a counselor as more human in the relationship and less threatening and remote (Watkins, 1990). An increase of trust and a sense of reassurance often promotes more intimate communication on the part of a client. In a less favorable direction, self-disclosures have been shown to have an adverse effect in treatment when the practitioner is perceived as insensitive or intrusive, thus raising doubt about his or her professional competency (Hill & Knox, 2002). In these instances, it is possible that a therapist's self-disclosure removes the focus from a client or burdens and confuses the individual. Self-disclosure by a counselor has also been found to reduce a client's perception of a practitioner's empathic understanding, trust, and capability (Curtis, 1982). Although there are contradictory findings in the professional literature regarding the therapeutic value of a practitioner's self-disclosure, it appears that the approach may either promote or impair empathic understanding in the treatment relationship.

From a subjective empathy perspective, a therapist may identify with a client's experience as a result of similar events in their respective backgrounds. It is also possible for a practitioner to immediately react to a client's disclosure with a felt-level response. As an example, in the continuing treatment illustration relating to Tonya, when she began to discuss her break-up with Larry, the counselor emotionally connected with her severance of a long-term relationship. Relating to an interpersonal empathy stance, the counselor immediately considered revealing to Tonya that they shared a similar experience in college. Tonya, however, was having little difficulty in expressing her feelings, and the counselor thought that a disclosure might have the effect of diverting or diminishing communication. The counselor was also aware that her experience was unlike Tonya's to the extent that it was she who had decided to end the relationship with her boyfriend. At a later point in treatment, after getting to know Tonya more fully, the counselor did disclose that she also had gone through the termination of a lengthy commitment. With regard to an objective empathy perspective, the counselor took into consideration some pertinent guidelines from the treatment literature. For instance, the self-disclosure of a therapist should be in the service of a client rather than serving the needs of the practitioner, and revelations are more effective when similar to the client's experiencing (Cormier & Nurius, 2003).

Another frequently cited guideline in the use of self-disclosure suggests that a client should have a readiness to cognitively and emotionally focus on a practitioner's remarks. The counselor who employs a self-disclosure when the client is highly agitated and distracted is demonstrating a lack of empathic understanding. Situations may also develop wherein a client seeks to elicit personal information from a therapist, and the practitioner will find it necessary to decide whether or not to communicate the material. In the event that the therapist chooses not to disclose, it is therapeutic to use a reflection in order to empathically acknowledge the client's reaction to not knowing (Goldstein, 1997). It is also possible that a counselor may find that compelling personal situations interfere with his or her ability to maintain an empathic connection with a client, and a decision needs to be made whether to disclose situational matters that are a distraction. As an example, a practitioner worried about the health of an elderly parent may decide to briefly mention the situation to a client.

A self-disclosure guideline that is often overlooked is that a counselor or a therapist must develop some understanding of a client before utilizing a self-disclosure. Typically, as treatment continues, a practitioner is able to employ self-disclosures that take into account the extended perspectives of a client, and this increases the likelihood of revelations that are attuned to an individual's pattern of experiencing. For instance, when working with early adolescents, a counselor frequently discloses that he disliked school prior to entering high school. As a result, a client may sense that the counselor understands him or her better because of their mutual feelings toward school. In contrast, another client may find the counselor's remarks to be threatening and invasive because of the lack of emotional readiness to be understood at that point in the treatment process. The use of self-disclosure in the form of self-involving statements may also be dependent on a practitioner's reactions to a client's behavior in treatment or to interactions within the therapeutic relationship (Watkins, 1990). A therapist, for example, becomes aware of her subjective reactions of irritability and states, "I think that I have been somewhat disagreeable with you so far today. Does this seem to be the case?" In another instance, a counselor relates, "I sense that you seem distracted and distant today, and this is not like you."

Questions

Practitioners frequently employ questions in counseling and psychotherapy, and the technique has a potential for use and misuse in treatment. The effectiveness of a question depends on various factors, such as the type of question and frequency of engagement (Cormier & Nurius, 2003; Sommers-Flanagan & Sommers-Flanagan, 2003). The counselor primarily asks a client a question in order to learn something about his or her situation (Tomm, 1988). Thus, the immediate purpose of asking a question is to develop or extend a practitioner's knowledge relating to a client. It is also possible for a therapist to pose a question with the intent of enhancing an empathic understanding of a client (Martin, 2000). In these instances, the client's perceptions may be unclear or confusing, and require that the therapist attempt to clarify the perspectives of the individual. As an example, an early adolescent is experiencing difficulty in mathematics and verbalizes a general disdain for the subject material. After reflecting the client's feelings, the school counselor states, "What is it about math that is hard for you?" As the discussion begins to focus on homework assignments, the counselor relates, "Is it that you find there are too many questions?" and "Is the assignment too long for you to finish?" In this context, the counselor's intention is to empathically explore vague or ambiguous client communications. An especially helpful question in this regard is, "Can you give me an example?" (Ivey & Ivey, 2003).

Of four types of questions that Tomm (1988) describes from a perspective of family therapy, circular questions, in particular, emphasize an empathic understanding of a client. A practitioner employs circular questions in an exploratory manner in order to gain insight into various facets of a client's experiencing. The primary goal is to clarify the interactional patterns of an individual that are largely unexpressed. For example, in a treatment situation a college student reports that he did not finish a mid-term examination and was angry at the instructor for giving him an unsatisfactory grade on the test. After acknowledging the client's feelings, the therapist states, "When you left the exam incomplete, what did you think that the professor would do?" In another instance, a middle-adulthood client expresses a high level of anxiety relating to his mother's physical ailments. During discussion, the practitioner asks, "Other than yourself, who else is troubled about your mother?" Soon after the client responds, the therapist asks a follow-up question. "When you compare your sister's concern with your own, how worried is your sister about your mother?" In these examples, the circular questions enable the client to make comparisons and evaluate his experiencing in an exploratory and empathic climate.

From a subjective empathy perspective, a counselor or a therapist should refrain from asking a question unless he or she has a purpose in mind (Cormier & Nurius, 2003). A misuse of questions occurs when a practitioner asks questions simply to satisfy his or her own curiosity or to fulfill a need for closure. In the absence of an empathic disposition at an interpersonal level, questions may be intrusive and threatening (Ivey & Ivey, 2003; Tomm, 1988). It is also possible for communication to assume a question-and-answer mode of exchange between a client and a therapist and diminish or negate a sense of empathic understanding. As an example, after a lengthy series of questions from a counselor, a client irritatingly states, "I don't want to talk anymore." In response, the counselor relates, "Why don't you want to talk?" In order to limit this type of exchange with a client, there are guidelines available to assist a practitioner from an objective level of empathic understanding. In this regard, referential sources suggest that effective questions should be relevant, timely, regulated, non-accusatory, and center on the needs and concerns of the client (Clark, 1989; Cormier & Nurius, 2003; Egan, 2002; Ivey & Ivey, 2003; Murphy & Dillon, 2003).

The Use of Touch

As an overt gesture by a counselor or a therapist, touch is a form of communication in the therapeutic process (Durana, 1998). In this regard, a practitioner's touch of a client has a potential to serve as an expression of caring and concern, or it can become gratuitous or exploitative. In recognizing the value of touch in counseling and psychotherapy, Corey, Corey, and Callahan (2003) stated, "There are also times when a touch that is given at the right moment can convey far more empathy than words can" (p. 285). As a natural and spontaneous expression of feeling, a therapist's touch of a client on his or her hand, shoulder, or mid and upper back may communicate a sense of support and reassurance in a treatment situation (Durana, 1998; Kertay & Reviere, 1993). In the experience of a client during periods of grief and trauma, isolation and loneliness, and depression and rejection, touch contributes to an expression of practitioner's empathic understanding and enables an individual to explore therapeutic issues at a deeper level (Durana, 1998; Horton, 1998). In other more uplifting occasions, a counselor is in a position to empathically acknowledge celebratory events in a client's experience such as securing a long-sought career position or the conception of a child after a lengthy period of attempting to conceive.

In contrast to the more advantageous uses of touch in counseling and psychotherapy, there are potentially damaging experiences where touch represents an empathic failure or a violation of client trust (Horton, 1998). In particular, a practitioner acting on sexual feelings and sexually exploiting a client is unethical and destructive (Corey et al., 2003). A client may also feel threatened by a therapist's unwanted touch due to a gender or power differential in a treatment relationship (Durana, 1998). In other instances, it is possible for a client to experience a counselor's touch as condescending or invasive of psychological boundaries. In order to reduce the misuse or abuse of touch in a treatment situation, a therapist's employment of multiple perspectives of empathy may be helpful. From a subjective empathy stance, momentary occurrences of identification with a client's experiencing provide an awareness of the individual's immediate and extended condition. This understanding enables a practitioner to maintain an empathic focus on the functioning of a client rather than on one's own issues and needs. An intuitive response in conjunction with a practitioner's felt-level experiencing contributes to an emotional attunement with a client that becomes manifest through the respectful use of touch. As an example, in the treatment illustration with Tonya, the counselor touched Tonya's hand when she proclaimed herself a "survivor." Furthermore, a thoughtful awareness of countertransference reactions decreases the likelihood of a practitioner acting out his or her feelings by inappropriately touching a client.

From an interpersonal empathy perspective, touch is more likely to be perceived as positive when the treatment relationship is sufficiently established and a practitioner has a more substantial understanding of a client (Horton, 1998). Knowledge of a client from a broader perspective also assists a counselor to anticipate the individual's readiness to touch and the potential for benefit or harm (Durana, 1998). A counselor or a therapist may also choose to accompany the touch of a client with a verbal explanation in order to clarify the meaning of the communication (Wilson, 1982). As an example, a practitioner responds to a middle-adulthood client who is experiencing a significant level of stress. As the therapist touches the client's hand, she states, "At this point it all seems overwhelming to you with so many pressures in your life." With respect to objective empathy, there are various guidelines in the professional literature relating to the effective use of touch in a treatment situation. In this regard, a practitioner's touch should only last for a few seconds. It should also be genuine and spontaneous, nonerotic, restricted to acceptable areas, and appropriate to the needs and readiness of a client (Corey, Corey, & Callahan, 2003; Durana, 1998; Horton, 1998; Kertay & Reviere, 1993; Willison & Masson, 1986; Wilson, 1982). In a final consideration from referential sources, clients with a history of sexual and physical abuse may react adversely to a practitioner's touch (Corey, Corey, & Callahan, 2003). At the same time, a judicious use of touch has been found to have a deconditioning and reparative effect with some clients with an abusive childhood history (Durana, 1998; Horton, 1998).

THE INTEGRATION STAGE, TECHNIQUES, AND EMPATHY

With a supportive relationship developed through empathic understanding in the initial period of the therapeutic process, the middle stage of counseling and psychotherapy focuses on integrating the functions of a client toward an increasingly coherent level. At this time, a practitioner assumes a more challenging posture with a client in order to explore conflictual material relating to an individual's belief structures. Examining ingrained convictions may be destabilizing for clients, and a therapist's empathic understanding is critical for working through personal issues of a long-standing nature. In this respect, the integration stage emphasizes second-order change by attempting to alter the fundamental structure of a client's belief system (Lyddon, 1990). In the context of an empathic and supportive therapeutic alliance, a treatment goal is to construct new and more purposeful client perceptions that can translate into advances in adaptive behavior. For some individuals, there may only be a minimal involvement in this phase, and with others with more extensive levels of pathology, the duration of treatment may be prolonged. Selected practitioner techniques that are appropriate in the integration stage, such as confrontation, cognitive restructuring, reframing, and interpretation can contribute to an in-depth exploration of a client's functioning. With each of the procedures it is possible to integrate empathic understanding in a way that enhances the effectiveness of the treatment process.

Confrontation

Although confrontation as a term suggests an aggressive overtone, in a therapeutic situation a practitioner may employ the technique in a supportive way in order to acknowledge discrepancies and contradictions in the behavior of a client (Welfel & Patterson, 2005). As a counselor or a therapist confronts a client, the practitioner is in a position to empathize with what it is like to be the individual in a challenging situation (Josephs, 1995). Without a sensitive attunement to the experiencing of a client, a confrontation is likely to provoke a defensive response by the individual and be detrimental to the treatment alliance (Erskine, Moursund, & Trautmann, 1999). In this regard, it is a sound direction for a practitioner to express a confrontation after the therapeutic relationship is reasonably well established in terms of trust and rapport. Generally, a counselor can expect a range of client reactions to a confrontation from denial to acknowledgement and acceptance (Cormier & Nurius, 2003; Ivey & Ivey, 2003; Young, 2005). In attempting to maintain an empathic stance, a therapist may utilize a reflection immediately after a client responds to a confrontation. In a therapy example, a middle-adulthood client discusses conflicts with his supervisor at work:

Client: He's always after me to get the projects completed, but it doesn't bother me that much.

Therapist: You are saying that the demands of your supervisor are not particularly affecting you, but as you say this your hands are shaking.

Client: Well, it's not easy, but I need the job. I feel pretty mixed up about all of this.

Therapist: This is confusing to you because you feel pulled in different directions and each of them seems important.

From a subjective empathy perspective, a counselor or a therapist may have difficulty confronting a client due to personal or countertransference issues. Accordingly, a practitioner may wish to avoid hurting or disturbing a client with a challenging remark that has the potential to disrupt the treatment relationship and, through a fear of being intrusive, withhold potentially therapeutic perspectives or information (Moses, 1988). In this respect, the failure of a therapist to confront when the client demonstrates self-defeating functioning inadvertently implies a condonment or support of the behavior (Tamminen & Smaby, 1981). For some practitioners, a particular outlook on life may contribute to a convictional bias that impedes their capacity to confront. As an example, a counselor maintains an ingrained conviction that relationships with others are generally harmonious, and the individual finds confrontational exchanges to be adverse.

With regard to an interpersonal empathy perspective, it is important for a therapist to recognize that a confrontation in the supportive context of the treatment relationship has the therapeutic potential to bring underlying patterns of dysfunctional behavior to a client's awareness that might otherwise remain undetected (Patton & Meara, 1992). Thus, in interactions with a client, a practitioner's "confrontation communicates the highest level of empathic understanding" (Ruble & Slivka, 1975, p. 14). In an opposite direction, it is possible for a counselor to become irritated by a client who repeatedly appears to avoid or evade issues. Consequently, a practitioner may begin to respond in judgmental and condescending ways (Leaman,

1978). To continue the illustration with the middle-adulthood client, consider the result if the counselor had said, "Oh, come on now. Your hands are shaking and it's obvious that you are really anxious about this." It is apparent that this type of statement would be unempathic and deflating to a client. With respect to an objective empathy stance, there are guidelines available in the professional literature that potentially contribute to more effective and empathic confrontations. In this regard, a practitioner may consider expressing a confrontation in a nonaccusatory, descriptive, and timely way that takes into account the immediate and extended perspectives of a client (Cormier & Nurius, 2003; Egan, 2002; Ivey & Ivey, 2003; Welfel & Patterson, 2005; Young, 2005).

Cognitive Restructuring

A purposeful direction for a counselor or a therapist to consider after clarifying a client's conflictive functioning is the technique of cognitive restructuring. Cognitive restructuring focuses on transforming a client's self-defeating beliefs in a more purposeful direction (Meichenbaum, 1977). As an approach that emphasizes second-order change, cognitive restructuring involves empathically identifying and altering a client's negative and dysfunctional self-statements (Hackney & Cormier, 2005). Clients under guidance actively construct counterstatements or *counters* that provide purposeful alternatives to maladaptive thought patterns and beliefs (Young, 2005). These counters or coping thoughts are incompatible with the more critical or faulty cognitions employed by the individuals (McMullin, 2000). As an example, a late-adulthood client named Mary chronically engages in self-talk represented by the anxiety-laden statement, "I continually worry about everything." Through an empathic examination of the implications of this verbalization, Mary identifies a counter that seems appropriate and viable: "I choose to worry about some things but not everything." Subsequently, through sustained practice outside of therapy and continuing treatment, the statement for Mary begins to assume a more convincing quality.

As a counselor or a therapist interacts with a client over an extended period of time, the practitioner experiences numerous instances of identification and imaginable activity involving the individual. This subjective empathic understanding is critical in providing an awareness of how a client broadly construes life and contributes to the formulation of a model of a client. From an interpersonal empathy stance, a practitioner is in a position to observe patterns of self-defeating statements expressed by a client in a treatment situation. As an example, clients often verbalize comments such as, "I can't do anything right," "I never get a break in life," and "I must do everything just right." From an objective empathy perspective, these reiterations are conceptualized as *basic mistakes* (Mosak & Maniacci, 1998), *irrational ideas* (Ellis, 2005), and *cognitive distortions* (Beck & Weishaar, 2005). An accurate grasp of the conceptions or constructs contributes to the formulation of counters that are pertinent to an individual. The constructs are also viable as a component of the model of a client that enables a practitioner to empathically understand an individual from a broader perspective. It is also possible to include in the model of a client particular schemas or fundamental convictions relating to how the individual construes life. With respect to the previous illustration involving Mary, specific schemas relating to herself and others are anxiety-laden. An awareness of these convictions enables a therapist to enhance an empathic understanding of how an individual functions according to his or her outlook on life.

Reframing

Reframing is another treatment technique that emphasizes an alternative perspective by modifying or restructuring a client's perceptions of a problem or a situation (Cormier & Nurius, 2003). In altering the frame in which a client perceives a particular condition, the meaning of specific assumptions and beliefs change and are placed in a new context (Sperry, Carlson, & Kjos, 2003). Reframing also involves shifting particular meanings of a client's experiencing in a more purposeful direction. In order to stimulate constructive change in a client's perceptions, it is necessary for a counselor or a therapist to empathically understand the individual from an immediate and extended basis. As a treatment example, a latency-age child named Jacob displaces hostile feelings on other children, and his current treatment focuses on bullying issues. From an extended empathic perspective, Jacob perceives strength and control as admirable personal qualities. In introducing a reframe, the practitioner invites Jacob to consider the viewpoint that a strong person is usually able to control one's feelings and not visit them on others who are less able to defend themselves. If Jacob begins to perceive his bullying as a sign of weakness, it is possible that his employment of displacement as a defense mechanism may assume a new and adverse meaning.

When a counselor or a therapist renders a reframe, the context and timing of the intervention often emerge through an intuitive reaction. From a subjective empathy perspective, a practitioner experiences a hunch that a particular reframe may be appropriate for a client. This notion may also include an imaginable element as the therapist anticipates how a client will respond to the reframe. For instance, an adolescent named Janice has been in treatment for disruptive behavior in a school and community setting and has been subject to a number of disciplinary proceedings. The therapist has an empathic understanding that Janice is averse to restrictions and controls on her behavior. In treatment, discussion focuses on various punishments that Janice has received for truancy from school and physical fights with her peers. In the context of this exchange, the practitioner invites Janice to consider a reframe that her quest to be free of restraints often results in an even greater reduction or diminution of her freedom. In this instance, Janice seems intrigued by the therapist's reframe from an interpersonal empathy stance. Janice and the therapist empathically explore the essence of a reframe that introduces the concept that it is possible to reduce potentially punitive actions in order to gain a more genuine and long-term level of personal freedom.

As the therapist interacts with Janice, she is aware of several guidelines involving reframing from an objective empathy perspective. Referential material from the treatment literature suggests that an effective reframe by a practitioner is seen as pertinent and plausible by the client, is proposed in an inviting and exploratory tone, and is rendered after grasping an extended understanding of a client (Clark, 1998b; Cormier & Nurius, 2003; Sperry, Carlson & Kjos, 2003). The professional literature also discusses a reframe as a relabeling or reclassification procedure. In this regard, as a semantic aspect of an interpretation, a new vocabulary or terminology may result in how phenomena are perceived by a client (Levy, 1963). The change in the meaning of the following terms, "stubborn" to "determined," "perfectionist" to "highly organized," and "protective" to "enabling," provide examples of reframing with significant behavioral implications. A spouse for example, perceives that she is "protecting" her family from the painful effects of her husband's alcoholism. A counselor's reframe of the term "protecting" to "enabling" suggests a different function with respect to the individual's behavior. In these instances, the use of a practitioner's reflection as a response to a client's reaction to a reframe provides a sense of empathic understanding.

Interpretation

As a technique in counseling and psychotherapy, interpretation emphasizes the consideration of material that is outside of a client's frame of reference by proposing causal relationships in an individual's experience. Through an interpretation, a therapist renders new or alternative perspectives by relating phenomena that had not previously been connected (Clark, 1995a; Hill, 2004; Levy 1963). Various theoretical orientations differ in terms of the importance that they ascribe to interpretations, but the intervention is used at least occasionally by nearly all practitioners (Seligman, 2004). A counselor or a therapist typically employs a conceptual formulation in conjunction with personal observations when expressing an interpretation. An interpretation has the potential to enhance an empathic understanding of a client or, on the other hand, diminish an individual's sense of being understood. As an example, a therapist renders an interpretation to a young adult that attributes the client's intensely competitive behavior to a long-term determination to surpass his older brother. The client thoughtfully responds to the interpretation and engages in a discussion about its implications. The therapist utilizes the interpretation only after an extensive exploration of the client's functioning in the context of positive treatment alliance. In contrast, a poorly timed or insensitive interpretation can have an adverse and deleterious effect. For instance, in the initial stage of treatment, a counselor employs an interpretation in the form of making a connection with an early-adulthood client's excessively anxious behavior with his history of child abuse even though there had only been a brief mention of abusive issues and the therapeutic relationship had not yet been established. As a consequence, the client becomes emotionally destabilized and fearful of further exposure to threatening issues.

The development of the framework for an interpretation may start early in treatment as a counselor or therapist empathically begins to formulate an extended understanding of client. Through discussions with a client, a practitioner participates in numerous interactions that involve a subjective empathy stance, and knowledge is derived from reciprocal processes. As an example, in initial treatment with a client named Wanda, the therapist identifies with her as she discusses emotionally laden topics. At the same time, the therapist observes that Wanda does not seem particularly anxious or emotionally distressed as she recalls in detail what seem to be disturbing events in her life. The practitioner also finds that his felt-level experiencing is also muted while listening to Wanda talk about affective issues. Over a period of time, a therapist is able to hypothesize generalizations about a client's functioning from an interpersonal empathy perspective. To continue with the case illustration relating to Wanda, the practitioner recognizes that she rarely emotes feelings during discussion of topics that typically evoke various degrees of affective reactions from individuals. This type of generalization involves relationship contingencies between events in a treatment situation (Levy, 1963).

In formulating and expressing an interpretation, a practitioner is able to utilize material available from referential sources from an objective empathy viewpoint. Theoretical conceptualizations in the form of constructions provide causal frameworks that are consistent with a client's behavior (Levy, 1963). For example, in Wanda's case, the therapist hypothesizes that Wanda employs the defense mechanism of isolation that involves severing verbalizations from associated affect (Clark, 1998a). Various guidelines are also available that contribute to an effective use of interpretation in the treatment process (Clark, 1995a; Gibbons, Crits-Christoph, & Apostal, 2004; Ivey & Ivey, 2003; Levy, 1963; Seligman, 2004; Weiner, 1998). In communicating an interpretation, a practitioner may suggest the proposition in a tentative form. This type of interpretation allows the client to disagree with the counselor or therapist or to partially or totally accept the practitioner's interpretation as accurate (Patton & Meara, 1992). To conclude with an empathic interpretation appropriate for the later stages of Wanda's treatment, the practitioner states, "Could it be that it is difficult for you to express your emotions because you learned early in life that in your family you had to keep your feelings inside?" It is also helpful after an interpretation is given that sufficient time be allowed for a client to explore and assimilate its meaning.

A misuse of empathy may also involve a seemingly correct or accurate interpretation offered before a client is emotionally ready to process the intervention (Szalita, 1981). In this regard, an interpretation may evoke intense or unfamiliar feelings or be overly intellectualized and distant from the emotional experiencing of a client (Schafer, 1959). It is also possible that an interpretation expressed by a practitioner at a particular time be perceived as unempathic by a client and at a later point in treatment be found to be empathic (Josephs, 1995). In these instances, a therapist's premature interpretation may evoke a defensive response that restricts the capacity of a client to consider an alternative point of view. Finally, an interpretation may involve relationships between a client's current and past functioning, or it may largely emphasize an analysis of current experiencing (Cashdan, 1988; Gibbons, Crits-Christoph, & Apostal, 2004). As an example, in a treatment situation, a client employs the defense mechanism of projective identification that entails a manipulation of the practitioner (Clark, 1995c; Ogden, 1982). As the therapist empathically associates the provocation with the client's efforts to seek relief from tension and conflict, the focus is on the individual's immediate functioning.

THE ACCOMPLISHMENT STAGE, TECHNIQUES, AND EMPATHY

As a client develops a more integrated level of functioning through the middle phase of treatment, therapeutic emphasis strategically shifts in the direction of behavioral change. In the final or accomplishment state, there is a focus on consolidating gains engendered through the therapy process and an effort is made to establish more adaptive client actions (Welfel & Patterson, 2005; Young, 2005). There are various techniques and interventions available to a practitioner that promote action-oriented change in a treatment situation (Hackney & Cormier, 2005). It is also possible for a counselor or therapist to employ an empathic disposition when utilizing a range of cognitive-behavioral or behavioral techniques. When considering possible interventions with a particular client, a counselor is able to engage multiple perspectives of empathy in order to determine appropriate and pertinent procedures. From a subjective empathy stance, a practitioner is in a position to momentarily identify with a client in terms of difficulties or challenges while in the process of taking action steps toward personal growth. In the context of this understanding, the therapist may experience an intuitive reaction that a particular technique seems appropriate for an individual. In turn, he or she briefly imagines what it would be like for a client to pursue a certain action.

As a counselor or a therapist interacts with a client, an interpersonal empathy stance acknowledges the receptivity of a client to a suggested technique. In this regard, a client may verbalize a reaction such as, "This makes sense to me, and I'd like to try it," or "I'm not sure if I can do it." As a therapist acknowledges a client's certainties or doubts, there is an emphasis on empathically understanding the individual's response. From an objective empathy perspective, a practitioner is able to use the extended understanding of a client that has been acquired over the course of the treatment process. This knowledge contributes to an appropriate identification of overt procedures and to any modification in an intervention that is appropriate for the individual. The counselor is also able to employ pertinent guidelines associated with the techniques available for therapeutic purposes. There are numerous action-oriented approaches that a practitioner may choose to employ in a treatment situation. The following three selected interventions have the potential to communicate a practitioner's empathic understanding while stimulating client behavioral change: *catching oneself, coping thoughts,* and *segmentation.* The procedures are pertinent when a client expresses or demonstrates a motivation to alter his or her behavior in a constructive direction.

Catching Oneself

When a client makes a commitment to change an undesirable behavior, *catching oneself* is a therapeutic technique that alerts the individual to internal cues that trigger the occurrence of an unwanted action (Oberst & Stewart, 2003). At a critical point of engaging a response, a client defers from following through with the behavior. Through a cued reminder, a client attempts to avoid acting on a repetitive cycle of negative functioning. As an example, a middle-adulthood client named Anna is attempting to break a pattern of alcohol abuse. When Anna feels the urge to drink, she takes a picture out of her pocket and looks at a snapshot of her children. The visual cue serves as a reminder of Anna's commitment to her family to stop drinking. In empathically understanding a client from an immediate and extended perspective, a practitioner is in a position to suggest a pertinent cue to a client that holds promise to stimulate a desirable response. Catching oneself has a potential for use with a range of adverse actions such as substance abuse, eating disorders, classroom inattention, defense mechanism engagement, and other functions that involve impulse control (Clark, 1998a.)

Coping Thoughts

Another action-oriented technique, *coping thoughts,* assists clients in following through with constructive efforts to break constricted or self-defeating patterns of behavioral functioning. An empathic understanding of a client enables a practitioner to assist the individual in identifying pertinent coping strategies that stimulate purposeful action. In this regard, J. S. Beck (1995) encourages clients to complete *coping cards* that list particular coping strategies. A client carries the small card on his or her person to read several times a day. The individual may also choose to place the card in a prominent place in the home or work site. As an example, a client diagnosed with an anxiety disorder writes an affirmation on a card, "I am a deserving person who chooses to take care of myself and worry less." In some instances, a client may find that a particular quotation serves as a source of inspiration to continue a constructive action pattern. The source of the quotation may emerge through discussion between a client and a counselor, or a therapist may suggest a quotation that is pertinent for a particular individual. For example, in a statement that is relevant to individuals with impulse-control issues, Pearl Buck (1942) wrote, "Every great mistake has a halfway moment, a split second when it can be recalled and perhaps remedied" (p. 117).

Segmentation

In a treatment situation, a client may be reluctant to attempt previously avoided or inhibited actions due to their perceived magnitude. In response to this potential impasse, a practitioner may empathically employ the therapeutic technique of segmentation. This process involves partializing challenging pursuits into small and manageable components. The premise behind segmentation is apparent in the 12-step programs for alcohol recovery through the maxim of "taking one step at a time" (Bristow-Braitman, 1995). When an individual divides large tasks into sequential and reachable segments, the endeavor frequently seems less daunting. In contrast, undertakings often appear burdensome when they are perceived from the perspective of the total effort required. In the counseling process, segmentation is also known as *Breaking It Down* (Clark, 1998a). As an action-oriented technique, a client pursues small or "baby steps" and is able to see the results of his or her efforts toward a desired goal. As an example, a middle-adulthood client named Ned has been terminated from a position that he had held for nearly 10 years. Ned feels overwhelmed at the prospect of beginning to look for work and has avoided the pursuit for several weeks. In response, the counselor introduces the technique of segmentation, and Ned expresses a sense of relief as he considers the approach. Subsequently, Ned decides that his first step in a job search is to write out his employment history.

SUMMARY

Empathy has a definable and purposeful role with a range of contemporary interventions in counseling and psychotherapy. Utilizing a three-stage conceptualization of the treatment process, it is possible to identify particular techniques in which a practitioner's employment of empathic understanding contributes to therapeutic gain and the enhancement of the working alliance. In the initial or relationship stage, reflection is a procedure that is most integral to empathy. Assessment, self-disclosure, questions, and the use of touch are other identifiable processes that utilize empathy in both their conceptualization and execution. A counselor or a therapist is able to employ empathy from subjective, interpersonal, and objective perspectives in advancing an understanding of a client. In the middle or integration stage, treatment emphasizes second-order change in stimulating the development of an individual. Confrontation, cognitive restructuring, reframing, and interpretation are selected interventions that involve a level of client challenge. At the same time, an empathic understanding of a client enables a counselor to maintain the therapeutic alliance even when communicating from outside of the person's frame of reference. In the final or accomplishment stage, there is a focus on action-oriented techniques that promote a client's adaptive functioning.

Chapter 9

Therapeutic Techniques and Empathy in Group Counseling and Psychotherapy

O wad some Power the giftie gie us to see oursels as ithers see us!

—R. Burns (1787/1897, p. 44)

In my first human services position as a school counselor, I regularly began to employ empathy with students in individual counseling sessions. Within a short period of time, I was given the opportunity to lead an early-adolescent counseling group. As I considered the various strategies available to me, I decided that here, too, empathy would be central in my treatment approach. After some initial assessment and preparation, the time arrived for my first group session. I felt my posture was well established and following 10 or 15 minutes of group member introductions, I was prepared to quickly demonstrate the full extent of my empathic understanding. All this was working well until one of the group participants called another student a derogatory name. Almost immediately, one of the other group members began to ridicule another individual, and suddenly empathy by itself did not seem to be a viable or sufficient process to get the students to settle down. I did not know it then, but I was struggling with the question of how a counselor or a therapist in a group experience is able to maintain an empathic disposition in the context of employing more directive interventions. To further complicate the situation, it was also unclear to me how to employ empathy with individual group members all at one time. It is one matter to utilize empathy with a single client, but quite another to attempt to engage empathic understanding with multiple individuals in a group setting.

Reflecting on my early group work, I realize that I lacked a conceptual and practical grasp of how to effectively demonstrate empathic understanding in group treatment, and only as my experience broadened did I slowly begin to comprehend how to integrate empathy into the group process. Much of this endeavor took place through trial and error, and only later was I able to find emerging material in the professional literature that brought more of a theoretical order to my approach. As I came to appreciate some of the challenges of attempting to employ empathy in a group setting, I also became convinced that empathic understanding was indispensable in working with groups in counseling and psychotherapy.

THERAPEUTIC TECHNIQUES IN GROUP COUNSELING AND PSYCHOTHERAPY

In individual treatment, a counselor or a therapist is in a position to communicate an expression of empathy to a single client in appropriate contexts. In a group experience, there is a marked expansion of the dynamics as a practitioner is able to express empathy toward a group member, to a subgroup of participants, or to the group as a whole (Agazarian, 1992; Schmid, 2001; Toseland & Rivas, 2005). In this regard, at a given time in a therapeutic group, a counselor may empathically interact with one, with several, or with all of the members. In a group counseling example, a practitioner empathizes with a group member who appears to be targeted as a scapegoat by several other adolescents in the group. The counselor acknowledges the feelings of threat and vulnerability that the ridiculed individual experiences both within and outside of the group. During this exchange, a subgroup of participants react in a negative manner to the practitioner's intervention, which they perceive as unjustified and overprotective. In their view, the targeted individual has set himself up for ridicule and rejection due to his immature and provocative actions. In this situation, if the counselor continues to empathize with the scapegoated member and does not empathically acknowledge the perceptions of the vocal subgroup, tensions and conflict within the group are likely to escalate (Clark, 2002c; Tuttman, 1993).

In group counseling and group psychotherapy, it is also possible for participants to offer an expression of empathy to each other. In this respect, a group member may convey an understanding to another individual or individuals that has potent therapeutic value (Scheidlinger, 1966; Stone & Whitman, 1980). A group therapist may contribute to this potentiality by modeling empathic interactions that are subsequently emulated by group participants. When group members are able to acknowledge the diverse backgrounds and perspectives of other group participants, there is a progressive movement toward more open communication and cohesion (Norcross, 2002; Stone & Whitman, 1980). In contrast, when group participants feel discounted or misunderstood, frequently there is a lack of connection to the group or to other group members. In a framework that is similar to individual treatment, a three-stage conceptualization of the group process enables a practitioner to use timely and pertinent interventions. In the initial or relationship stage, there is an emphasis on empathically understanding individuals in the group and establishing a level of cohesiveness. The middle or integration stage focuses on addressing the conflictual functioning of group participants in the context of supportive relationships. In the final or accomplishment stage, group members attempt to encourage each other towards more adaptive actions.

THE RELATIONSHIP STAGE, GROUP TECHNIQUES, AND EMPATHY

In the initial period of group counseling and group psychotherapy, individual members are often tentative and uncertain about what the group process entails. In other instances, group participants may be defensive as they experience a sense of threat and vulnerability (Brabender, 2002; Clark, 1992, 1997). In these common occurrences, a group therapist's use of empathy can contribute to a group member feeling understood and can promote a climate of trust and support. In a group situation, there are several interventions accessible to a practitioner in which empathy is integral to the procedures. A number of the techniques that a counselor may employ are the same approaches available for use in individual treatment. With consideration as to how the interventions relate to the group process, the procedures potentially provide versatile therapeutic directions. The selected techniques include reflection, assessment, self-disclosure, questions, and the use of touch. In addition, there are other interventions that are applicable only in a group experience involving multiple individuals. Empathy is central to the effective employment of the procedures that also contribute to the development of cohesiveness in a group. Among the selected group techniques that a practitioner may utilize are universality, linking, blocking, and modification. Although these interventions are prominent in the initial stage of treatment, they also have a treatment utility throughout the group process.

Universality

In group counseling and psychotherapy, participants frequently feel that they are unique in terms of particular difficulties and problems. In maintaining this assumption, the individuals typically feel different from or unlike other persons or others in the group. As a group practitioner becomes aware of a member's feelings of isolation and aloneness, it is possible to employ the group technique or skill of universality. This procedure enables a therapist to empathically promote the realization that a group member shares common perspectives and problems with others (Corey & Corey, 2006; Posthuma, 2002). Frequently, group participants experience a sense of relief when they recognize that their feelings and thoughts are not unique or aberrant. As a therapeutic group factor, universality diminishes feelings of alienation while contributing to the development of cohesion and trust (Yalom, 2005). Universality focuses on recognizing underlying issues and common themes that relate to group participants. It is also possible that when individuals participate in a group that addresses their primary concerns, they may experience a sense of universality with other members. For example, children who are ridiculed in a school situation realize that they are not the only ones who are subject to teasing and taunting once they have joined a group of students with similar problems.

As an example of universality in the relationship stage of treatment, a group member named Sylvia experiences a sense of inadequacy and resentment because she has to participate in a mandated group for persons convicted for driving under the influence. In the initial group session, the adult members appear hesitant or reluctant to join in discussion. From a subjective empathy perspective, the group therapist experiences a felt-level reaction of hostility and embarrassment. The practitioner also identifies with the members' feelings of inadequacy and intuitively decides to address their common experiencing through the group technique of universality. After Sylvia hesitantly expresses resentment about being required to attend the group, the therapist responds from an interpersonal empathy stance, "You feel resentful about being forced to come to the group, and it doesn't make sense to you. You are probably not alone in feeling this way." At this point, the practitioner waits to see if other members affirm similar views.

It is also possible for the therapist to ask in an inviting tone, "Does anyone else feel this way?" Subsequently, the practitioner may empathically address deeper concerns of the group participants that also touch on universal themes. For instance, the members may believe that participation in the group reflects on their adequacy as a person, or there may be common fears of being apprehended again for drunk driving.

Linking

Linking is an approach that is similar to universality, but differs in that it involves the practitioner's connecting what one group participant says to the meaning of another member's statements (Jacobs, Masson, & Harvill, 2002; Posthuma, 2002). In this regard, a counselor or a therapist empathically points out to particular individuals concerns or perspectives that they share in common (Gladding, 2003). Linking has a potential to strengthen the bonds between group participants and to facilitate the development of group cohesion. In employing linking as a technique or a skill, a practitioner must be alert to cues that are suggestive of how certain members experience a mutuality in their viewpoints. More often, a therapist may recall discussion material that relates one member to another in terms of common issues or themes. In other instances, a counselor may observe that a group member reacts nonverbally by nodding or leaning forward as another participant expresses remarks.

As a practitioner employs linking, he or she demonstrates an empathic understanding of particular group members and promotes an encompassing involvement of the other group participants (Morran, Stockton, & Whittingham, 2004; Posthuma, 2002). As an example of linking in a young-adulthood group, a therapist empathically responds to Linda after she expresses fears about starting a new job. The practitioner relates, "This is a scary thing for you because there is so much that seems unfamiliar or new." After Linda responds to this reflection, the therapist states to another group member, "Joe, this seems to be similar to something you had to deal with when you relocated to the city."

Blocking

At various times in group counseling and psychotherapy, a group member may express statements that are detrimental to the other group participants, and it may then become necessary for a practitioner to block the individual's communication. Blocking is a practitioner technique or skill that prevents the continuation of a group member's undesirable, unethical, or inappropriate verbalizations (Bloch & Crouch, 1985; Trotzer, 1999). It becomes the responsibility of a counselor or a therapist to restrict a group member's statements without attacking the personhood of the individual (Corey & Corey, 2006). In this regard, it is necessary at times for a therapist to empathically intervene in order to reduce the potential for psychologically harmful interactions of group members.

As an example of blocking in an initial group therapy session for substance abuse treatment, Greg confronts another member, Joanne, and "demands" that she be honest with the group about her drug use. Up until this early point in treatment, Joanne had denied any serious abuse of substances. As Greg berates Joanne, she appears emotionally shaken and threatened. At that point, with no other members offering comment, the therapist finds it necessary to block or cut off Greg's psychological assault on Joanne. At the same time, the practitioner is sensitive to the need to empathically acknowledge Greg's position in order to prevent the possibility that he feels discounted or may subsequently escalate his verbal attack. The following dialogue highlights the therapist's blocking interaction.

Joanne: I'm not like the rest of you. I manage things, and I don't have a problem with drugs.

Greg: Oh, come off it. You have an out-of-control habit, and you know it. You're pathetic.

Joanne: I don't know what to say (in a soft, shaky voice).

Greg: I see how afraid you are. It is so obvious that you are lying.

Therapist: Greg, you feel strongly about what you just said. At the same time, no one will feel much support in our group if I allow you to continue this way.

Joanne: I can't say anymore.

Therapist: Joanne, it seems that Greg caught you off guard, and you're feeling pretty vulnerable right now.

In this group illustration of a member "stripping" another participant's defenses, the therapist utilizes the intervention of blocking (Clark, 1992). From a subjective empathy perspective, the therapist momentarily identifies with each group member involved in the interaction. She also experiences a felt-level response to the intense feelings of both individuals in the group. The practitioner intuitively reacts to the rapidly escalating exchange by deciding to employ blocking. From an interpersonal empathy stance, the practitioner visually observes the emotional intensity manifest in the group member's reactions and empathically intervenes in a supportive tone. Counterproductive interactions that are appropriate for a therapist to block include physical or emotional threats, invasions of privacy, and expressions containing damaging insults or ridicule (Corey & Corey, 2006). It is also important for a counselor or a therapist to be aware of countertransference reactions that may restrict discussion of particular topics that relate to his or her unresolved issues (Flapan & Fenchel, 1984; Goodman, Marks, & Rockberger, 1964; Hayes, 1995). With respect to blocking, a therapist may overuse this intervention if he or she experiences conflictive feelings when a group member expresses strong negative feelings toward other group participants. In these instances, a practitioner may attempt to maintain a cooperative and emotionally restrained group climate through an excessive use of blocking (Schwartz & Wolf, 1964).

Modification

Although blocking may be helpful in responding to detrimental behavior, group members frequently evoke some degree of constructive intent in their interactions with other group participants. In this regard, there is an intermediate position in which an individual's evaluative statements to another member contain both counterproductive and constructive qualities. In response to this dynamic, it is possible for a practitioner to utilize the group skill of modification, which involves empathically requesting a group participant to restate unacceptable feedback to another member that contains potentially therapeutic content (Clark, 1995b). For example, in an eating disorder treatment group, Zelda harshly says to Stephanie, "You are such a waste. You just sit there week after week and you don't say anything. I know you have something to offer the group, but you never talk." In response, after empathizing with Stephanie's feelings, the counselor says to Zelda, "I think that you have something constructive to share, but the way you are putting it makes it difficult for Stephanie to listen to you. Can you say what you mean in a more acceptable way?" Zelda pauses and then responds, "Well, what I mean is that I think you have something to add to the group, but you never say anything."

From a subjective empathy stance, a counselor or a therapist initially becomes aware of a group member's communication containing a mixed message in terms of purposeful content. When observing an exchange between two group participants, the practitioner recognizes an opportunity to employ modification. This occurs through an intuitive reaction and may involve felt-level experiencing on the part of the therapist. From an interpersonal empathy perspective, the counselor follows a logical sequence by empathically acknowledging the emotional response of the group participant receiving an unacceptable message. The therapist then affirms the provider of the feedback for his or her potentially constructive intent while observing the negative effect on the receiver. The sequence concludes by asking the initiator to restate the communication in more palatable terms. A group practitioner should attempt to express a modification in a supportive and convincing way and avoid a critical or condescending tone (Clark, 1995b, 1997; Gladding, 2003). It is also helpful to encourage other group members to react to the altered exchange in order to elicit more purposeful and supportive communication. In time, group participants may begin to employ modification on their own. In such instances, a group member might respond to another individual's feedback, "Hey, that is hard to take. Can't you say it without the put-down?"

Further Group Techniques

In the previous chapter, selected therapeutic techniques were introduced in the context of individual treatment. It is also possible for a practitioner to utilize these same interventions in group counseling and psychotherapy by directing his or her empathic understanding toward particular members, subgroups, and the group as a whole. Reflection, assessment, self-disclosure, questions, and the use of touch contribute to promoting cohesion in groups through an empathic understanding of individual participants.

Reflection. In individual counseling and psychotherapy, reflection is a prominent practitioner technique. Similarly, in a group situation, reflection is a primary intervention for a counselor or a therapist, and it is also possible for other group members to utilize the skill. In this regard, a therapist should not take full responsibility for employing reflection, as others are potentially capable of acknowledging the feelings and meanings of participants in a group (Burlingame, Fuhriman, & Johnson, 2002; Chen & Rybak, 2004). A counselor is in a position to model the effective use of reflection in a way that serves to promote group member competency in its application. In this regard, peer-directed empathic communication provides maturational opportunities for both individuals employing reflection and for the recipients of the interactions (Stone & Whitman, 1980). As participants in group counseling and psychotherapy engage one another through exchanges involving reflection, there frequently is a broadening of appreciation and insight into developmental experiences that contribute to an understanding of members' current condition or situation (Giesekus & Mente, 1986; Yalom, 2005). In the context of encounter groups, Rogers (1970) spoke to this point when he stated, "My attempt to understand the exact meaning of what the person is communicating is the most important and most frequent of my behaviors in a group" (p. 51).

When utilizing a reflection on an individual basis, a practitioner enables a group participant to formulate an accurate expression of his or her inner experiencing. Even though the direction of a therapist's comments may be toward a particular group member, reflection often has a salutary effect on the entire group (Stone & Whitman, 1980). What transpires as a comment directed at other group members is simultaneously experienced as an empathic message to all of the participants. Consequently, this interaction often produces a calming influence in the group. As an example, a middle-adulthood client named Vernon recently joined a group that has been in existence for a number of months. Vernon appears anxious in an initial group session and does not join in any of the discussion. In response to Vernon's reactions, the therapist empathically states, "It is not easy to come into a group with people that you do not know, and who have been meeting for some time."

In other instances, a counselor's use of reflection involves a small group of members. The practitioner is able to observe that several group participants share a common experience, and that a reflection is timely and appropriate. For instance, in a children's group, a group member, Sally, begins to cry as she talks about her parent's recent separation. Two other participants, Nancy and Jill, appear to be near tears as they react to Sally's painful account. With no other group members appearing ready to speak, the counselor looks toward Nancy and Jill and states, "You feel sad when listening to Sally because you know she hurts so much inside." It is also possible for a practitioner to utilize a reflection that empathically acknowledges the experiencing of all of a group's members. After Jill and Nancy respond to the practitioner's reflection, all of the group participants join in a discussion that is supportive of Sally. As the individuals actively express their feelings, the counselor employs a reflection, "It's a relief for all of you to be able to talk to Sally and to support her." In this context, Stone and Whitman (1980) make a relevant point that as a practitioner listens to group members make sequential associations, the collective reactions of the whole group function almost as if one person is talking. In this regard, the therapist attunes to the shared feelings that reverberate in the group atmosphere, which may or may not be directly expressed. In turn, the counselor is in a position to employ a reflection in an attempt to capture the group participants' experiencing as a component of a single unit.

Assessment. When working with a client in individual treatment, a counselor or a therapist may use a range of appraisal instruments that enhance an empathic understanding of the person. As a practitioner evaluates a client for possible inclusion in a therapeutic group, he or she may also call on various objective and projective procedures. When considering a client for group counseling and psychotherapy, it is also possible for a therapist to assess the individual's empathic capacities (Kleinberg, 1991; Stone & Whitman, 1980). The appraisal of a client's ability to empathically relate with others enables a practitioner to decide whether a group is an appropriate modality for the person. In this regard, consideration of a client's empathic ability may be an important predictor of a person's progress in a group experience and may constitute a factor in indicating the potential for therapeutic success of the group (de Carufel & Piper, 1988). In this respect, a therapist evaluates a prospective member in terms of a sound "fit" for a particular treatment group (Rutan & Stone, 2001). There may be instances, for example, wherein an individual feels alienated from others to the point that he or she is unable to identify with other people. In these less frequent cases, it may be judicious not to include the person in a group situation. From an ethical vantage point, Rutan and Stone (2001) suggested that a person who is either unable or unwilling to adhere to a level of confidentiality may not be an appropriate candidate for a group.

Self-Disclosure. In group counseling and psychotherapy, a practitioner may give consideration to disclosing personal experiences and perspectives in order to enhance an empathic understanding of group members. An occasional and timely self-disclosure by a counselor or a therapist also has the potential to serve as a model for other group members (Ivey, Pedersen, & Ivey, 2001; Jacobs, Masson, & Harvill, 2002; Yalom, 2005). As an example, in a substance abuse treatment group, a young-adulthood member states that he is doubtful that the group will help him. In response, after reflecting the individual's feelings, the therapist states, "I sometimes find myself skeptical about things until I see that they might work." It is also possible for a group practitioner to direct his or her disclosure to a member subgroup. For example, in a group for children whose parents are in the process of separating or divorcing, two group participants state that they miss having both of their parents at home. After empathically acknowledging the children's sense of loss, the counselor relates that she had similar feelings when her parents separated when she was a child. The counselor remembered wishing that they could be together again, even though they had frequent arguments. A therapist's self-disclosure may also be communicated to the group as a whole. As an example, an adult group has been meeting for over 4 months. Although the group has reached an appropriate time to consider termination, the members are reluctant to address the possibility of ending the group. In response, the therapist states, "We have touched on the idea of bringing our time together to a close. Sometimes at times like this I have difficulty in letting go of relationships with people who are important to me. It's as if I wish that things could just stay the same."

As with a number of other group techniques or skills, a practitioner is able to empathically express self-disclosures from multiple perspectives. From a subjective empathy stance, a counselor or a therapist momentarily identifies with a group member's experiencing and imagines what it is like to be in a similar situation. The therapist may resonate with a felt-level response and intuitively react by bringing to mind a personal experience or perspective that has some relevance to the immediate discussion. With respect to an interpersonal empathy perspective, a practitioner may recognize that a group member or members are at an emotional impasse and a self-disclosure seems appropriate. Observing that no other group members appear ready or willing to respond, the counselor acknowledges the feelings of the group participants prior to relating a self-disclosure. From an objective perspective, in a caution to group practitioners, Morran, Stockton, and Whittingham (2004) stated that, "Leaders should avoid self-disclosures that are designed to only impress members, gain sympathy, or unburden personal problems" (p. 99). In this respect, a therapist's awareness of countertransference reactions may reduce the possibility of his or her personal issues interfering with an appropriate use of self-disclosure in group counseling and psychotherapy (Flapan & Fenchel, 1984; Schwartz & Wolf, 1964). Finally, a counselor or a therapist may also employ self-involving statements that communicate the practitioner's reactions to group members' behavior within the treatment relationship (Watkins, 1990).

Questions. In group counseling and psychotherapy, a practitioner's questions can contribute to therapeutic progress when effectively utilized. Indiscriminate and excessively frequent questioning, however, have a potential to erode a group's cohesiveness and undermine empathic interactions (Clark, 1989; Corey & Corey, 2006; Ivey, Pedersen, & Ivey, 2001; Posthuma, 2002). In particular, less experienced counselors and therapists may use questions as a means of controlling a group by directing inquiries to individual members. As group participants observe a practitioner's frequent employment of questions, they often assume that the exchange represents the primary means of communication; consequently, the members begin to ask numerous questions. At times, group members' questioning can be inappropriate or insensitive and divert a group in unproductive directions. As an example, in an adolescent counseling group several members ask another group participant, Aaron, unregulated and irrelevant questions. Aaron had just informed the group that his parents had recently separated, and he was still in a state of shock about it. All of the questions were asked within a time span of 20 seconds.

Denise: Why did they break up?
Robert: Did your father have an affair?
Jerry: You're not sure; but did your dad have any affairs before?

In this example, group members' misplaced questions were asked out of curiosity rather than to assist Aaron. In instances of this type, it is often necessary for a practitioner to block potentially detrimental questions in order to protect the privacy of a group member.

As in individual treatment, it is possible for a counselor or a therapist to employ questions in order to enhance the empathic understanding of a client. As group participants observe a therapist, they may begin to emulate a skill that empathically focuses on the needs of a person or persons. From an individual empathy stance, questions can serve to expand an awareness of a group member's functioning. For instance, a practitioner asks particular members, "What is it like for you to enter a group that has been meeting for some time?" "What are you experiencing right now as the group focuses on you?" "How do you find relief from the stresses and tensions in your life?" These types of inquiries may be asked in a supportive and inviting tone, and as open questions they typically elicit expansive responses from group members.

A therapist may also direct his or her questions to several group participants. For example, in an anxiety disorders group, two adult members appear hesitant to join in discussions. In response, the therapist asks the individuals, "What do you think might happen to you if you do begin to talk about yourself in the group?" This type of question is more likely to be effective if it is preceded by a reflection such as, "Having to talk about yourself is not easy at this point, and you are both hesitant to jump right in." In terms of directing a question to the whole group, certain *overhead questions* may elicit purposeful discussion (Dinkmeyer & Muro, 1979). As an example, a therapist states, "What is happening in the group right now?" In another instance, a counselor relates, "We do not seem to be listening to each other today. Does it seem that way to you?"

The Use of Touch

In individual treatment, a counselor or a therapist may convey empathic understanding to a client through the use of touch. In group counseling and psychotherapy, a practitioner is in a position to empathically utilize touch and model an appropriate use of the intervention to group members. At the same time, however, unlike in dyadic treatment, a therapist's use of touch is witnessed by others, and a counselor often needs to assume a mobile position in order to touch a person or persons (Corey, Corey, & Callahan, 2003). In these instances, the intentionality and propriety of a practitioner's employment of touch may be more readily assessed by group participants. As an example, Tara is terminating from an adult group in which she has been a member for over 4 months. Toward the end of the session, as Tara is saying goodbye, the therapist gets out of her chair and goes over to briefly hug Tara. The other group participants follow the practitioner's lead and, in turn, also hug Tara. In this interaction, the use of touch by the therapist and others in the group expresses an empathic understanding and appears ethically acceptable. It also seems that not touching in this situation might convey a lack of empathy and miss an opportunity to acknowledge the personhood of the group member.

A practitioner's use of touch in group requires consideration of a number of variables in order to empathically employ the technique. A counselor or a therapist needs to be aware that certain group members may be uncomfortable with touch. Although individual group participants may change their readiness to be touched as a group evolves, a lack of respect for physical boundaries can be unempathic and emotionally damaging. This is a particular concern in the use of group exercises involving the employment of touch, and participants should be given an option to choose to participate in the activities (Jacobs et al., 2002). In another direction, the use of touch in groups, such as a hug at the end of each group meeting, can take on a ritualistic or perfunctory quality and diminish its therapeutic potency. At other times, a counselor or a therapist may be personally uncomfortable with touch in a group situation, and the practitioner may choose to convey this to the group (Durana, 1998). In this regard, in the absence of a self-disclosure, group members may assume that a therapist's nonuse of touch represents a lack of empathic understanding. Finally, in group counseling and psychotherapy, participants may spontaneously use touch that is appropriate or inappropriate (Stone & Whitman, 1980). In situations involving the misuse of touch, it is necessary for a practitioner to empathically block unacceptable member interactions in order to maintain the integrity of a group.

THE INTEGRATION STAGE, GROUP TECHNIQUES, AND EMPATHY

In the middle or integration stage of group counseling and psychotherapy, it is possible for a practitioner to employ selected techniques or skills that are also applicable in individual treatment. In a group context, however, other group members in addition to the counselor or a therapist may participate in the engagement of particular interventions. At this point in group development, a relatively supportive climate is usually established, and group members have made progress toward acquiring an extended understanding of each other. Under these conditions, the group practitioner and group participants are in an advantageous position to contribute to the engagement of more challenging procedures. Among the selected techniques that are pertinent at this stage of the group experience are confrontation, cognitive restructuring, reframing, and interpretation.

Confrontation

As a type of feedback, confrontation enables group members to become aware of behavioral incongruities in their functioning (Corey, Corey, Callahan, & Russell, 2004; Posthuma, 2002). The group practitioner and more advanced participants may demonstrate the employment of confrontation in a way that balances challenge with empathic understanding. Even though a single member may be subject to a confrontation, other group members often gain an awareness of their experiencing by observing or interacting with the confrontation process. As an example, in an adult therapy group, Donna frequently monopolizes the group by repeatedly talking and drawing attention to herself. Although Donna has gained some awareness of this behavior in the initial stage of treatment, she continues to talk excessively. At one point, Donna comments at length about her recent hospitalization and surgery, and no other group members join in the discussion. In response, the therapist states, in a supportive tone, "Donna, you said last week that you should talk less in group, but now you are talking more than anyone else." In reaction to this confrontation, Donna replies, "You are right. I do need to talk less, but nobody else is saying anything, so somebody has to carry the ball." The therapist concludes the interaction by empathically stating, "It seems to you that you need to keep talking because somebody has to be responsible for keeping the conversation going."

It is also possible for a practitioner to express a confrontation to members of a subgroup or to the entire group. To continue the illustration with Donna, after she describes the extent of her recent operation, several of the group participants begin to complain about Donna's monopolizing the group discussion. In response, the therapist states, "A few of you are saying that you are tired of hearing Donna talk, but at the same time, nobody in the group is bringing up other matters that we can discuss." Again, the practitioner utilizes a reflection in response to group member reactions to his or her confrontation. Although confrontations bring an awareness to the group of contradictory member functioning, some group counselors or therapists may be reluctant or hesitant to confront. Practitioners may not wish to disrupt or jeopardize a positive climate in the group for the sake of challenging participant behavior. At the same time, a failure to confront may keep the focus of a group at a superficial level and restrict the potential for empathic understanding. A counselor's avoidance of confrontation in group may also involve countertransference reactions that require exploration in order to expand his or her capacity to address emotionally conflictive issues (Flapan & Fenchel, 1984; Schwartz & Wolf, 1964).

Cognitive Restructuring

At times it is necessary in group counseling and psychotherapy to go beyond clarifying a group member's contradictory behavior in order to promote constructive change in the functioning of an individual. As a group technique or skill, cognitive restructuring involves transposing dysfunctional and self-defeating beliefs in the direction of more constructive perspectives (Gladding, 2003; Posthuma, 2002; Toseland & Rivas, 2005). With the consistent support and challenge of the group, it becomes possible for individual participants to develop more purposeful assumptions or convictions.

As an example, to continue with the group illustration involving Donna, it becomes apparent to the other members at this stage of group development that she has unfulfilled needs for recognition and admiration. This awareness was gained through discussion conducted in the context of empathic understanding rather than from a chastisement of Donna for her monopolistic behavior (Stone & Whitman, 1980). In this regard, Donna began to recognize her exhibitionistic and narcissistic functioning in a supportive and nondeprecatory group climate. In this period, the group therapist introduced the technique of cognitive restructuring and explained to the group how it may be helpful for Donna. Initially, the group participants assisted Donna in recognizing her maladaptive convictions. In particular, several group members suggested that she placed too much importance on being liked. After further discussion on this point, Donna identified a core belief: "It is very important for me to be liked by almost everyone." Through further group interaction, Donna was able to arrive at an alternative counterstatement or a counter that involved a more purposeful self-statement: "I want to be liked, but I can't force myself on people." Donna practiced employing the counter both in and outside of the group and continued to discuss the implications of her evolving perspectives with the empathic understanding of other group members.

Reframing

Reframing is a less extensive group technique or skill when compared with cognitive restructuring and relates primarily to transposing the meanings of group members' experiences through a relabeling or reclassification procedure (Clark, 1998b). As a semantic aspect of interpretation, reframing involves formulating and substituting new frames of reference in the place of constricted perspectives (Ivey, Pedersen, & Ivey, 2001; Levy, 1963). In this regard, a group practitioner or other group members may communicate a reframe that presents alternative meanings to problems or experiences. The diverse cultural backgrounds of participants in many therapeutic groups contribute to a potential for enriching the perceptions of other members in a constructive direction. It is helpful to propose a reframe in an inviting and supportive tone and to base the content of the intervention on an extended empathic understanding of an individual.

As an example of reframing in continuing the illustration involving Donna, at one point she states, "I know that I have done a better job about not talking as much in the group, but I do miss the attention." In response, the group therapist empathically relates, "You don't get as much attention from the group, and this is a loss for you. I'm wondering though if it is possible for you to look at this change in a different way. It seems that the group is now listening more for the quality rather than the quantity of what you say." Donna is given sufficient time to process this reframe and is intrigued by the implications of the new perspective. Subsequently, several other group members acknowledge the viability of this alternative point of view.

Although reframing is most often directed at a particular group member, it is also possible for the intervention to be communicated to a subgroup or to the group as a whole. For example, on an individual basis, a group member expresses a sense of embarrassment for having cried in front of the group. In response, another group participant reframes the individual's crying as an ability to express emotion. On a subgroup level, two group participants state that they are anxious about having to leave the group at a subsequent point. After acknowledging the members' feelings, the counselor relates that their disclosures provide an awareness to the group about the importance of devoting sufficient time to termination concerns. From a whole-group level, most of the members of a substance abuse treatment group express discomfort about its designation as an "addict group." After a discussion, the participants relabeled their group as "in recovery."

Interpretation

An interpretation as a proposition emphasizes understanding causal relationships that explain the development or the purpose of an individual's behavior (Clark, 1993; Levy, 1963). Through an interpretation, a group member construes a new frame of reference and is able to relate the meaning of his or her current functioning to immediate or past experiences (Ivey, Pedersen, & Ivey, 2001). Group members, in addition to the practitioner, are able, with varying degrees of proficiency, to express an interpretation. Group participants may also be capable of collaboratively processing an interpretation in order to clarify its implications (Stone & Whitman, 1980). Although criticisms of interpretation as a group intervention focus on its intellectualized quality, the procedure has been found to promote emotional involvement and the expression of feelings among group participants (Clark, 1994b; Yalom, 2005). It is necessary, however, for the group to have an extended understanding of an individual's functioning in order to empathically evaluate and discuss the meaning of the interpretation as it relates to the group member or members. As group participants develop new and more constructive perspectives through the use of interpretations, they potentially assume a position to act in more adaptive ways.

In the rendering of an interpretation, each group member hears the communication and may be affected differently by it (Rutan & Stone, 2001).

As an example, in the continuing group illustration involving Donna, even though she has made gains in an awareness of her excessive need for attention and recognition, her tendency toward monopolistic behavior continues. In this regard, immediately after Donna speaks at some length, the therapist empathically begins to express an interpretation. "When you have an opportunity to talk in front of the group, it is difficult for you to refrain, even though you sense that you may be talking too much." After a pause, Donna responds to this generalization, "It is really hard for me to let go of being the center of attention. Yet, I know that I overdo this." After reflecting Donna's conflictive feelings, the practitioner continues the interpretation with a construction stated in a tentative way: "I'm wondering if it is possible that this relates to what it was like for you in growing up. You have shared with us a sense that when you were younger you often felt bypassed and unimportant. Could it be that as a result of feeling overlooked, you searched for and found a way to get attention the way you do today?" After Donna responds to the interpretation, other group members may then empathically join in the discussion and possibly relate how they had been affected by the interpretative interactions.

At a later point in treatment, the therapist employs an interpretation involving two other group members who experience difficulty in expressing anger or other emotions that may be perceived as exhibiting a lack of self-control. Even during periods when Donna elicited hostility from most of the group for her monopolistic behavior, the two members did not criticize her. Through an interpretation, the therapist empathically connected the participants' functioning to behaviors they seemed to find adaptive in their early development. At times, the direction of an interpretation is toward the entire group, and most often the intervention is rendered by the practitioner. To conclude with a group-as-a-whole illustration, the therapist expresses an interpretation as the group is about to conceptually move into the final stage of treatment. The therapist states, "I have the impression that at this point in our group we are spending most of our time on matters that seem quite important to each of you. Is it possible that the group has become a place that offers you a chance to be heard that is not as readily available elsewhere, and you want to take advantage of it in the time we have left together?" This interpretation reflects the therapist's subjective empathy perspective, as she intuitively senses that the group is tacitly avoiding the issue of eventual termination. In a felt-level experiencing, the practitioner fleetingly imagines the participants being in situations without the support of the group. From an interpersonal empathic stance, the therapist responds to participants as they react to the interpretation.

THE ACCOMPLISHMENT STAGE, GROUP TECHNIQUES, AND EMPATHY

The consolidation of insights and new perspectives acquired through the treatment process generally occurs in the final stage of group counseling and psychotherapy. With an enhanced self-understanding, individual group participants are in a more favorable position to focus on adaptive actions. Through collaborative endeavors, the group frequently serves as a vehicle for constructive behavioral change. Typically, in the last stage of group treatment, group members also reflect on therapeutic gains made by individual members and address termination issues. Discussion and recognition of positive change in group member functioning provides an opportunity for the group participants to empathically acknowledge each others' growth and development. The termination of a group also enables a practitioner and other group participants to empathically express an understanding of the variety of ways in which the individuals are experiencing the end of a group (Rutan & Stone, 2001). During this period, with its emphasis on promoting and recognizing member change and movement toward termination, a counselor or a therapist also needs to be aware of possible countertransference reactions. Some practitioners may experience difficulties in terminating a group because the finality of the process triggers unresolved issues of abandonment or personal rejection (Flapan & Fenchel, 1984). An awareness of this dynamic may reduce the possibility that countertransference issues will interfere with empathically acknowledging and accepting progressive change in the independence of group members or compound their issues in separating from the group. In this period, various action-oriented techniques may be proposed by a practitioner or other group participants in the context of empathic understanding. A number of interventions that are useful in individual treatment are also applicable to group situations.

Catching Oneself

After a practitioner introduces an action-oriented group technique to a group member, other group participants frequently provide encouragement for the individual to follow through with the intervention. In the case of *catching oneself,* a group counselor or therapist invites individuals to consider the technique as a means to control or change undesirable behavior (Oberst & Stewart, 2003). After briefly describing the procedure, the practitioner asks a group member to identify a cue that may be used as a reminder to avoid a particular action. The group can be helpful to assist a person in selecting a relevant cue and clarifying contexts for using the signal device. As an example, in the continuing case illustration relating to Donna, she, with the assistance of the group, identifies a cued reminder that she plans to employ in order to avoid the occurrence of an unwanted action. In Donna's case, she decides to use a humorous picture of wide red lips and smiling teeth in order to limit her monopolizing tendencies. At the moment that Donna begins to sense that she is about to talk too much, she takes a quick look at the picture. In a subsequent group session, when Donna takes the picture out of her pocket in order to look at it, she and the other group members have an empathic laugh. Donna also uses the cue device outside of the group and discusses its implementation with the other group participants.

Segmentation

As group members observe that particular techniques prove to be helpful, they may also express an interest in trying any one or several of the approaches. Segmentation is another group procedure that emphasizes an action orientation by partializing challenging pursuits into small and manageable components (Clark, 1998a). Group participants at times magnify the demands of behavioral change, and breaking down tasks into "baby steps" often makes the total effort seem less daunting. In a group example, two members express a sense of discouragement with respect to limited gains that they have made in changing ingrained patterns of passive behavior and the avoidance of interpersonal conflict. In response, after acknowledging the feelings of the individuals, the practitioner suggests that they consider using segmentation. After a discussion of the procedure, the group participants decide to attempt to act assertively and try to employ the intervention with its "one-day-at-a-time" mentality. In the next group session, the individuals discuss their efforts, and the other group members express an empathic understanding of their pursuits.

SUMMARY

In group counseling and psychotherapy, there are numerous practitioner techniques or skills in which empathy has an integral role. The complement of group members provides a means for expanding the communication of empathic understanding beyond the capacity of a group counselor or therapist. Utilizing a three-stage conceptualization of the group process, various techniques contribute to therapeutic gain. In the initial or relationship stage of group development, several interventions are pertinent to both individual and group treatment. In other instances, specific procedures are only applicable to the group experience. In the middle or integration stage, particular interventions with an empathic focus are common to dyadic and group modalities. The final or accomplishment stage emphasizes the use of a range of action-oriented approaches that contribute to behavioral change of group participants.

Chapter 10

Empathy in Counseling and Psychotherapy: A Case Study

> *Empathy, like life itself, is perpetual discovery, even on a small scale.*
>
> —Szalita (1976, p. 144)

When I listened to Carl Rogers talk about empathy over 30 years ago, I thought at that time there was little more for me to learn about the construct. In the years that have followed, my treatment experience with a diverse range of clients and my increased familiarity with the vast literature on empathy in a therapeutic context have demonstrated how presumptuous I was early in my career. Today, I continue my efforts to refine my knowledge about the various dimensions and potency of empathy and empathic understanding in presenting a common ground for practitioners. In this regard, there seem to be few major areas in counseling and psychotherapy that do not involve empathy when a counselor or a therapist is prepared to assume an empathic disposition. Such topics as the treatment alliance, theoretical orientations, multicultural forces, assessment, therapeutic techniques, countertransference, ethics, and defense mechanisms are integral to the utilization of empathy. When employing empathy from a multiperspective stance, the construct assumes an even broader and more expansive quality. In concluding this text with a case study, it is my intention to touch on some of the topics and processes that demonstrate the value and the complexities of empathy in counseling and psychotherapy. The case example expands on a brief illustration relating to a client from a previous publication (Clark, 2002b).

EMPATHY IN A CASE STUDY

My introduction to the background of 15-year-old Crystal Lynn took place at a staff meeting in a school program for at-risk adolescents. Crystal was entering the placement from a public high school and was scheduled to meet with me on a weekly basis for individual counseling. Crystal's education record reflected a pattern of disciplinary infractions including classroom misbehavior and truancies. Her academic progress was inconsistent, and she had been absent from school for an excessive number of days in recent years. Crystal had a court referral for shoplifting and marijuana use. At the time of treatment, Crystal was residing with her mother and her mother's boyfriend. Crystal's father died when she was a child. A psychological report indicated that Crystal's behavior had been consistently impulsive and immature, and the clinician determined a diagnosis of Conduct Disorder with an onset in adolescence (*DSM-IV-TR*). In the report, a rather singular statement caught my eye primarily because of its unprofessional quality. The clinician wrote, "Crystal tends to demonstrate goofy behavior." Crystal's background was not unlike many other adolescents with whom I had worked, and in some ways her issues were less extensive. As I was leaving the staff meeting, a social worker mentioned to me that Crystal was talented in art. Although I had not yet met Crystal, I was beginning to form a model of a client in my mind from an objective empathy stance.

EMPATHY IN THE THERAPEUTIC PROCESS

Relationship Stage

When Crystal appeared at my office door for her initial treatment session, I was struck by her appearance, in a full-length multicolored dress and with abundant auburn hair. In addition, Crystal wore several strings of beads around her neck and she was displaying a nose ring. She immediately began throwing two colored balls in the air and announced with delight that it was her 16th birthday. As I was about to acknowledge her excitement on her birthday, Crystal asked if she could return to her classroom in order to practice juggling. At this point, my empathic stance was disengaged as

I said, "I am afraid that this is not an option." Within moments, Crystal started rolling the balls across my desk, and I reflected her feelings about this activity being an escape for her to play with the balls. This exchange ended with Crystal casually telling me that I could use a "little loosening up." As I usually do in my first meeting, I brought up the subject of confidentiality and ways that we could structure our time together. Crystal appeared bored with this and once again asked whether she could return to her class. I did not wish to conclude our time together on a negative note, so I asked Crystal about her interest in art. Crystal responded with enthusiasm and she described a project that she was currently completing. As our session was drawing to a close, we touched on the topic of how she apparently does not like to be told what to do or how to behave. Our scheduled time ran out, and Crystal quickly left my office without further comment.

When I had a few moments to reflect on the session with Crystal, I felt somewhat dissatisfied. I was caught off guard by her request to return to class and my "not an option" comment lacked empathy. I did acknowledge that Crystal found relief by playing with the balls, but then I lost her interest with my discussion on confidentiality and structuring future sessions. Although these matters are important and need to be addressed, they could have waited until I began to grasp a sense of Crystal's experiencing. What I had largely failed to do, however, was to relate to Crystal from a subjective empathy stance by resonating with Crystal's excitement about her birthday. At another level, as I interacted with Crystal, I was conscious of the observation in the psychological report relating to her "goofy" behavior, and I did not wish to get drawn into immature antics. This thought seemed to inhibit my personal reactions to Crystal from a subjective empathy mode. When Crystal rolled the balls across my desk, I did sense her emotional release, and I reflected her feelings from an interpersonal empathy perspective. Drawing on information that I had learned about Crystal in the staff meeting, I made an effort to utilize an objective empathy stance when making reference to her artwork and restrictions on her behavior. The session did end on a perhaps more engaging note with the focus on Crystal's disdain for being told how to behave.

After a week went by and my second session with Crystal was about to begin, I was determined to engage her more in terms of my subjective empathic reactions. It did not take Crystal long to test my empathy stance, as she entered my office carrying a purple vase and began to drop small beads into the vessel. I acknowledged the fun that Crystal was having with the activity as it gave her an opportunity to relax. As she played with the materials, our discussion began to focus on Crystal's art projects and as Crystal talked, I slowly began to experience some of her pleasure in creating a piece of sculpture. I easily imagined an image of Crystal spending lengthy periods with her creative endeavors and losing track of time and her surroundings. From an interpersonal perspective, I was aware that our communication was mutually engaging, and the time seemed right to request that Crystal begin an assessment task.

Up to this point, I had a fair amount of objective data relating to Crystal, but I was lacking an understanding of her phenomenological functioning. Consequently, I thought that Crystal would respond positively to a request to draw a human figure as a part of a relatively brief projective assessment battery. In response to my request, Crystal eagerly sketched a small female figure and scribbled lines around its body. After Crystal finished the drawing, I asked her to respond to a 25-item sentence completion task that I have used with children and adolescents for many years (Clark, 1998a). Several of Crystal's responses revealed her personality dynamics as she thoughtfully considered each sentence stem. As an example, "I feel . . . I don't know." "I regret . . . getting caught." "I am best when . . . I am free." "I failed . . . nothing." "School . . . is the same old boring thing."

Immediately after Crystal finished the sentence completion tasks, I asked her, as a projective technique, to describe one of her early recollections. Without hesitation, Crystal stated, "I was at a birthday party, and the kids were running all over the place. One of the boys threw ice cream at another kid, and it was so funny." In response to follow-up questions, Crystal also recalled the blue and orange balloons attached to the chairs. The boy throwing the ice cream was the most vivid part of the memory, and she felt "excited" at that point. Crystal's second memory involved her mother: "I took some candy from a counter in a store and walked out. My mother told me that I shouldn't take the candy, but she was kind of smiling and didn't make me put it back." Responding to follow-up questions, Crystal added that the candy was red hot balls, and her mother's smile entailed the most vivid part of the memory. When her mother smiled, Crystal felt "relieved and happy." As our counseling session was drawing to a close, Crystal related a third early memory that was similar to her initial recollection involving peers in a disruptive and "exciting" experience.

After Crystal left my office, I had time to consider her assessment materials, and I began by evaluating her early recollection responses (Clark, 2002b). I appraised each memory from a multiple perspective stance, and gave consideration first to Crystal's early memory of "stealing" candy from the store. From a subjective empathy perspective, I momentarily identified with Crystal and felt tension and relief in her interaction with her mother. At the same time, I intuitively sensed a disregard for self-restraint and responsibility suggested by the memory. In terms of an interpersonal empathic stance, I considered thematic variables and details in assessing Crystal's phenomenological experiencing. I identified themes of defiance relating to the self and evidence that, to Crystal, others are enabling, and events are exciting. With respect to details, the color of the hot balls stood out. The mention of color possibly reflects Crystal's aesthetic appreciation or an artistic interest. From an objective perspective, considering Crystal's diagnosis of conduct disorder, research studies suggest that a pattern of rule breaking without sanction frequently occurs in populations demonstrating conduct disturbances and juvenile delinquency (Bruhn & Davidow, 1983; Davidow & Bruhn, 1990).

In addition to evaluating the two other early recollections that had similar content to her first memory, I assessed Crystal's human figure drawing and the sentence completion tasks. Crystal's artistic ability was apparent in her drawing, with an elevated page placement of a small figure and scribblings. In terms of interpretation, her drawing suggests a reduced self-concept, a perception of an unpredictable environment, and regressive tendencies (Handler, 1996). Crystal's sentence stem responses involve a lack of restraint and the possible employment of denial as a defense. From the assessment material and previously collected data, I was able to construct the following hypotheses relating to Crystal's perception of the self, others, and events: "I am free to act as I chose." "Others enable me to do as I wish." "Events are exciting when they involve rule-breaking." This framework contributed to the development of a *model of a client* as treatment progressed. It was important for me to keep in mind that the assessment findings are tentative and are subject to revision and refinement.

As Crystal was about to arrive for her third therapy session, I felt that as a result of the assessment process, I had more of an understanding of her outlook on life. As Crystal stood by my office door, she was playing with a yo-yo and having a difficult time manipulating the toy. After briefly watching Crystal, I asked her if I could give the yo-yo a try. Taking an opportunity to reveal an aspect of myself, I eagerly demonstrated a couple of tricks. Crystal was gleeful with my performance, but then I realized that I was engaging in an exhibitionistic activity and gave her back the yo-yo. She asked me about my experience with the yo-yo, and in the spirit of self-disclosure, I told Crystal about a couple of contests that I had won as a young person. After a few minutes, Crystal asked me a thought-provoking question about why I gave up the yo-yo when I seemed to enjoy it so much.

I was not sure how to respond, but I mentioned something about assuming new responsibilities as I grew up. In the context of this discussion, I asked Crystal what enjoyable activities she had given up as she got older. Although Crystal could not immediately identify any activities, she seemed intrigued by my question, and we subsequently returned to this topic at later points in the treatment process. As this discussion slowed down, Crystal abruptly asked me if I "do dreams?" She had a dream the previous night and wanted to talk about it. I was able to respond to Crystal's narration of her dream from a multiperspective empathic stance, and it occurred to me that our treatment alliance was building (Clark, 1999b). The reverie-like quality of dreams seemed to relate to Crystal's lifestyle or convictions about life, and she shared several dreams with me over the course of our time together.

On one morning of the following week, I received an unexpected telephone call from the director of our treatment program who informed me that Crystal's mother had suffered a heart attack and was in the hospital. Mrs. Lynn, who is extremely overweight, was taken by an ambulance from her home the previous evening. As it turned out, she experienced severe gastrointestinal problems and was released from the hospital after a brief stay. When I saw Crystal a few days later, unlike her behavior in our previous meetings, she appeared somber and subdued as she began to talk.

CL: She could have died, and I was so scared.
AC: Your mother is so important to you, and it frightens you to think that you might have lost her.

At this point, Crystal began to tremble and cry. Empathically, from an *experience-near* posture, Crystal's fear and disbelief briefly resonated within me. When I oscillated to an *experience-distant* perspective, it occurred to me that under the circumstances, Crystal's general orientation toward escape and denial was unworkable. When her mother left to go to the hospital, it was indisputable that her life was in jeopardy. As I happened to gaze down at Crystal's hands, they were shaking and looked small to me, and my experiencing was of a profound sense of aloneness and vulnerability. I briefly touched the back of Crystal's hand and said, "You are shaken and feeling alone deep inside." In my view, Crystal was experiencing a *marker of vulnerability* that was intense and threatening. Our discussion continued as I primarily reflected Crystal's feelings and meanings. There were no "light" moments in our exchanges, and our time together concluded with a minute or two of silence.

A few days after the session, the teacher from our school program told me that Crystal's behavior had markedly changed, and that she had become emotionally withdrawn in the classroom. It seemed likely to both of us that Mrs. Lynn's health scare triggered Crystal's apathetic behavior. Our next treatment session began with Crystal looking down at the floor without her usual eye contact. We sat together in silence until I expressed a reflection.

AC: You find this so hard, and you have a lot of feelings built up inside of you.
CL: I guess, whatever.
AC: It all doesn't make much sense to you.
CL: I don't know.

It appeared that my reflections were not working because Crystal was emotionally indifferent. Crystal's speech was flat, and her responses were terse during most of the meeting. At the same time, her behavior was quite similar to that of many other adolescents with whom I had worked in terms of being emotionally withdrawn and relatively unresponsive. I felt that it was important to try to elicit some feelings from Crystal, so I asked her about her dreams; however, even this typically evocative topic did little to stimulate Crystal to express herself or to initiate conversation. At one point, I even asked Crystal if she would like to try a hand-strengthening exerciser that I keep in my desk. She declined. Our time together ended as in our previous meeting in silence; this time, however, Crystal's emotional expression was largely absent.

When I had an opportunity to reflect on the treatment session, I felt that it had not gone well. What had become of my model of a client? I had anticipated that at some point Crystal would show something of her playful self. After all, her mother's sickness was not life threatening, and she even went bowling with Crystal a few days after her hospitalization. Only after giving further thought to our interactions, however, did I realize that my empathic understanding was largely mobilized from an extended perspective. I was ready for Crystal's frivolous character to materialize so that we could get back on track with emotionally laden interactions. What I had failed to do was to allow Crystal's experiencing of disequilibrium to resonate within me from a subjective empathy stance. Instead, I had permitted the client model to drive my expectations for her behavior. To look at it in another way, I became more of an observer in the relationship than a participant with respect to my sensibilities. Yet, to give myself some credit, I was aware that I had little basis on which to respond in terms of Crystal's emotional functioning, and I had tried to convey an empathic understanding from an interpersonal perspective.

During the week, I received a telephone call from Mrs. Lynn informing me that Crystal was upstairs in her bedroom with her boyfriend, and she thought that they were smoking marijuana. She asked me what should be done about it. I was not sure what to tell her and mentioned something about confronting Crystal when her boyfriend left. A few days after the incident, Crystal appeared in my office carrying two pieces of cake and said, "You looked kind of sad the last time we met, and I thought you could use some cheering up." I was not sure if this was an empathic statement or the use of projection, but in either case, I enjoyed eating the cake. On an emotional level, Crystal was expressive and demonstrated little of the dysphoria from the previous week. When I pointed this out, Crystal said that she just needed a little time to adjust to the possibility that her mother could have died. This made sense to me, and we briefly discussed her feelings. Just before I was about to raise the matter of the telephone call from Crystal's mother, Crystal began complaining about some of her teachers.

CL: They are always after me and on my case.
AC: On your case?
CL: I mean it's all work, and all we do is go from one project to another. I'm sick of it.
AC: It seems tiresome to you, and there is not much fun in all of it.
CL: That's it. It was such a good time today when we celebrated Joe's birthday.
AC: As with days like today, you would like to have more occasions in school when things can be more enjoyable.

In this interaction, as we talked, I found it helpful to evoke an image of one of Crystal's early recollections that seemed most clearly to capture or represent the dynamics of her outlook on life. I refer to this selection as a *prime early recollection,* and in Crystal's case I chose the "stealing" episode with her mother. By calling to mind the prime early recollection, I was able to enhance my empathic understanding through a felt-level experiencing of the evocative memory. In another direction, as we continued to discuss Crystal's feelings about school, I began to recognize that it was time for me to shift to a more challenging posture. At the same time, I needed to maintain a consistency in my empathic disposition. Until this point, I had been largely supportive and understanding with respect to Crystal's perspectives, and we had developed a reasonable level of trust and open communication. Practically speaking, I was also not sure how to fully address the situation regarding Mrs. Lynn's telephone call or Crystal's classroom views without considering broader dimensions of her behavior.

Integration Stage

As we entered the middle phase of treatment, I was aware that although progress had been made toward establishing a therapeutic alliance, there had been little change in Crystal's core convictions or her outlook on life. Without an effort to stimulate *second-order change,* aspects of Crystal's self-defeating perceptions would largely remain the same. In my next meeting with Crystal, I planned to be more active in challenging her dysfunctional views. It would not be difficult to identify Crystal's conflictual functioning because various inconsistencies had become apparent in the initial therapy stage. Crystal's most common conflict seemed to occur in terms of her involvement in some type of violation of conditions or situations that represent standards of behavior.

It did not take long for Crystal to arrive at a perspective that offered a potential for a confrontation as she began to speak even before sitting down.

CL: I can't believe it. A few days ago my mother got after me for being in my room with a friend.
AC: I'm not sure if I'm following you.
CL: Well, after my boyfriend left sometime after midnight, she started yelling at me for no reason at all.
AC: This doesn't make any sense to you. You just said, though, that you were in your bedroom with your boyfriend.
CL: So what? What's the big deal?
AC: In your view, your mother overreacted. I'm finding this a little unlike your mother, though, because she seems so easy-going.
CL: She is, but this time she got ripped.
AC: This time?
CL: Well, OK, we were smoking a little, but it was no big thing.
AC: It sounds like you want to be able to do something that almost any parent would object to, but you are upset when your mother complains.

Through various points in the middle phase of treatment, I employed a confrontation to clarify contradictions and inconsistencies in Crystal's behavior. This was an uneven process, and Crystal accused me of "taking the fun out of everything." Yet, it seemed to me that Crystal perceived to some degree that my challenges were made with a supportive and empathic intent.

Through the treatment experience, my empathic understanding was extended through discussions with Crystal relating to her childhood and adolescence. Crystal's father died when she was 6 years old, and she only had a vague remembrance of his presence. Soon after her father's death, Crystal and her mother moved in with her grandmother, Agnes, due to financial problems. Agnes seemed to be a stabilizing influence in Crystal's life and she was able to recall positive interactions and feelings of admiration toward Agnes. From a self psychology perspective, Agnes seemed to provide functions for Crystal to meet her selfobject needs for mirroring and idealization. Agnes, however, experienced a serious illness and died when Crystal was 10 years old. Crystal's mother already had problems with alcohol, and the loss of her mother led to more serious episodes of drinking. It was soon after Agnes's death that Crystal intensified her acting out behavior and became truant from school. This information was essential for establishing a developmental and extended perspective relating to Crystal's functioning. In this regard, her use of denial as a defense mechanism became more understandable given the precarious quality of her caregiving and the significant losses in Crystal's life.

Throughout our discussions, Crystal would periodically express faulty beliefs relating to aspects of her outlook on life. In initiating cognitive restructuring, I attempted to challenge aspects of her ingrained convictions.

CL: I'm sick of Mr. Boyd. I hate being in his class.
AC: You're tired of being told what to do.
CL: Yes. He just doesn't get it. I can do whatever I want.
AC: Even though you feel strongly about that, it also seems that you pay a price for being free to do what you want to do.
CL: It's his fault. I didn't start the trouble.
AC: I don't want to lose track of the bigger picture here. I'm talking about how often you say that you are free to do what you want to do, but then you seem to lose your freedom because of your actions. Does this make sense to you?

I did not fully articulate my point, but Crystal picked up on the thought and collaboratively we began to clarify one of Crystal's core beliefs, and how it seemed to play out in her life.

CL: I do get tired of getting into trouble so much.
AC: How much does this have to do with your pushing the limits and trying to get away with things?
CL: It's not all my fault, but I know what you mean.
AC: This is a lot for you to think about, and it seems that you are looking at something pretty new to you.
CL: It is kind of new, but I have thought about this before.

As we continued aspects of this discussion over the next two or three sessions, Crystal began to consider the possibility that she could be more free with a greater acceptance of certain restrictions and limits. Together we struck upon the idea that artists are free to create, but only within the particular limits and demands of their medium. Building on this observation, Crystal playfully identified a counterstatement or a counter that she practiced articulating during the week. The counter related: "Like an artist, I choose to be free and disciplined."

The possibility that Crystal was making even minor changes in the direction of understanding the self-defeating quality of avoiding restraints on her behavior was encouraging to me. As I attempted to empathically understand Crystal's experiencing, it occurred to me how difficult it is to effect purposeful change in an individual's outlook on life. As an example, at one point Crystal said that things were not working out, and nobody was giving her a chance to try out some things.

CL: A kid in class heard me talking about my counter and he told the other kids about it.
AC: This is embarrassing to you because of the way things turned out.
CL: Well, of course. Then they started calling me all of my old names like, "Crystal Clown" and "Crystal Ball."
AC: You have been trying to get away from these names, and now it kind of hurts when you hear them again.
CL: What's the use? Maybe I am just goofy.
AC: You are telling yourself some negative thoughts. I wonder whether it might be possible for you to hear your name in a different way?
CL: What do you mean?
AC: Well, a crystal is usually a hard material like a piece of jewelry that can take a lot.
CL: Do you know that my grandmother gave me my name?
AC: I didn't know that. She was special to you.

CL: She was, but I still don't get your point.
AC: It is something like this. When someone says your name, can you hear it as something strong and precious as your grandmother saw you? The put-down names may still come with it for a while.
CL: I'm not so sure. Let's talk some more about this. I wonder if . . .

In this instance, I utilized a reframe that occurred to me in an intuitive reaction, and Crystal's reference to her grandmother strengthened the intervention.

On the occasion of our 10th counseling session, there was a noticeable mutuality to our interactions. For Crystal, the idea that behavioral limits and restrictions had the potential for increasing her choices and freedom had become a prominent focus in our discussion. In this context, Crystal asked a probing question, "Why is it that I am always looking for excitement?" In response, we explored developmental aspects of this generalization.

AC: This is something that has been a part of your life for about as long as you can remember.
CL: Well, it is, and I find myself getting in trouble because of it.
AC: It seems like the excitement of trying to get away with things provides you with something that is not immediately available elsewhere.
CL: What do you mean?
AC: Could it be that breaking the rules is the way that you have found to get excitement for a long time and it almost always works?
CL: This may be, but I don't want to get nailed for things.
AC: Is it possible then that it is particularly exciting when you get involved in rule-breaking and you can get away with it?
CL: Well, I do like the excitement, but I'm getting sick of getting in trouble.

We continued to discuss the implications of the interpretation and how it might be possible for Crystal to find excitement or even enjoyment without becoming involved in disciplinary infractions. At a later point, another interpretation focused on relating Crystal's current behavior to the relative absence of limit-setting in her childhood.

AC: You are saying that there was a lot going on after your father died, and perhaps your mother was not as emotionally available to you.

CL: A lot of times I felt like nobody was watching out for me, or even cared if I was around.

AC: This gives you a feeling of being unimportant. I'm wondering if there is a link between the way you look for excitement by breaking rules, and what it was like for you growing up as a child. Could it be that with all the strains in your mother's life at the time and without much limit-setting, you often found yourself in rule-breaking situations?

This interpretation made sense to Crystal, and it led us into a further exploration of her childhood and its influence on her current behavior. Through this process, Crystal's motivation for behavioral change was becoming apparent as we progressed to the final stage of treatment.

Accomplishment Stage

With some movement toward Crystal developing insight into her core beliefs, it was time to turn our full attention to fostering more adaptive actions. In our 12th session, Crystal led into this possibility by stating:

CL: Things have improved, but I'm still having some problems. I sometimes find myself slipping and wanting to cut class or get high.

AC: You have made progress, but at times it is hard to let go of old habits.

CL: Yeah. The other day, I just didn't feel like going to class, so I skipped out.

AC: When you say this, you sound a little disappointed in yourself. I'm wondering if it would help if you had a reminder to keep you from slipping back during those times.

CL: What are you saying?

AC: What if you used a cue or a reminder that you can carry with you that will alert you to keep on track?

CL: How could I do this?

AC: Is there something that you could look at or touch that will cue you to control your behavior?

CL: I'm not sure. I can't think of anything.

AC: Something just occurred to me. I know that you cared a lot about your grandmother. What if you looked at her photograph to alert you not to do something that doesn't help you?

CL: I do have some pictures of her but I would feel kind of funny taking it out. Remember what happened when the kids heard about my counter and ended up laughing at me. I have a better idea. My grandmother gave me a necklace with a blue opal on it, and she said it would protect me. I only wear it when I go on an airplane, and I've only done that once in my life. What if I wear the necklace and touch the opal to remind me to behave?

AC: The opal necklace is important to you, and nobody would even know what you are doing when you touch it.

Crystal found the amulet helpful, and she regularly used the cuing device. We continued to focus on action-oriented techniques in this period as we progressed toward termination. The reports that I received from Crystal's teachers and her social worker were fairly positive, and her school attendance had improved. I had an opportunity to visit one of Crystal's classes, and she proudly showed me a few of her art projects. At this point, it was enjoyable and even gratifying for me to meet with Crystal, but these are not justifiable reasons to continue treatment. I know that I have some difficulty in terminating with clients with whom I have an emotional connection, and I need to be aware of countertransference reactions in this regard. In our last and 16th session, to my surprise and delight, Crystal demonstrated her recently acquired skill with the yo-yo. It occurred to me that Crystal was true to herself in enjoying the activity, but she had also shown some measure of discipline in mastering the toy. I expressed my empathic understanding of her effort in developing a level of proficiency with the yo-yo because I know that it is difficult to learn. In response, Crystal stated, "Not really. I was just having fun."

References

Abend, S. M. (1986). Countertransference, empathy and the analytic ideal: The impact of life stresses on analytic capability. *Psychoanalytic Quarterly, 55,* 563–575.

Ackerman, S. J., & Hilsenroth, M. J. (2003). A review of therapist characteristics and techniques positively impacting the therapeutic alliance. *Clinical Psychology Review, 23,* 1–33.

Adler, A. (1927). *Understanding human nature* (W. B. Wolfe, Trans.). New York: Greenberg.

Adler, A. (1935). The structure of neurosis. *International Journal of Individual Psychology, 1,* 3–12.

Adler, A. (1936). Compulsion neurosis. *International Journal of Individual Psychology, 2,* 3–22.

Adler, A. (1937). Significance of early recollections. *International Journal of Individual Psychology,* 3, 283–287.

Adler, A. (1958). *What life should mean to you.* New York: G. P. Putnam. (Original work published 1931)

Adler, A. (1969). *The science of living* (H. L. Ansbacher, Ed.). Garden City, NY: Anchor Books. (Original work published 1929)

Agazarian, Y. M. (1992). Contemporary theories of group psychotherapy: A systems approach to the group-as-a-whole. *International Journal of Group Psychotherapy, 42,* 177–203.

Agosta, L. (1984). Empathy and intersubjectivity. In J. Lichtenberg, M. Bornstein, & D. Silver (Eds.), *Empathy I* (pp. 43–61). Hillsdale, NJ: The Analytic Press.

Aiken, L. R. (2003). *Psychological testing and assessment.* Boston: Allyn & Bacon.

Alexander, F., & French, T. (1946). *Psychoanalytic therapy.* New York: Ronald Press.

Alexson, J. A. (2005). *Counseling and development in a multicultural society* (3rd ed.). Belmont, CA: Brooks/Cole.

American Psychiatric Association. (2000). *Diagnostic and statistical manual of mental disorders—text revision* (4th ed.). Washington, DC: Author.

Ansbacher, H. L. (1990). Alfred Adler's influence on the three leading cofounders of humanistic psychology. *Journal of Humanistic Psychology, 30,* 45–53.

Ansbacher, H. L. (1992). Alfred Adler's concepts of community feeling and of social interest and the relevance of community feeling for old age. *Individual Psychology: The Journal of Adlerian Theory, Research & Practice, 48,* 402–412.

Ansbacher, H. L., & Ansbacher, R. (Eds.). (1956). *The individual psychology of Alfred Adler: A systematic presentation in selections from his writings.* New York: Basic Books.

Aring, C. D. (1958). Sympathy and empathy. *Journal of the American Medical Association, 167,* 448–452.

Aron, L., & Harris, A. (Eds.). (1993). *The legacy of Sándor Ferenczi.* Hillsdale, NJ: The Analytic Press.

Arlow, J. A. (1979). The role of empathy in the psychoanalytic process. *Bulletin, The Association for Psychoanalytic Medicine, 18,* 64–69.

Auld, F., Hyman, M., & Rudzinski, D. (2005). *Resolution of inner conflict: An introduction to psychoanalytic therapy* (2nd ed.). Washington, DC: American Psychological Association.

Avenanti, A., Bueti, D., Galati, G., & Aglioti, S. M. (2005). Transcranial magnetic stimulation highlights the sensorimotor side of empathy for pain. *Nature Neuroscience, 8,* 955–960.

Bachelor, A., & Horvath, A. (1999). The therapeutic relationship. In M. A. Hubble, B. L. Duncan, & S. D. Miller (Eds.), *The heart and soul of change: What works in therapy* (pp. 133–178). Washington, DC: American Psychological Association.

Bachrach, H. M. (1976). Empathy: We know what we mean, but what do we measure? *Archives of General Psychiatry, 33,* 35–38.

Baker, E. K. (2003). *Caring for ourselves: A therapist's guide to personal and professional well-being.* Washington, DC: American Psychological Association.

Balint, M. (1967). Sandor Ferenczi's technical experiments. In B. B. Wolman (Ed.), *Psychoanalytic techniques: A handbook for the practicing psychoanalyst* (pp. 147–167). New York: Basic Books.

Barkham, M. (1988). Empathy in counseling and psychotherapy: Present status and future directions. *Counseling Psychology Quarterly, 1,* 407–428.

Barrett-Lennard, G. T. (1976). Empathy in human relationships: Significance, nature and measurment. *Australian Psychologist, 11,* 173–184.

Barrett-Lennard, G. T. (1981). The empathy cycle: Refinement of a nuclear concept. *Journal of Counseling Psychology, 28,* 91–100.

Barrett-Lennard, G. T. (1993). The phases and focus of empathy. *British Journal of Medical Psychology, 66,* 3–14.

Barrett-Lennard, G. T. (1998). *Carl Roger's helping system: Journey and substance.* London: Sage.

Barrett-Lennard, G. T. (2003). *Steps on a mindful journey: Person-centered expressions.* Ross-on-Wye, UK: PCCS Books.

Basch, M. F. (1983). Empathic understanding: A review of the concept and some theoretical considerations. *Journal of the American Psychoanalytic Association, 31,* 101–126.

Beck, A. T., Rush, A. J., Shaw, B. F., & Emery, G. (1979). *Cognitive therapy of depression.* New York: Guilford.

Beck, A. T., & Weishaar, M. (2005). Cognitive therapy. In R. J. Corsini & D. Wedding (Eds.), *Current psychotherapies* (7th ed., pp. 238–268). Belmont, CA: Brooks/Cole.

Beck, J. S. (1995). *Cognitive therapy: Basics and beyond.* New York: Guilford.

Beech, C., & Brazier, D. (1996). Empathy for a real world. In R. Hutterer, G. Pawlowsky, P. F. Schmid, & R. Stipsits (Eds.), *Client-centered and experiential psychotherapy: A paradigm in motion* (pp. 331–346). New York: Peter Lang.

Benedek, T. (1953). Dynamics of the transference. *Bulletin of the Menninger Clinic, 17,* 201–208.

Bennett, M. J. (2001). *The empathic healer: An endangered species.* Belmont, MA: Academic Press.

Beres, D. (1968). The role of empathy in psychotherapy and psychoanalysis. *Journal of the Hillside Hospital, 17,* 362–369.

Beres, D., & Arlow, J. A. (1974). Fantasy and identification in empathy. *Psychoanalytic Quarterly, 43,* 26–50.

Berger, D. M. (1984). On the way to empathic understanding. *American Journal of Psychotherapy, 38,* 111–119.

Berger, D. M. (1987). *Clinical empathy.* Northvale, NJ: Jason Aronson.

Berne, E. (1961). *Transactional analysis in psychotherapy.* New York: Grove Press.

Binder, U. (1998). Empathy and empathy development with psychotic clients. In B. Thorne & E. Lambers (Eds.), *Person-centered therapy: A European perspective* (pp. 216–230). London: Sage.

Black, D. M. (2004). Sympathy reconfigured: Some reflections on sympathy, empathy, and the discovery of values. *International Journal of Psycho-Analysis, 85,* 579–596.

Bloch, S., & Crouch, E. (1985). *Therapeutic factors in group psychotherapy.* New York: Oxford University Press.

Blum, H. P. (1982). Theories of the self and psychoanalytic concepts: Discussion. *Journal of the American Psychoanalytic Association, 30,* 959–978.

Bohart, A. C. (1991). Empathy in client-centered therapy: A contrast with psychoanalysis and self psychology. *Journal of Humanistic Psychology, 31,* 34–48.

Bohart, A. C. (1999). Intuition and creativity in psychotherapy. *Journal of Constructivist Psychology, 12,* 287–311.

Bohart, A. C. (2004). How do clients make empathy work? *Person-Centered and Experiential Psychotherapies, 3,* 102–116.

Bohart, A. C., Elliot, R., Greenberg, L. S., & Watson, J. C. (2002). Empathy. In J. Norcross (Ed.), *Psychotherapy relationships that work: Therapist contributions and responsiveness to patients* (pp. 89–108). New York: Oxford University Press.

Bohart, A. C., & Greenberg, L. S. (1997). Empathy: Where are we and where do we go from here. In A. C. Bohart & L. S. Greenberg (Eds.), *Empathy reconsidered: New directions in psychotherapy* (pp. 419–449). Washington, DC: American Psychological Association.

Bohart, A. C., Magallanes, M., Guzman, R., Smiljanich, K., Aguallo, S., & Humphrey, A. (1993). Emphasizing the future in empathy responses. *Journal of Humanistic Psychology, 33,* 12–29.

Bohart, A. C., & Rosenbaum, R. (1995). The dance of empathy: Empathy diversity and technical eclecticism. *The Person-Centered Journal, 2,* 5–29.

Bolognini, S. (1997). Empathy and "empathism." *International Journal of Psycho-Analysis, 78,* 279–293.

Book, H. E. (1988). Empathy: Misconceptions and misuses in psychotherapy. *American Journal of Psychiatry, 145,* 420–424.

Book, H. E. (1991). Is empathy cost efficient? *American Journal of Psychiatry, 145,* 21–30.

Bouchard, M.-A., Normandin, L., & Séguin, M.-H. (1995). Countertransference as instrument and obstacle: A comprehensive and descriptive framework. *Psychoanalytic Quarterly, 44,* 717–745.

Boy, A. V., & Pine, G. J. (1982). *Client-centered counseling: A renewal.* Boston: Allyn & Bacon.

Bozarth, J. D. (1984). Beyond reflection: Emergent modes of empathy. In R. F. Levant & J. M. Shlien (Eds.), *Client-centered therapy and the person-centered approach: New directions in theory, research, and practice* (pp. 59–75). New York: Praeger.

Bozarth, J. D. (1997). Empathy from the framework of client-centered theory and the Rogerian hypothesis. In A. C. Bohart & L. S. Greenberg (Eds.), *Empathy reconsidered: New directions in psychotherapy* (pp. 81–102). Washington, DC: American Psychological Association.

Bozarth, J. D. (1998). *Person-centered therapy: A revolutionary paradigm.* Ross-on-Wye, UK: PCCS Books.

Brabender, V. (2002). *Introduction to group therapy.* New York: John Wiley & Sons.

Brammer, L. M., & MacDonald, G. (2003). *The helping relationship: Process and skills* (8th ed.). Boston: Allyn & Bacon.

Breggin, P. R. (1997). *The heart of being helpful: Empathy and the creation of the healing presence.* New York: Springer.

Breggin, P. R. (2002). Empathic self-transformation in therapy. In P. R. Breggin, G. Breggin, & F. Bemak (Eds.), *Dimensions of empathic therapy* (pp. 177–189). New York: Springer.

Brink, D. C., & Farber, B. A. (1996). A scheme of Rogers' clinical responses. In B. A. Farber, D. C. Brink, & P. M. Raskin (Eds.), *The psychotherapy of Carl Rogers: Cases and commentary* (pp. 15–24). New York: Guilford.

Bristow-Braitman, A. (1995). Addiction recovery: 12-step programs and cognitive-behavioral psychology. *Journal of Counseling & Development, 73,* 414–418.

Brodley, B. T. (1996). Empathic understanding and feelings in client-centered therapy. *Person-Centered Journal, 3,* 22–30.

Brodley, B. T. (1999). Reasons for responses expressing the therapist's frame of reference in client-centered therapy. *Person-Centered Journal, 6,* 4–27.

Bromberg, P. M. (1980). Empathy, anxiety and reality: A view from the bridge. *Contemporary Psychoanalysis, 16,* 223–236.

Bruhn, A. R., & Davidow, S. (1983). Earliest memories and the dynamics of delinquency. *Journal of Personality Assessment, 47,* 476–482.

Buber, M. (1957). Elements of the interhuman. *Psychiatry, 20,* 105–113.

Buber, M. (1958). *I and thou* (2nd ed.; R. G. Smith, Trans.). New York: Charles Schibner's Sons.

Buber, M., & Rogers, C. R. (1960). Dialogue between Martin Buber and Carl Rogers. *Psychologia, 3,* 208–221.

Buck, P. S. (1942). *What America means to me.* New York: The John Day Company.

Buie, D. H. (1981). Empathy: Its nature and limitations. *Journal of the American Psychoanalytic Association, 29,* 281–307.

Burkard, A. W., & Knox, S. (2004). Effect of therapist color-blindness on empathy and attributions in cross-cultural counseling. *Journal of Counseling Psychology, 51,* 387–397.

Burlingame, G. M., Fuhriman, A., & Johnson, J. E. (2002). Cohesion in group psychotherapy. In J. C. Norcross (Ed.), *Psychotherapy relationships that work: Therapist contributions and responsiveness to patients* (pp. 71–87). New York: Oxford University Press.

Burns, D. D., & Nolen-Hoeksema, S. (1992). Therapeutic empathy and recovery from depression in cognitive-behavioral therapy: A structural equation model. *Journal of Consulting and Clinical Psychology, 60,* 441–449.

Burns, R. (1897). *The complete poetical works of Robert Burns* (W. E. Henley & T. F. Henderson, Eds.). Boston: Houghton Mifflin. (Original work published 1787)

Carkhuff, R. R. (1969). *Helping and human relations (Vols. 1 and 2).* New York: Holt, Rinehart and Winston.

Carkhuff, R. R. (1987). *The art of helping* (6th ed.). Amherst, MA: Human Resource Development Press.

Carkhuff, R. R., & Berenson, B. G. (1977). *Beyond counseling and therapy* (2nd ed.). New York: Holt, Rinehart and Winston.

Carlozzi, A. F., Bull, K. S., Stein, L. B., Ray, K., & Barnes, L. (2002). Empathy theory and practice: A survey of psychologists and counselors. *The Journal of Psychology, 136,* 161–170.

Cashdan, S. (1988). *Object relations therapy: Using the relationship.* New York: W. W. Norton.

Cates, J. A. (1999). The art of assessment in psychology: Ethics, expertise, and validity. *Journal of Clinical Psychology, 55,* 631–641.

Chen, M., & Rybak, C. J. (2004). *Group leadership skills: Interpersonal process in group counseling and therapy.* Belmont, CA: Thompson Brooks/Cole.

Chismar, D. (1988). Empathy and sympathy: The important difference. *Journal of Value Inquiry, 22,* 257–266.

Chung, R. C-Y., & Bemak, F. (2002). The relationship of culture and empathy in cross-cultural counseling. *Journal of Counseling & Development, 80,* 154–159.

Clark, A. J. (1989). Questions in group counseling. *Journal for Specialists in Group Work, 14,* 121–124.

Clark, A. J. (1991). The identification and modification of defense mechanisms in counseling. *Journal of Counseling & Development, 69,* 231–236.

Clark, A. J. (1992). Defense mechanisms in group counseling. *Journal for Specialists in Group Work, 17,* 151–160.

Clark, A. J. (1993). Interpretation in group counseling: Theoretical and operational issues. *Journal for Specialists in Group Work, 18,* 174–181.

Clark, A. J. (1994a). Early recollections: A personality tool for elementary school counselors. *Elementary School Guidance and Counseling, 29,* 92–101.

Clark, A. J. (1994b). Working with dreams in group counseling: Advantages and challenges. *Journal of Counseling & Development, 73,* 141–144.

Clark, A. J. (1995a). An examination of the technique of interpretation in counseling. *Journal of Counseling & Development, 73,* 489–495.

Clark, A. J. (1995b). Modification: A leader skill in group work. *Journal for Specialists in Group Work, 20,* 14–17.

Clark, A. J. (1995c). Projective identification in counselling: Theoretical and therapeutic considerations. *Canadian Journal of Counselling, 29,* 37–49.

Clark, A. J. (1995d). Projective techniques in the counseling process. *Journal of Counseling & Development, 73,* 311–316.

Clark, A. J. (1995e). Techniques in the counseling process with adolescents. In K. V. Chandras (Ed.), *Handbook on counseling adolescents, adults and older persons* (pp. 13–22). Alexandria, VA: American Counseling Association.

Clark, A. J. (1997). Projective identification as a defense mechanism in group counseling and therapy. *Journal for Specialists in Group Work, 22,* 85–96.

Clark, A. J. (1998a). *Defense mechanisms in the counseling process.* Thousand Oaks, CA: Sage.

Clark, A. J. (1998b). Reframing: A counseling technique in group counseling. *Journal for Specialists in Group Work, 23,* 66–73.

Clark, A. J. (1999a). Safeguarding tendencies: A clarifying perspective. *The Journal of Individual Psychology, 55,* 72–81.

Clark, A. J. (1999b). Theoretical and practical issues in working with children's dreams in counseling. *Journal of Humanistic Education and Development, 37,* 160–168.

Clark, A. J. (2000). Safeguarding tendencies: Implications for the counseling process. *The Journal of Individual Psychology, 56,* 192–204.

Clark, A. J. (2001). Early recollections: A humanistic assessment in counseling. *Journal of Humanistic Counseling, Education and Development, 40,* 96–104.

Clark, A. J. (2002a). The defense never rests. In L. B. Golden (Ed.), *Case studies in child and adolescent counseling* (3rd ed., pp. 48–59). Upper Saddle River, NJ: Merrill/Prentice Hall.

Clark, A. J. (2002b). *Early recollections: Theory and practice in counseling and psychotherapy.* New York: Brunner-Routledge.

Clark, A. J. (2002c). Scapegoating: Dynamics and interventions in group counseling. *Journal of Counseling & Development, 80,* 276–281.

Clark, A. J. (2004a). Empathy: Implications of three ways of knowing in counseling. *Journal of Humanistic Counseling, Education and Development, 43,* 141–151.

Clark, A. J. (2004b). On the meaning of color in early recollections. *The Journal of Individual Psychology, 60,* 141–154.

Cochran, J. L., & Cochran, N. H. (2006). *The heart of counseling: A guide to developing therapeutic relationships.* Belmont, CA: Thompson Brooks/Cole.

Constantine, M. G. (2001). Multicultural training, theoretical orientation, empathy, and multicultural case conceptualization ability in counselors. *Journal of Mental Health Counseling, 23,* 357–372.

Cooper, A. M. (1983). The place of self psychology in the history of depth psychology. In A. Goldberg (Ed.), *The future of psychoanalysis: Essays in honor of Heinz Kohut* (pp. 3–17). New York: International Universities Press.

Cooper, M. (2001). Embodied empathy. In S. Haugh & T. Merry (Eds.), *Rogers' therapeutic conditions: Evolution, theory and practice. Vol. 2: Empathy* (pp. 218–229). Ross-on-Wye, UK: PCCS Books.

Corcoran, K. J. (1981). Experiential empathy: A theory of a felt-level experience. *Journal of Humanistic Psychology, 21,* 29–37.

Corey, G. (2005). *Theory and practice of counseling and psychotherapy* (7th ed.). Belmont, CA: Thompson Brooks/Cole.

Corey, G., Corey, M. S., & Callahan, P. (2003). *Issues and ethics in the helping professions* (6th ed.). Belmont, CA: Thompson Brooks/Cole.

Corey, G., Corey, M. S., Callahan, P., & Russell, J. M. (2004). *Group techniques* (3rd ed.). Belmont, CA: Thompson Brooks/Cole.

Corey, M. S., & Corey, G. (2006). *Groups: Process and practice* (7th ed.). Belmont, CA: Thompson Brooks/Cole.

Cormier, S., & Hackney, H. (2005). *Counseling strategies and interventions* (6th ed.). Boston: Allyn & Bacon.

Cormier, S., & Nurius, P. S. (2003). *Interviewing and change strategies for helpers: Fundamental skills and cognitive behavioral interventions* (5th ed.). Belmont, CA: Brooks/Cole.

Cox, L., & Lyddon, W. J. (1997). Constructivist conceptions of self: A discussion of emerging identity constructs. *Journal of Constructivist Psychology, 10,* 201–219.

Crutchfield, L. B., Baltimore, M. L., Felfeli, M., & Worth, S. (2000). Empathic responding skills across counselor education tracks: A comparison study. *Journal of Humanistic Counseling, Education and Development, 38,* 162–169.

Curtis, J. M. (1982). The effect of therapist self-disclosure on patients' perceptions of empathy, competence and trust in an analogue psychotherapeutic interaction. *Psychotherapy: Theory, Research and Practice, 19,* 54–62.

Dana, R. H. (2000). Culture and methodology in personality assessment. In I. Cuéllar & F. A. Paniagua (Eds.), *Handbook of multicultural mental health: Assessment and treatment of diverse populations* (pp. 97–129). San Diego, CA: Academic Press.

Davidow, S., & Bruhn, A. R. (1990). Earliest memories and the dynamics of delinquency: A replication study. *Journal of Personality Assessment, 54,* 601–616.

Davis, M. H. (1996). *Empathy: A social psychological approach.* Boulder, CO: Westview Press.

Day, H. I., & Chambers, J. (1991). Empathy and burnout in rehabilitation counselors. *Canadian Journal of Rehabilitation, 5,* 33–44.

Day, S. X. (2004). *Theory and design in counseling and psychotherapy.* Boston: Lahaska Press/Houghton Mifflin.

de Carufel, F. L., & Piper, W. E. (1988). Group psychotherapy or individual psychotherapy: Patient characteristics as predictive factors. *International Journal of Group Psychotherapy, 38,* 169–188.

Decety, J., & Jackson, P. L. (2004). The functional architecture of human empathy. *Behavioral and Cognitive Neuroscience Reviews, 3,* 71–100.

de Forest, I. (1954). *The leaven of love: A development of the psychoanalytic theory and technique of Sándor Ferenczi.* New York: Harper & Brothers.

Deutsch, F., & Madle, R. A. (1975). Empathy: Historic and current conceptualizations, measurement, and a cognitive theoretical perspective. *Human Development, 18,* 267–287.

Dinkmeyer, D. C., & Muro, J. J. (1979). *Group counseling: Theory and practice* (2nd ed.). Itasca, IL: F. E. Peacock.

Dinkmeyer, D. C., Jr., & Sperry, L. (2000). *Counseling and psychotherapy: An integrated, individual psychology approach* (3rd ed.). Upper Saddle River, NJ: Prentice-Hall.

Dreikurs, R. (1967). *Psychodynamics, psychotherapy, and counseling: Collected papers.* Chicago: Alfred Adler Institute of Chicago.

Dryden, W. (1990). *Rational-emotive counselling in action.* London: Sage.

Duan, C., & Hill, C. E. (1996). The current state of empathy research. *Journal of Counseling Psychology, 43,* 261–274.

Duan, C., Rose, T. B., & Kraatz, R. A. (2002). Empathy. In G. S. Tryon (Ed.), *Counseling based on process research: Applying what we know* (pp. 197–231). Boston: Allyn & Bacon.

Duffy, M., Gillig, S. E., Tureen, R. M., & Ybarra, M. A. (2002). A critical look at the *DSM-IV. The Journal of Individual Psychology, 58,* 363–373.

Dupont, J. (1988). Ferenczi's "madness." *Contemporary Psychoanalysis, 24,* 250–161.

Durana, C. (1998). The use of touch in psychotherapy: Ethical and clinical guidelines. *Psychotherapy, 35,* 269–280.

Dymond, R. F. (1950). Personality and empathy. *Journal of Consulting Psychology, 14,* 343–350.

Eagle, M., & Wolitzky, D. L. (1997). Empathy: A psychoanalytic perspective. In A. C. Bohart & L. S. Greenberg (Eds.), *Empathy reconsidered: New directions in psychotherapy* (pp. 217–244). Washington, DC: American Psychological Association.

Edwards, D. J. A., Dattilio, F. M., & Bromley, D. B. (2004). Developing evidence-based practice: The role of case-based research. *Professional Psychology: Research and Practice, 35,* 589–597.

Egan, G. (2002). *The skilled helper: A problem-management and opportunity-development approach to helping* (7th ed.). Pacific Grove, CA: Brooks/Cole.

Ehmann, V. E. (1971). Empathy: Its origin, characteristics, and process. *Perspectives in Psychiatric Care, 9,* 72–80.

Eisenberg, N., & Strayer, J. (Eds.). (1987). *Empathy and its development.* New York: Cambridge University Press.

Eisengart, S. P., & Faiver, C. M. (1996). Intuition in mental health counseling. *Journal of Mental Health Counseling, 18,* 41–52.

Elliot, R., Greenberg, L. S., & Lietaer, G. (2004). Research on experiential psychotherapies. In M. J. Lambert (Ed.), *Bergin and Garfield's handbook of psychotherapy and behavior change* (5th ed., pp. 493–539). New York: John Wiley & Sons.

Ellis, A. (1959). Requisite condition for basic personality change. *Journal of Consulting Psychology, 23,* 538–540.

Ellis, A. (2005). Rational emotive behavior therapy. In R. J. Corsini & D. Wedding (Eds.), *Current psychotherapies* (7th ed., pp. 166–201). Belmont, CA: Brooks/Cole.

Emery, E. J. (1987). Empathy: Psychoanalytic and client centered. *American Psychologist, 42,* 513–516.

Enns, C. Z. (2004). *Feminist theories and feminist psychotherapies: Origins, themes, and diversity* (2nd ed.). New York: Haworth.

Epp, L. R. (2002). Self-understanding: The path to empathy. In P. R. Breggin, G. Breggin, & F. Bemak (Eds.), *Dimensions of effective empathy* (pp. 154–161). New York: Springer.

Erskine, R. G. (1993). Inquiry, attunement, and involvement in the psychotherapy of dissociation. *Transactional Analysis Journal, 23,* 184–190.

Erskine, R. G., Moursund, J. P., & Trautmann, R. L. (1999). *Beyond empathy: A therapy of contact-in-relationship.* New York: Brunner-Routledge.

Evans, K. M., Kincade, E. A., Marbley, A. F., & Seem, S. R. (2005). Feminism and feminist therapy: Lessons from the past and hopes for the future. *Journal of Counseling & Development, 83,* 269–277.

Ewen, R. B. (2003). *An introduction to theories of personality* (6th ed.). Mahwah, NJ: Lawrence Erlbaum Associates.

Fall, K. A., Holden, J. M., & Marquis, A. (2004). *Theoretical models of counseling and psychotherapy.* New York: Brunner-Routledge.

Feiner, A. H. (1979). Countertransference and the anxiety of influence. In L. Epstein & A. H. Feiner (Eds.), *Countertransference* (pp. 105–128). New York: Jason Aronson.

Feiner, K., & Kiersky, S. (1994). Empathy: A common ground. *Psychoanalytic Dialogues, 4,* 425–440.

Feller, C. P., & Cottone, R. R. (2003). The importance of empathy in the therapeutic alliance. *Journal of Humanistic Counseling, Education and Development, 42,* 53–61.

Fenichel, O. (1953). *The collected papers of Otto Fenichel: First Series* (D. Rapaport, Ed.). New York: W. W. Norton.

Ferenczi, S. (1955). The elasticity of psychoanalytic technique. In M. Balint (Ed.), *Final contributions to the problems and methods of psychoanalysis by Sándor Ferenczi, M.D.* (Vol. 3, pp. 87–102). New York: Basic Books. (Original work published 1928)

Ferenczi, S. (1955). The principle of relaxation and neocatharsis. In M. Balint (Ed.), *Final contributions to the problems and methods of psychoanalysis by Sándor Ferenczi, M.D.* (Vol. 3, pp. 108–125). New York: Basic Books. (Original work published 1929)

Ferenczi, S. (1955). Child analysis in the analysis of adults. In M. Balint (Ed.), *Final contributions to the problems and methods of psychoanalysis by Sándor Ferenczi, M.D.* (Vol. 3, pp. 126–142). New York: Basic Books. (Original work published 1931)

Ferenczi, S. (1955). The confusion of tongues between adults and children: The language of tenderness and of passion. In M. Balint (Ed.), *Final contributions to the problems and methods of psychoanalysis by Sándor Ferenczi, M.D.* (Vol. 3, pp. 156–167). (Original work published 1933)

Ferenczi, S. (1988). *The clinical diary of Sándor Ferenczi* (J. Dupont, Ed. & M. Balint & N. Z. Jackson, Trans.). Cambridge, MA: Harvard University Press.

Finn, S. E., & Tonsager, M. E. (1997). Information-gathering and therapeutic models of assessment: Complementary paradigms. *Psychological Assessment, 9,* 374–385.

Flapan, D., & Fenchel, G. H. (1984). Countertransference in group psychotherapy. *Group, 8,* 17–29.

Fliess, R. (1942). The metapsychology of the analyst. *The Psychoanalytic Quarterly, 11,* 211–227.

Fox, R. E., & Goldin, P. C. (1964). The empathic process in psychotherapy: A survey of theory and research. *Journal of Nervous and Mental Disease, 138,* 324–331.

Frankl, V. E. (1959). *Man's search for meaning: An introduction to logotherapy.* New York: Simon & Schuster.

Free, N. K., Green, B. L., Grace, M. C., Chernus, L. A., & Whitman, R. M. (1985). Empathy and outcome in brief focal dynamic therapy. *American Journal of Psychiatry, 142,* 917–921.

Freud, A. (1966). *The ego and the mechanisms of defense* (Rev. ed.). New York: International Universities Press. (Original work published 1936)

Freud, S. (1953). Three essays on the theory of sexuality. In J. Strachey (Ed. & Trans.), *The standard edition of the complete psychological works of Sigmund Freud* (Vol. 7, pp. 135–243). London: Hogarth. (Original work published 1905)

Freud, S. (1955a). Group psychology and the analysis of the ego. In J. Strachey (Ed. & Trans.), *The standard edition of the complete psychological works of Sigmund Freud* (Vol. 18, pp. 65–143). London: Hogarth. (Original work published 1921)

Freud, S. (1955b). The Moses of Michelangelo. In J. Strachey (Ed. & Trans.), *The standard edition of the complete psychological works of Sigmund Freud* (Vol. 13, pp. 211–238). London: Hogarth. (Original work published 1914)

Freud, S. (1957). The future prospects of psycho-analytic therapy. In J. Strachey (Ed. & Trans.), *The standard edition of the complete psychological works of Sigmund Freud* (Vol. 11, pp. 139–151). London: Hogarth. (Original work published 1910)

Freud, S. (1958). Recommendations to physicians practicing psychoanalysis. In J. Strachey (Ed. & Trans.), *The standard edition of the complete psychological works of Sigmund Freud* (Vol. 12, pp. 111–120). London: Hogarth. (Original work published 1912)

Freud, S. (1959). Inhibitions, symptoms and anxiety. In J. Strachey (Ed. & Trans.). *The standard edition of the complete psychological works of Sigmund Freud* (Vol. 20, pp. 87–172). London: Hogarth. (Original work published 1926)

Freud, S. (1960). Jokes and their relation to the unconscious. In J. Strachey (Ed. & Trans.), *The standard edition of the complete psychological works of Sigmund Freud* (Vol. 8, pp. 9–236). London: Hogarth. (Original work published 1905)

Freud, S. (1962a). The neuro-psychoses of defense. In J. Strachey (Ed. & Trans.). *The standard edition of the complete psychological works of Sigmund Freud* (Vol. 3, pp. 45–61). London: Hogarth. (Original work published 1894)

Freud, S. (1962b). Further remarks on the neuro-psychoses of defence. In J. Strachey (Ed. & Trans.), *The standard edition of the complete psychological works of Sigmund Freud* (Vol. 3, pp. 162–185). London: Hogarth. (Original work published 1896)

Fromm-Reichmann, F. (1950). *Principles of intensive psychotherapy.* Chicago: The University of Chicago Press.

Garb, H. N. (1997). Race bias, social class bias, and gender bias in clinical judgment. *Clinical Psychology: Science and Practice, 4,* 99–120.

Garb, H. N., Wood, J. M., Lilienfeld, S. O., & Nezworski, M. T. (2002). Effective use of projective techniques in clinical practice: Let the data help with selection and interpretation. *Professional Psychology: Research and Practice, 33,* 454–463.

Gardner, J. R. (1991). The application of self psychology to brief psychotherapy. *Psychoanalytic Psychology, 8,* 477–500.

Garduk, E. L., & Haggard, E. A. (1972). Immediate effects on patients of psychoanalytic interpretations. *Psychological Issues, 7,* 1–84.

Gazzola, N., & Stalikas, A. (1997). An investigation of counselor interpretations in client-centered therapy. *Journal of Psychotherapy Integration, 7,* 313–327.

Gazzola, N., & Stalikas, A. (2003). Can Carl Rogers teach us anything about interpretation? *Person-Centered and Experiential Psychotherapies, 2,* 242–257.

Gedo, J. E. (1986). *Conceptual issues in psychoanalysis: Essays in history and method.* Hillsdale, NJ: The Analytic Press.

Gelso, C. J., & Carter, J. A. (1985). The relationship in counseling and psychotherapy: Components, consequences, and theoretical antecedents. *The Counseling Psychologist, 13,* 155–243.

Gelso, C. J., & Hayes, J. A. (2002). The management of countertransference. In J. C. Norcross (Ed.), *Psychotherapy relationships that work: Therapist contributions and responsiveness to patients* (pp. 267–283). New York: Oxford University Press.

Gendlin, E. T. (1961). Experiencing: A variable in the process of therapeutic change. *American Journal of Psychotherapy, 15,* 233–245.

Gendlin, E. T. (1962). *Experiencing and the creation of meaning: A philosophical and psychological approach to the subjective.* New York: The Free Press.

Gendlin, E. T. (1978). *Focusing.* New York: Everest House.

Gendlin, E. T. (1998). *Focusing-oriented psychotherapy: A manual of the experiential method.* New York: Guilford.

Gergen, K. J., Lightfoot, C., & Sydow, L. (2004). Social construction: Vistas in clinical child and adolescent psychology. *Journal of Clinical Child and Adolescent Psychology, 33,* 389–399.

Gibbons, M. B. C., Crits-Christoph, P., & Apostal, P. (2004). Constructing interpretations and assessing their accuracy. In D. P. Harman (Ed.), *Core processes in brief psychodynamic psychotherapy* (pp. 145–163). Mahwah, NJ: Lawrence Erlbaum Associates.

Giesekus, U., & Mente, A. (1986). Client empathic understanding in client-centered therapy. *Person-Centered Review, 1,* 163–171.

Gill, M. M. (1994). Heinz Kohut's self psychology. In A. Goldberg (Ed.), *A decade of progress: Progress in self psychology* (Vol. 10, pp. 197–211). Hillsdale, NJ: The Analytic Press.

Gladding, S. T. (2002). *Family therapy: History, theory, & process* (3rd ed.). Upper Saddle River, NJ: Merrill/Prentice Hall.

Gladding, S. T. (2003). *Group work: A counseling specialty* (4th ed.). Upper Saddle River, NJ: Pearson Education.

Gladding, S. T. (2005). *Counseling theories: Essential concepts and applications.* Upper Saddle River, NJ: Pearson Education.

Gladstein, G. A. (1977). Empathy and counseling outcome: An empirical and conceptual review. *The Counseling Psychologist, 6,* 70–79.

Gladstein, G. A. (1983). Understanding empathy: Integrating counseling, developmental, and social psychology perspectives. *Journal of Counseling Psychology, 30,* 467–482.

Gladstein, G. A., & Associates. (1987). *Empathy and counseling: Explorations in theory and research.* New York: Springer-Verlag.

Gladwell, M. (2005). *Blink: The power of thinking without thinking.* New York: Little, Brown.

Glauser, A. S., & Bozarth, J. D. (2001). Person-centered counseling: The culture within. *Journal of Counseling & Development, 79,* 142–147.

Goldberg, A. (Ed.). (1978). *The psychology of the self: A casebook.* New York: International Universities Press.

Goldberg, A. (1980). Compassion, empathy and understanding. In J. Mishne (Ed.), *Psychotherapy and training in clinical social work* (pp. 231–240). New York: Gardner Press.

Goldberg, A. (1983). On the scientific status of empathy. *Annual of Psychoanalysis, 11,* 155–169.

Goldberg, A. (1988). Changing psychic structure through treatment: From empathy to self-reflection. *Journal of the American Psychoanalytic Association, 36,* 211–224.

Goldberg, A. (1999). Between empathy and judgment. *Journal of the American Psychoanalytic Association, 47,* 351–364.

Goldstein, A. P., & Michaels, G. Y. (1985). *Empathy: Development, training, and consequences.* Hillsdale, NJ: Lawrence Erlbaum Associates.

Goldstein, E. G. (1997). To tell or not to tell: The disclosure of events in the therapist's life to the patient. *Clinical Social Work Journal, 25,* 41–58.

Goodheart, C. D. (2004). Evidence-based practice and the endeavor of psychotherapy. *The Independent Practitioner, 24,* 6–10.

Goodman, A. (1992). Empathy and inquiry: Integrating empathic mirroring in an interpersonal framework. *Contemporary Psychoanalysis, 28,* 631–646.

Goodman, M., Marks, M., & Rockberger, H. (1964). Resistance in group psychotherapy enhanced by the countertransference reactions of the therapist: A peer group experience. *International Journal of Group Psychotherapy, 14,* 332–343.

Goodyear, R. K. (1979). Inference and intuition as components of empathy. *Counselor Education and Supervision, 18,* 214–222.

Greenberg, L. S., Rice, L. N., & Elliot, R. (1993). *Facilitating emotional change: The moment-by-moment process.* New York: Guilford.

Greenson, R. R. (1960). Empathy and its vicissitudes. *International Journal of Psycho-Analysis, 41,* 418–424.

Greenson, R. R. (1967). *The technique and practice of psychoanalysis* (Vol. 1). New York: International Universities Press.

Guistolise, P. (1996). Failures in the therapeutic relationship: Inevitable *and* necessary. *Transactional Analysis Journal, 26,* 284–288.

Haaga, D. A. F., Rabois, D., & Brody, C. (1999). Cognitive behavior therapy. In M. Hersen & A. S. Bellack (Eds.), *Handbook of comparative interventions for adult disorders* (2nd ed., pp. 48–61). New York: John Wiley & Sons.

Haase, R., & Tepper, D., Jr. (1972). Nonverbal components of empathic communication. *Journal of Counseling Psychology, 19,* 417–424.

Hackney, H. (1978). The evolution of empathy. *Personnel and Guidance Journal, 57,* 35–38.

Hackney, H. L., & Cormier, L. S. (2005). *The professional counselor: A process guide to helping* (5th ed.) Boston: Allyn & Bacon.

Halpern, J. (1993). Empathy: Using resonance emotions in the service of curiosity. In H. M. Spiro, M. G. McCrea Curnen, E. Peschel, & D. St. James (Eds.), *Empathy and the practice of medicine: Beyond pills and the scalpel* (pp. 160–173). New Haven, CT: Yale University Press.

Ham, M. D-C. (1989). Empathic understanding: A skill for "joining" with immigrant families. *Journal of Strategic and Systemic Therapies, 8,* 36–40.

Handler, L. (1996). The clinical use of figure drawings. In C. S. Newmark (Ed.), *Major psychological assessment instruments* (2nd ed., pp. 206–293). Boston: Allyn & Bacon.

Hansen, J. T. (2000). Psychoanalysis and humanism: A review and critical examination of integrationist efforts with some proposed resolutions. *Journal of Counseling & Development, 78,* 21–28.

Hansen, J. T. (2003). Including diagnostic training in counseling curricula: Implications for professional identity development. *Counselor Education and Supervision, 43,* 96–107.

Hartley, G. D. (1995). Empathy in the counseling process: The role of counselor understanding in client change. *Journal of Humanistic Education and Development, 34,* 13–23.

Haugh, S., & Merry, T. (2001). *Rogers' therapeutic conditions: Evolution, theory, and practice: Vol. 2. Empathy.* Ross-on-Wye, UK: PCCS Books.

Havens, L. L. (1974). The existential use of the self. *American Journal of Psychiatry, 131,* 1–10.

Haverkamp, B. E. (1993). Confirmatory bias in hypothesis testing for client-identified and counselor self-generated hypotheses. *Journal of Counseling Psychology, 40,* 303–315.

Hayes, J. A. (1995). Countertransference in group psychotherapy: Waking a sleeping dog. *International Journal of Group Psychotherapy, 45,* 521–535.

Hayes, J. A., McCraken, J. E., McClanahan, M. K., Hilt, C. E., Harp, J. S., & Carozzoni, P. (1998). Therapist perspectives on countertransference: Qualitative data in search of a theory. *Journal of Counseling Psychology, 45,* 468–482.

Haynal, A. (1993). Ferenczi and the origins of psychoanalytic technique. In L. Aron

& A. Harris (Eds.), *The legacy of Sándor Ferenczi* (pp. 53–74). Hillsdale, NJ: The Analytic Press.

Heimann, P. (1950). On counter-transference. *International Journal of Psycho-Analysis, 31,* 81–84.

Hill, C. E. (2004). *Helping skills: Facilitating exploration, insight, and action* (2nd ed.). Washington, DC: American Psychological Association.

Hill, C. E., & Knox, S. (2002). Self-disclosure. In J. C. Norcross (Ed.), *Psychotherapy relationships that work: Therapist contributions and responsiveness to patients* (pp. 255–265). New York: Oxford University Press.

Hoffman, D. (2003). Sándor Ferenczi and the origins of humanistic psychology. *Journal of Humanistic Psychology, 43,* 59–86.

Hoffman, M. L. (2000). *Empathy and moral development: Implications for caring and justice.* New York: Cambridge University Press.

Holaday, M., Smith, D. A., & Sherry, A. (2000). Sentence completion tests: A review of the literature and results of a survey of members of the Society of Personality Assessment. *Journal of Personality Assessment, 74,* 371–383.

Horton, J. (1998). Further research on the patient's experience of touch in psychotherapy. In E. W. L. Smith, P. R. Clance, & S. Imes (Eds.), *Touch in psychotherapy: Theory, research, and practice* (pp. 127–141). New York: Guilford.

Hunsdahl, J. B. (1967). Concerning einfühlung (empathy): A concept analysis of its origin and early development. *Journal of the History of the Behavioral Sciences, 3,* 180–191.

Ibrahim, F. A. (1985). Effective cross-cultural counseling and psychotherapy: A framework. *The Counseling Psychologist, 13,* 625–638.

Ibrahim, F. A. (1991). Contribution of cultural worldview to generic counseling and development. *Journal of Counseling & Development, 70,* 13–19.

Ivey, A. E. (1987). The multicultural practice of therapy: Ethics, empathy, and dialectics. *Journal of Social and Clinical Psychology, 5,* 195–204.

Ivey, A. E., D'Andrea, M., Ivey, M. B., & Simek-Morgan, L. (2002). *Theories of counseling and psychotherapy: A multicultural perspective* (5th ed.). Boston: Allyn & Bacon.

Ivey, A. E., & Ivey, M. B. (1998). Reframing *DSM-IV:* Positive strategies from developmental counseling and therapy. *Journal of Counseling & Development, 76,* 334–350.

Ivey, A. E., & Ivey, M. B. (2003). *Intentional interviewing and counseling: Facilitating client development in a multicultural society* (5th ed.). Pacific Grove, CA: Thompson Brooks/Cole.

Ivey, A. E., Pedersen, P. B., & Ivey, M. B. (2001). *Intentional group counseling: A microskills approach.* Pacific Grove, CA: Brooks/Cole.

Jacobs, D., & Williams, V. (1983). Clinical theory and scientism: Empathy research as a case study. *Journal of Humanistic Psychology, 23,* 79–96.

Jacobs, E. E., Masson, R. L., & Harvill, R. L. (2002). *Group counseling: Strategies and skills* (4th ed.). Pacific Grove, CA: Brooks/Cole.

Jaffe, D. S. (1986). Empathy, counteridentification, countertransference: A review with some personal perspectives on the "analytic instrument." *Psychoanalytic Quarterly, 55,* 215–243.

Jenkins, A. H. (1997). The empathic context in psychotherapy with people of color. In A. Bohart & L. Greenberg (Eds.), *Empathy reconsidered: New directions in psychotherapy* (pp. 321–342). Washington, DC: American Psychological Association.

Jones, E. (1933). Obituary: Sándor Ferenczi, 1873–1933. *International Journal of Psycho-Analysis, 14,* 463–466.

Jordan, J. V. (2001). A relational-cultural model: Healing through mutual empathy. *Bulletin of the Menninger Clinic, 65,* 92–104.

Jordan, J. V., Surrey, J. L., & Kaplan, A. G. (1991). Women and empathy: Implications for psychological development and psychotherapy. In J. V. Jordan, A. G. Kaplan, J. B. Miller, I. P. Stiver, & J. L. Surrey (Eds.), *Women's growth in connection. Writings from the Stone Center* (pp. 27–50). New York: Guilford.

Josephs, L. (1995). *Balancing empathy and interpretation: Relational character analysis.* Northvale, NJ: Jason Aronson.

Jourard, S. M. (1959). I–thou relationship versus manipulation in counseling and psychotherapy. *Journal of Individual Psychology, 15,* 174–179.

Jourard, S. M. (1964). *The transparent self: Self-disclosure and well-being.* New York: Van Nostrand Reinhold.

Kahn, E. (1985). Heinz Kohut and Carl Rogers: A timely comparison. *American Psychologist, 40,* 893–904.

Kahn, E. (1989). Carl Rogers and Heinz Kohut: On the importance of valuing the self. In D. W. Detrick & S. P. Detrick (Eds.), *Self psychology: Comparisons and contrasts* (pp. 213–228). Hillsdale, NJ: The Analytic Press.

Kalisch, B. J. (1973). What is empathy? *American Journal of Nursing, 73,* 1548–1552.

Katz, R. L. (1963). *Empathy: Its nature and uses.* New York: The Free Press.

Keefe, T. (1976). Empathy: The critical skill. *Social Work, 21,* 10–14.

Keijsers, G. P. J., Schaap, C. P. D. R., & Hoogduin, C. A. L. (2000). The impact of interpersonal patient and therapist behavior on outcome in cognitive-behavior therapy: A review of empirical studies. *Behavior Modification, 24,* 264–297.

Keil, W. W. (1997). Hermeneutic empathy in client-centered therapy. In E. Ulrich, H. Pabst, & G. W. Speierer (Eds.), *The power of the person centered approach: New challenges–perspectives–answers* (pp. 65–80). Köln: GwG-Verlag.

Kelly, E. W., Jr. (1997). Relationship-centered counseling: A humanistic model of integration. *Journal of Counseling & Development, 75,* 337–343.

Kernberg, O. F. (1979). Notes on empathy. *Bulletin, The Association of Psychoanalytic Medicine, 18,* 75–80.

Kertay, L., & Reviere, S. L. (1993). The use of touch in psychotherapy: Theoretical and ethical considerations. *Psychotherapy, 30,* 32–40.

Kirschenbaum, H. (2004). Carl Roger's life and work: An assessment on the 100th anniversary of his birth. *Journal of Counseling & Development, 82,* 116–124.

Kleinberg, J. L. (1991). Teaching beginning group therapists to incorporate a patient's empathic capacity in treatment planning. *Group, 15,* 141–151.

Kohut, H. (1959). Introspection, empathy, and psychoanalysis. An examination of the relationship between mode of observation and theory. *Journal of the American Psychoanalytic Association, 7,* 459–483.

Kohut, H. (1971). *The analysis of the self.* New York: International Universities Press.

Kohut, H. (1977). *The restoration of the self.* Madison, CT: International Universities Press.

Kohut, H. (1982). Introspection, empathy, and the semi-circle of mental health. *International Journal of Psycho-Analysis, 63,* 395–407.

Kohut, H. (1984). *How does analysis cure?* (A. Goldberg & P. E. Stepansky, Eds.). Chicago: International Universities Press.

Kohut, H. (1990). Introspection and empathy: Further thoughts about their role in psychoanalysis. In P. H. Ornstein (Ed.), *The search for the self: Selected writings of Heinz Kohut: 1978–1981* (Vol. 3, pp. 83–101). Madison, CT: International Universities Press.

Kohut, H. (1991). On empathy. In P. H. Ornstein (Ed.), *The search for the self: Selected writings of Heinz Kohut: 1978–1981* (Vol. 4, pp. 525–535). Madison, CT: International Universities Press.

Kohut, H., & Wolf, E. S. (1978). The disorders of the self and their treatment: An outline. *International Journal of Psycho-Analysis, 59,* 413–425.

Kottler, J. A., Montgomery, M. J., & Marbley, A .F. (1998). Three variations on a theme: The power of pure empathy. *Journal of Humanistic Education and Development, 37,* 39–46.

Lafferty, P., Beutler, L. E., & Crago, M. (1989). Differences between more and less effective psychotherapists: A study of select therapist variables. *Journal of Consulting and Clinical Psychology, 57,* 76–80.

LaFountain, R. M. (1996). Social interest: A key to solutions. *Individual Psychology: The Journal of Adlerian Theory, Research & Practice, 52,* 150–157.

Lambert, M. J., & Barley, D. E. (2002). Research summary on the therapeutic relationship and psychotherapy. In J. C. Norcross (Ed.), *Psychotherapy relationships that work: Therapist contributions and responsiveness to patients* (pp. 17–32). New York: Oxford University Press.

Lang, J. A. (1994). Is empathy always "nice?": Empathy, sympathy, and the psychoanalytic situation. In E. S. More & M. A. Milligan (Eds.), *The empathic practitioner: Empathy, gender, and medicine* (pp. 98–112). New Brunswick, NJ: Rutgers University Press.

Leaman, D. R. (1978). Confrontation in counseling. *Personnel and Guidance Journal, 56,* 630–633.

Leider, R. J. (1996). The psychology of the self (self psychology). In E. Nersessian & R. G. Kopff (Eds.), *Textbook of psychoanalysis* (pp. 127–164). Washington, DC: American Psychiatric Press.

Levy, L. H. (1963). *Psychological interpretation.* New York: Holt, Rinehart & Winston.

Levy, S. T. (1985). Empathy and psychoanalytic technique. *Journal of the American Psychoanalytic Association, 33,* 353–379.

Lichtenberg, J. D. (1981). The empathic mode of perception and alternative vantage points for psychoanalytic work. *Psychoanalytic Inquiry, 1,* 329–355.

Little, C., Packman, J., Smaby, M. H., & Maddux, C. D. (2005). The skilled counselor training model: Skills acquisition, self-assessment, and cognitive complexity. *Counselor Education and Supervision, 44,* 189–200.

Lorand, S. (1966). Sándor Ferenczi: Pioneer of pioneers. In F. Alexander, S. Eisenstein, & M. Grotjahn (Eds.), *Psychoanalytic pioneers* (pp. 14–35). New York: Basic Books.

Lyddon, W. J. (1990). First- and second-order change: Implications for rationalist and constructivist cognitive therapies. *Journal of Counseling & Development, 69,* 122–127.

MacIsaac, D. S. (1997). Empathy: Heinz Kohut's contribution. In A. C. Bohart & L. S. Greenberg (Eds.), *Empathy reconsidered: New directions in psychotherapy* (pp. 245–264). Washington, DC: American Psychological Association.

Mahoney, M. J. (2000). Core ordering and disordering processes: A constructive view of psychological development. In R. A. Neimeyer & J. D. Raskin (Eds.), *Constructions of disorder: Meaning-making frameworks in psychotherapy* (pp. 43–62). Washington, DC: American Psychological Association.

Mahoney, M. J. (2003). *Constructive psychotherapy: A practical guide.* New York: Guilford.

Mahrer, A. R., Dessaulles, A., Gervaize, P. A., & Nadler, W. P. (1987). An indictment of interpretation: The elevated role of therapist as grand interpreter. *Psychotherapy in Private Practice, 5,* 39–51.

Manaster, G. J., & Corsini, R. J. (1982). *Individual psychology: Theory and practice.* Itasca, IL: F. E. Peacock.

Marcia, J. (1987). Empathy and psychotherapy. In N. Eisenberg & J. Strayer (Eds.), *Empathy and its development* (pp. 81–102). New York: Cambridge University Press.

Margulies, A. (1984). Toward empathy: The uses of wonder. *American Journal of Psychiatry, 141,* 1025–1033.

Margulies, A. (1989). *The empathic imagination.* New York: W. W. Norton.

Marks, S. E., & Tolsma, R. J. (1986). Empathy research: Some methodological considerations. *Psychotherapy, 23,* 4–20.

Martin, D. G. (2000). *Counseling and therapy skills* (2nd ed.), Prospect Heights, IL: Waveland Press.

Masson, J. M. (1984). *The assault on truth: Freud's suppression of the seduction theory.* New York: Farrar, Straus & Giroux.

May, R. (1939). *The art of counseling: How to gain and give mental health.* New York: Abingdon-Cokesbury Press.

May, R., & Yalom, I. (2005). Existential psychotherapy. In R. J. Corsini & D. Wedding (Eds.), *Current psychotherapies* (7th ed., pp. 269–298). Belmont, CA: Brooks/Cole.

McMullin, R. E. (2000). *The new handbook of cognitive therapy techniques.* New York: W. W. Norton.

Mearns, D. (2003). *Developing person-centred counselling* (2nd ed.). London: Sage.

Mearns, D., & Thorne, B. (1988). *Person-centered counseling in action.* Newbury Park, CA: Sage.

Meichenbaum, D. (1977). *Cognitive-behavior modification: An integrative approach.* New York: Plenum.

Meier, S. T., & Davis, S. R. (2005). *The elements of counseling* (5th ed.). Belmont, CA: Brooks/Cole.

Meissner, W. W. (1972). Notes on identification: III. The concept of identification. *The Psychoanalytic Quarterly, 41,* 224–260.

Meissner, W. W. (1996). *The therapeutic alliance.* New Haven, CT: Yale University Press.

Messer, S. B. (2004). Evidence-based practice: Beyond empirically supported treatments. *Professional Psychology: Research and Practice, 35,* 580–588.

Miller, J. B. (1986). *Toward a new psychology of women* (2nd ed.). Boston, MA: Beacon Press.

Miller, K. I., Stiff, J. B., & Ellis, B. H. (1988). Communication and empathy as precursors to burnout among human service workers. *Communication Monographs, 55,* 250–265.

Miller, J. B., & Stiver, I. P. (1997). *The healing connection: How women form relationships in therapy and in life.* Boston: Beacon Press.

Mitchell, S. A. (1988). *Relational concepts in psychoanalysis: An integration.* Cambridge, MA: Harvard University Press.

Mitchell, S. A. (1993). *Hope and dread in psychoanalysis.* New York: Basic Books.

Mitchell, S. A. (1997). *Influence and autonomy in psychoanalysis.* Hillsdale, NJ: The Analytic Press.

Mitchell, S. A., & Black, M. J. (1995). *Freud and beyond: A history of modern psychoanalytic thought.* New York: Basic Books.

Modell, A. H. (1979). Empathy and the failure of empathy. *Bulletin, The Association for Psychoanalytic Medicine, 18,* 70–75.

Morran, D. K., Stockton, R., & Whittingham, M. H. (2004). Effective leader interventions for counseling and psychotherapy groups. In J. L. DeLucia-Waack, D. Gerrity, C. R. Kalodner, & M. T. Riva (Eds.), *Handbook of group counseling and psychotherapy* (pp. 91–103). Thousand Oaks, CA: Sage.

Mosak, H. H. (1958). Early recollections as a projective technique. *Journal of Projective Techniques, 22,* 302–311.

Mosak, H. H. (2005). Adlerian psychotherapy. In R. J. Corsini & D. Wedding (Eds.), *Current psychotherapies* (7th ed., pp. 52–95). Belmont, CA: Brooks/Cole.

Mosak, H. H., & Maniacci, M. P. (1998). *Tactics in counseling and psychotherapy.* Itasca, IL: F. E. Peacock.

Mosak, H. H., & Maniacci, M. P. (1999). *A primer of Adlerian psychology: The analytic-behavioral-cognitive psychology of Alfred Adler.* Philadelphia: Brunner/Mazel.

Moses, I. (1988). The misuse of empathy in psychoanalysis. *Contemporary Psychoanalysis, 24,* 577–594.

Moursund, J. P., & Erskine, R. G. (2004). *Integrative psychotherapy: The art and science of relationship.* Pacific Grove, CA: Brooks/Cole.

Murdock, N. L. (2004). *Theories of counseling and psychotherapy: A case approach.* Upper Saddle River, NJ: Pearson Education.

Murphy, B. C., & Dillon, C. (2003). *Interviewing in action: Relationship, process, and change* (2nd ed.). Pacific Grove, CA: Brooks/Cole.

Murstein, B. I., & Pryer, R. S. (1959). The concept of projection: A review. *Psychological Bulletin, 56,* 353–374.

Myers, S. (2000). Empathic listening: Reports on the experience of being heard. *Journal of Humanistic Psychology, 40,* 148–173.

Neimeyer, R. A. (1995). Constructivist psychotherapies: Features, foundations, and future directions. In R. A. Neimeyer & M. J. Mahoney (Eds.), *Constructivism in psychotherapy* (pp. 11–38). Washington, DC: American Psychological Association.

Nicoll, W. G. (1999). Brief therapy strategies and techniques. In R. E. Watts & J. Carlson (Eds.), *Interventions and strategies in counseling and psychotherapy* (pp. 15–30). Philadelphia: Accelerated Development/Taylor & Francis.

Noonan, K. A. (1981). *Coping with illness.* Albany, NY: Delmar.

Norcross, J. C. (2002). Empirically supported therapy relationships. In J. C. Norcross (Ed.), *Psychotherapy relationships that work: Therapist contributions and responsiveness to patients* (pp. 3–16). New York: Oxford University Press.

Nystul, M. S. (2003). *Introduction to counseling: An art and science perspective* (2nd ed.). Boston: Allyn & Bacon.

Oberst, U. E., & Stewart, A. E. (2003). *Adlerian psychotherapy: An advanced approach to individual psychology.* New York: Brunner-Routledge.

Ogden, T. H. (1982). *Projective identification and psychotherapeutic technique.* New York: Jason Aronson.

O'Hara, M. M. (1984). Person-centered Gestalt: Toward a holistic synthesis. In R. Levant & J. Shlien (Eds.), *Client-centered therapy and the person-centered approach: New directions in theory, research and practice* (pp. 203–221). New York: Praeger.

Olinick, S. L. (1969). On empathy, and regression in service of the other. *British Journal of Medical Psychology, 42,* 41–49.

Olinick, S. L. (1984). A critique of empathy and sympathy. In J. Lichtenberg, M. Bornstein, & D. Silver (Eds.), *Empathy I* (pp. 137–166). Hillsdale, NJ: The Analytic Press.

Ornstein, A. (1984). Psychoanalytic psychotherapy: A contemporary perspective.

In P. E. Stepansky & A. Goldberg (Eds.), *Kohut's legacy: Contributions to self psychology* (pp. 171–181). Hillsdale, NJ: The Analytic Press.

Ornstein, A. (1994). Empathy, the interpretive process and the relativity of psychoanalytic cure. *Canadian Journal of Psychoanalysis, 2,* 103–117.

Ornstein, P. H. (1979). Remarks on the control position of empathy in psychoanalysis. *Bulletin, The Association for Psychoanalytic Medicine, 18,* 95–108.

Ornstein, P. H., & Ornstein, A. (1980). Formulating interpretations in clinical psychoanalysis. *International Journal of Psycho-Analysis, 61,* 203–211.

Orr, D. W. (1954). Transference and countertransference: A historical survey. *Journal of the American Psychoanalytic Association, 2,* 621–670.

Packer, M. J. (1985). Hermeneutic inquiry in the study of human conduct. *American Psychologist, 40,* 1081–1093.

Paivio, S. C., & Laurent, C. (2001). Empathy and emotional regulation: Reprocessing memories of childhood abuse. *Journal of Clinical Psychology, 57,* 213–226.

Parker, C. A. (1955). Empathy. *Personnel and Guidance Journal, 34,* 89–93.

Patterson, C. H. (1984). Empathy, warmth, and genuineness in psychotherapy: A review of reviews. *Psychotherapy, 21,* 431–438.

Patton, M. J., & Meara, N. M. (1992). *Psychoanalytic counseling.* New York: John Wiley & Sons.

Peabody, S. A., & Gelso, C. J. (1982). Countertransference and empathy: The complex relationship between two divergent concepts in counseling. *Journal of Counseling Psychology, 29,* 240–245.

Pearson, Q. M. (1999). Integrative empathy: Training counselors to listen with a theoretical ear. *The Journal of Humanistic Counseling, Education and Development, 38,* 13–18.

Pedersen, P. B., Draguns, J. G., Lonner, W. J., & Trimble, J. E. (Eds.). (2002). *Counseling across cultures* (5th ed.). Thousand Oaks, CA: Sage.

Peloquin, S. M. (1995). The fullness of empathy: Reflections and illustrations. *The American Journal of Occupational Therapy, 49,* 24–31.

Pepinsky, H. B., & Pepinsky, P. B. (1954). *Counseling: Theory and practice.* New York: Ronald Press.

Persons, J. B., & Burns, D. D. (1985). Mechanisms of action of cognitive therapy: The relative contributions of technical and interpersonal interventions. *Cognitive Therapy and Research, 9,* 539–551.

Petitmengin-Peugeot, C. (1999). The intuitive experience. *Journal of Consciousness Studies, 6,* 43–77.

Petro, C. S., & Hansen, J. C. (1977). Counselor sex and empathic judgment. *Journal of Counseling Psychology, 24,* 373–376.

Pigman, G. W. (1995). Freud and the history of empathy. *International Journal of Psycho-Analysis, 76,* 237–256.

Poland, W. S. (1984). On empathy in and beyond analysis. In J. Lichtenberg, M. Bornstein, & D. Silver (Eds.), *Empathy I* (pp. 331–349). Hillsdale, NJ: The Analytic Press.

Post, S. L. (1980). Origins, elements, and functions of therapeutic empathy. *International Journal of Psycho-Analysis, 61,* 277–293.

Post, S. L., & Miller, J. P., Jr. (1984). Apprehensions of empathy. In J. Lichtenberg, M. Bornstein, & D. Silver (Eds.), *Empathy I* (pp. 217–235). Hillsdale, NJ: The Analytic Press.

Posthuma, B. W. (2002). *Small groups in counseling and therapy: Process and leadership* (4th ed.). Boston: Allyn & Bacon.

Powers, R. L., & Griffith, J. (1987). *Understanding life-style: The psycho-clarity process.* Chicago: The Americas Institute of Adlerian Studies.

Presbury, J. H., Echterling, L. G., & McKee, J. E. (2002). *Ideas and tools for brief counseling.* Upper Saddle River, NJ: Merrill Prentice Hall.

Rachman, A. W. (1988). The rule of empathy: Sandor Ferenczi's pioneering contributions to the empathic method in psychoanalysis. *Journal of the American Academy of Psychoanalysis, 16,* 1–27.

Rachman, A. W. (1989). Ferenczi's contributions to the evolution of a self psychology framework in psychoanalysis. In D. W. Detrick & S. P. Detrick (Eds.), *Self psychology: Comparisons and contrasts* (pp. 89–109). Hillsdale, NJ: The Analytic Press.

Rachman, A. W. (1997). *Sándor Ferenczi: The psychotherapist of tenderness and passion.* Northvale, NJ: Jason Aronson.

Racker, H. A. (1953). A contribution to the problem of counter-transference. *International Journal of Psycho-Analysis, 34,* 313–324.

Rangell, L. (1982). The self in psychoanalytic theory. *Journal of the American Psychoanalytic Association, 30,* 863–891.

Raskin, N. J. (2001). The history of empathy in the client-centered movement. In S. Haugh & T. Merry (Eds.), *Rogers' therapeutic conditions: Evolution, theory and practice. Vol. 2: Empathy* (pp. 1–15). Ross-on-Wye, UK: PCCS Books.

Raskin, N. J., & Rogers, C. R. (2005). Person-centered therapy. In R. J. Corsini & D. Wedding (Eds.), *Current psychotherapies* (7th ed., pp. 130–165). Belmont, CA: Brooks/Cole.

Raue, P. J., & Goldfried, M. R. (1994). The therapeutic alliance in cognitive-behavior therapy. In A. O. Horvarth & L. Greenberg (Eds.), *The working alliance: Theory, research and practice* (pp. 131–152). New York: John Wiley & Sons.

Rea, B. D. (2001). Finding our balance: The investigation and clinical application of intuition. *Psychotherapy, 38,* 97–106.

Redfern, S., Dancey, C. P., & Dryden, W. (1993). Empathy: Its effect on how counsellors are perceived. *British Journal of Guidance and Counselling, 21,* 300–309.

Reich, A. (1951). On counter-transference. *International Journal of Psycho-Analysis, 32,* 3–7.

Reich, A. (1960). Further remarks on countertransference. *International Journal of Psycho-Analysis, 41,* 389–395.

Reik, T. (1948). *Listening with the third ear: The inner experience of a psychoanalyst.* Garden City, NY: Garden City Books.

Ridley, C. R., & Udipi, S. (2002). Putting cultural empathy into practice. In P. B. Pedersen, J. G. Draguns, W. J. Lonner, & J. E. Trimble (Eds.), *Counseling across cultures* (5th ed., pp. 317–333). Thousand Oaks, CA: Sage.

Robinson, T. L. (2005). *The convergence of race, ethnicity, and gender: Multiple identities in counseling* (2nd ed.). Upper Saddle River, NJ: Pearson Education.

Rogers, C. R. (1942). *Counseling and psychotherapy: Newer concepts in practice.* Boston: Houghton Mifflin.

Rogers, C. R. (1949). The attitude and orientation of the counselor in client-centered therapy. *Journal of Consulting Psychology, 13,* 82–94.

Rogers, C. R. (1951). *Client-centered therapy: Its current practice, implications, and theory.* Boston: Houghton Mifflin.

Rogers, C. R. (1954). The case of Mrs. Oak: A research analysis. In C. R. Rogers & R. F. Dymond (Eds.), *Psychotherapy and personality change: Co-ordinated research studies in the client-centered approach* (pp. 259–348). Chicago: The University of Chicago Press.

Rogers, C. R. (1957). The necessary and sufficient conditions of therapeutic personality change. *Journal of Consulting Psychology, 21,* 95–103.

Rogers, C. R. (1959). A theory of therapy, personality, and interpersonal relationships, as developed in the client-centered framework. In S. Koch (Ed.), *Psychology: A study of science, Vol. 3: Formulations of the person and the social context* (pp. 184–256). New York: McGraw-Hill.

Rogers, C. R. (1961). *On becoming a person: A therapist's view of psychotherapy.* Boston: Houghton Mifflin.

Rogers, C. R. (1964). Toward a science of the person. In T. W. Wann (Ed.), *Behaviorism and phenomenology: Contrasting bases for modern psychology* (pp. 109–140). Chicago: University of Chicago Press.

Rogers, C. R. (1965). The therapeutic relationship: Recent theory and research. *Australian Journal of Psychology, 17,* 95–108.

Rogers, C. R. (1966). Client-centered therapy. In S. Arieti (Ed.), *American handbook of psychiatry* (Vol. 3, pp. 183–200). New York: Basic Books.

Rogers, C. R. (1969). Two divergent views. In R. May (Ed.), *Existential psychology* (2nd ed., pp. 84–98). New York: Random House.

Rogers, C. R. (1970). *Carl Rogers on encounter groups.* New York: Harper & Row.

Rogers, C. R. (1975). Empathic: An unappreciated way of being. *The Counseling Psychologist, 5,* 2–10.

Rogers, C. R. (1980). *A way of being.* Boston: Houghton Mifflin.

Rogers, C. R. (1986a). Reflection of feelings. *Person-Centered Review, 1,* 375–377.

Rogers, C. R. (1986b). Rogers, Kohut, and Erickson: A personal perspective on some similarities and differences. *Person-Centered Review, 1,* 125–140.

Rogers, C. R., & Dymond, R. F. (Eds.). (1954). *Psychotherapy and personality change: Co-ordinated research studies in the client-centered approach.* Chicago: The University of Chicago Press.

Rogers, C. R., Gendlin, E. T., Kiesler, D. J., & Truax, C. (Eds.). (1967). *The therapeutic relationship and its impact: A study of psychotherapy with schizophrenics.* Madison, WI: University of Wisconsin Press.

Rogers, C. R., & Sanford, R. C. (1985). Client-centered psychotherapy. In H. I. Kaplan & B. J. Sadock (Eds.), *Comprehensive textbook of psychiatry/IV* (Vol. 2, pp. 1374–1388). Baltimore: Williams & Wilkins.

Rosenberger, E. W., & Hayes, J. A. (2002). Therapist as subject: A review of the empirical countertransference literature. *Journal of Counseling & Development, 80,* 264–270.

Rothstein, A. (1980). Toward a critique of the psychology of the self. *Psychoanalytic Quarterly, 49,* 423–455.

Rowe, C. E., Jr., & MacIsaac, D. S. (1989). *Empathic attunement: The "technique" of psychoanalytic self psychology.* Northvale, NJ: Jason Aronson.

Ruble, R. A., & Slivka, S. (1975). To confront or not confront: Is that the question? *The School Counselor, 23,* 10–15.

Rud, C. (1993). Empathy: The adventure of being present. *Person-Centered and Experiential Psychotherapies, 2,* 162–171.

Rutan, J. S., & Stone, W. N. (2001). *Psychodynamic group psychotherapy* (3rd ed.). New York: Guilford.

Safran, J. D., & Segal, Z. V. (1990). *Interpersonal process in cognitive therapy.* New York: Basic Books.

St. Clair, M., & Wigren, J. (2004). *Object relations and self psychology: An introduction* (4th ed.). Belmont, CA: Brooks/Cole.

Santayana, G. (1935). *The life of reason or the phases of human progress. Vol. 3: Reason in science.* New York: Charles Scribner's Sons. (Original work published 1905)

Sawyier, F. H. (1975). A conceptual analysis of empathy. *The Annual of Psychoanalysis, 3,* 37–47.

Schafer, R. (1959). Generative empathy in the treatment situation. *Psychoanalytic Quarterly, 28,* 342–373.

Schlesinger, H. J. (1981). The process of empathic response. *Psychoanalytic Inquiry, 1,* 393–416.

Scheidlinger, S. (1966). The concept of empathy in group psychotherapy. *International Journal of Group Psychotherapy, 16,* 413–424.

Schiller, F. (1985). *Friedrich Schiller: Poet of freedom.* New York: New Benjamin Franklin House. (Original work published 1795)

Schmid, P. F. (2001). Comprehension: The art of not knowing. Dialogical and ethical perspectives on empathy as dialogue in personal and person-centred relationships. In S. Haugh & T. Merry (Eds.), *Rogers' therapeutic conditions: Evolution, theory and practice. Vol. 2: Empathy* (pp. 53–71). Ross-on-Wye, UK: PCCS Books.

Schmid, P. F. (2003). The characteristics of a person-centered approach to therapy and counseling: Criteria for identity and coherence. *Person-Centered and Experiential Psychotherapies, 2,* 104–120.

Schuster, R. (1979). Empathy and mindfulness. *Journal of Humanistic Psychology, 19*, 71–77.

Schwaber, E. (1981). Empathy: A mode of analytic listening. *Psychoanalytic Inquiry, 1*, 357–392.

Schwartz, E. K., & Wolf, A. (1964). On countertransference in group psychotherapy. *The Journal of Psychology, 57*, 131–142.

Sciarra, D. T. (1999). *Multiculturalism in counseling.* Itasca, IL: F. E. Peacock.

Segal, N. P. (1981). Narcissism and adaptation to indignity. *International Journal of Psycho-Analysis, 62*, 465–476.

Seligman, L. (2004). *Technical and conceptual skills for mental health professionals.* Upper Saddle River, NJ: Pearson Education.

Seruya, B. B. (1997). *Empathic brief psychotherapy.* Northvale, NJ: Jason Aronson.

Shapiro, T. (1974). The development and distortions of empathy. *Psychoanalytic Quarterly, 43*, 4–25.

Shapiro, T. (1981). Empathy: A critical reevaluation. *Psychoanalytic Inquiry, 1*, 423–448.

Sharf, R. S. (2004). *Theories of psychotherapy and counseling: Concepts and cases* (3rd ed.). Pacific Grove, CA: Brooks/Cole.

Sharma, R. M. (1992). Empathy—A retrospective on its development in psychotherapy. *Australian and New Zealand Journal of Psychiatry, 26*, 377–390.

Shedler, J., Mayman, M., & Manis, M. (1993). The illusion of mental health. *American Psychologist, 48*, 1117–1131.

Shostrum, E. T., Shostrum, S. K., & Ratner, H. (1977). *Three approaches to psychotherapy II. Part 1. Carl Rogers. Client-centered therapy* [Video recording]. (Available from Psychological and Educational Films, PMB #252, East Coast Highway, Corona Del Mar, CA 92625)

Silverstein, M. L. (1999). *Self psychology and diagnostic assessment: Identifying selfobject functions thorough psychological testing.* Mahwah, NJ: Lawrence Erlbaum Associates.

Singer, B. A., & Luborsky, L. (1977). Countertransference: The status of clinical versus quantitative research. In A. S. Gurman & A. M. Razin (Eds.), *Effective psychotherapy: A handbook of research* (pp. 433–451). New York: Pergamon Press.

Snyder, M. (1992). The relationship enhancement model of family therapy: A systematic eclectic approach. *Journal of Family Psychotherapy, 2*, 1–26.

Sommers-Flanagan, J., & Sommers-Flanagan, R. (2003). *Clinical interviewing* (3rd ed.). New York: John Wiley & Sons.

Sonstegard, M. A., & Bitter, J. A. (2004). *Adlerian group counseling and therapy: Step-by-step.* New York: Brunner-Routledge.

Spence, D. P. (1982). *Narrative truth and historical truth: Meaning and interpretation in psychoanalysis.* New York: W. W. Norton.

Spencer, J. H., & Balter, L. (1984). Empathy and the analyzing instrument. In J. Lichtenberg, M. Bornstein, & D. Silver (Eds.), *Empathy II* (pp. 289–307). Hillsdale, NJ: The Analytic Press.

Spengler, P. M., Strohmer, D. C., Dixon, D. N., & Shivy, V. A. (1995). A scientist-practitioner model of psychological assessment: Implications for training, practice and research. *The Counseling Psychologist, 23,* 506–534.

Sperry, L., Carlson, J., & Kjos, D. (2003). *Becoming an effective therapist.* Boston: Allyn & Bacon.

Spitz, R. A. (1956). Countertransference: Comments on its varying role in the analytic situation. *Journal of the American Psychoanalytic Association, 4,* 256–265.

Stanton, M. (1991). *Sándor Ferenczi: Reconsidering active intervention.* Northvale, NJ: Jason Aronson.

Stern, D. B. (1988). Not misusing empathy. *Contemporary Psychoanalysis, 24,* 598–611.

Stewart, D. A. (1955). Empathy, common ground of ethics and of personality theory. *The Psychoanalytic Review, 42,* 131–141.

Stewart, D. A. (1956). *Preface to empathy.* New York: Philosophical Library.

Stolorow, R. D. (1986). Critical reflections on the theory of self psychology: An inside view. *Psychoanalytic Inquiry, 6,* 387–402.

Stone, W. N., & Whitman, R. M. (1980). Observations on empathy in group psychotherapy. In L. R. Wolberg & M. L. Aronson (Eds.), *Group and family therapy 1980* (pp. 102–117). New York: Brunner/Mazel.

Strunk, O., Jr., (1957). Empathy: A review of theory and research. *Psychological Newsletter, 9,* 47–57.

Strupp, H. H. (1996). Some salient lessons from research and practice. *Psychotherapy, 33,* 135–138.

Sullivan, H. S. (1953). *The interpersonal theory of psychiatry.* New York: W. W. Norton.

Sullivan, H. S. (1954). *The psychiatric interview* (H. S. Perry & M. L. Gawel, Eds.). New York: W. W. Norton.

Szalita, A. B. (1976). Some thoughts on empathy. *Psychiatry,* 39, 142–152.

Szalita, A. B. (1981). The use and misuse of empathy in psychoanalysis and psychotherapy. *The Psychoanalytic Review, 68,* 3–21.

Tamminen, A. W., & Smaby, M. H. (1981). Helping counselors learn to confront. *Personnel and Guidance Journal, 60,* 41–45.

Tansey, M., & Burke, W. (1989). *Understanding countertransference: From projective identification to empathy.* Hillsdale, NJ: The Analytic Press.

Teich, N. (1992a). Backgrounds: Origins, locations, and multiple definitions of empathy. In N. Teich (Ed.), *Rogerian perspectives: Collaborative rhetoric for oral and written communication* (pp. 241–247). Norwood, NJ: Ablex.

Teich, N. (1992b). Heinz Kohut: Empathy in and beyond psychoanalysis. In N. Teich (Ed.), *Rogerian perspectives: Collaborative rhetoric for oral and written communication* (pp. 257–272). Norwood, NJ: Ablex.

Teich, N. (1992c). Rogerian empathy. In N. Teich (Ed.), *Rogerian perspectives: Collaborative rhetoric for oral and written communication* (pp. 249–256). Norwood, NJ: Ablex.

Thompson, C. (1944). Ferenczi's contribution to psychoanalysis. *Psychiatry, 7,* 245–252.

Thoreau, H. D. (1968). *The writings of Henry David Thoreau. Vol. 2. Walden.* New York: Ames Press. (Original work published 1854)

Thorne, B. (2003). *Carl Rogers* (2nd ed.). Thousand Oaks, CA: Sage.

Tobin, D. J. (2003). Countertransference and the hidden client in counselor training and supervision. *The Journal of the Pennsylvania Counseling Association, 5,* 19–29.

Tobin, S. A. (1991). A comparison of psychoanalytic self psychology and Carl Rogers's person-centered therapy. *Journal of Humanistic Psychology, 31,* 9–33.

Tolan, J. (2003). *Skills in person-centred counselling and psychotherapy.* London: Sage.

Tomm, K. (1988). Interventive interviewing: Part III. Intending to ask lineal, circular, strategic, or reflexive questions. *Family Process, 27,* 1–15.

Toseland, R. W., & Rivas, R. F. (2005). *An introduction to group work practice* (5th ed.). Boston: Allyn & Bacon.

Treurniet, N. (1980). On the relation between the concepts of self and ego in Kohut's psychology of the self. *International Journal of Psycho-Analysis, 61,* 325–333.

Troemel-Ploetz, S. (1980). "I'd come to you for therapy": Interpretation, redefinition and paradox in Rogerian therapy. *Psychotherapy: Theory, Research and Practice, 17,* 246–257.

Trotzer, J. P. (1999). *The counselor and the group: Integrating theory, training, and practice* (3rd ed.). Philadelphia: Accelerated Development/Taylor & Francis.

Truax, C. B., & Carkhuff, R. R. (1967). *Toward effective counseling and psychotherapy: Training and practice.* Chicago: Aldine.

Trusty, J., Ng, K-M., & Watts, R. E. (2005). Models of effects of adult attachment on emotional empathy of counseling students. *Journal of Counseling & Development, 83,* 66–77.

Turock, A. (1978). Effective challenging through additive empathy. *Personnel and Guidance Journal, 57,* 144.

Tuttman, S. (1993). Countertransference and transference in groups. In H. I. Kaplan & B. J. Sadock (Eds.), *Comprehensive group psychotherapy* (3rd ed., pp. 98–105). Baltimore: Williams & Wilkins.

Van Balen, R. (1990). The therapeutic relationship according to Carl Rogers, only a climate? A dialogue? Or both? In G. Lietaer, J. Rombauts, & R. Van Balen (Eds.), *Client-centered and experiential psychotherapy in the nineties.* Leuven, Belgium: Leuven University Press.

van Kaam, A. L. (1959). Phenomenal analysis: Exemplified by a study of the experience of "really feeling understood." *Journal of Individual Psychology, 15,* 66–71.

van Kaam, A. (1969). *Existential foundations of psychology.* Garden City, NY: Image Books.

Van Wagoner, S. L., Gelso, C. J., Hayes, J. A., & Diemer, R. A. (1991). Countertransference and the reputedly excellent therapist. *Psychotherapy, 28,* 411–421.

Vanaerschot, G. (1990). The process of empathy: Holding and letting go. In G. Lietaer, J. Rombauts, & R. Van Balen (Eds.), *Client-centered and experiential psychotherapy in the nineties* (pp. 269–293). Leuven, Belgium: Leuven University Press.

Vanaerschot, G. (1997). Empathic resonance as a source of experience-enhancing interventions. In A. C. Bohart & L. S. Greenberg (Eds.), *Empathy reconsidered: New directions in psychotherapy* (pp. 141–165). Washington, DC: American Psychological Association.

Wallace, E. R. (1985). *Historiography and causation in psychoanalysis: An essay on psychoanalytic and historical epistemology.* Hillsdale, NJ: Lawrence Erlbaum Associates.

Wallerstein, R. S. (1983). Self psychology and "classical" psychoanalytic psychology: The nature of their relationship. *Psychoanalysis and Contemporary Thought, 6,* 553–593.

Wampold, B. E. (2001). *The great psychotherapy debate: Models, methods, and findings.* Mahwah, NJ: Lawrence Erlbaum Associates.

Warner, M. S. (1989). Empathy and strategy in the family system. *Person-Centered Review, 4,* 324–343.

Warner, M. S. (1996). How does empathy cure? A theoretical consideration of empathy, processing and personal narrative. In R. Hutterer, G. Pawlowsky, P. F. Schmid, & R. Stipsits (Eds.), *Client-centered and experiential psychotherapy: A paradigm in motion* (pp. 127–143). New York: Peter Lang.

Watkins, C. E., Jr. (1990). The effects of counselor self-disclosure: A research review. *The Counseling Psychologist, 18,* 477–500.

Watkins, C. E., Jr. (2000). Some final thoughts about using tests and assessment procedures in counseling. In C. E. Watkins, Jr. & V. L. Campbell (Eds.), *Testing and assessment in counseling practice* (2nd ed., pp. 547–555). Mahwah, NJ: Lawrence Erlbaum Associates.

Watson, J. C. (2002). Re-visioning empathy. In D. J. Cain & J. Seeman (Eds.), *Humanistic psychotherapies: Handbook of research and practice* (pp. 445–471). Washington, DC: American Psychological Association.

Watson, J. C., Goldman, R., & Vanaerschot, G. (1998). Empathic: A postmodern way of being? In L. S. Greenberg, J. C. Watson, & G. Lietaer, (Eds.), *Handbook of experiential psychotherapy* (pp. 61–81). New York: Guilford.

Watts, R. E. (1996). Social interest and the core conditions: Could it be that Adler influenced Rogers? *Journal of Humanistic Education and Development, 34,* 165–170.

Watts, R. E., & Pietrzak, D. (2000). Adlerian "encouragement" and the therapeutic process of solution-focused brief therapy. *Journal of Counseling & Development, 78,* 442–447.

Watts, R. E., & Shulman, B. H. (2003). Integrating Adlerian and constructive therapies: An Adlerian perspective. In R. E. Watts (Ed.), *Adlerian, cognitive, and constructivist psychotherapies: An integrative dialogue* (pp. 9–37). New York: Springer.

Weigert, E. (1962). Sympathy, empathy and freedom in therapy. In L. Salzman & J. H. Masserman (Eds.), *Modern concepts in psychoanalysis* (pp. 143–159). New York: Philosophical Library.

Weiner, I. B. (1998). *Principles of psychotherapy* (2nd ed.). New York: John Wiley & Sons.

Welfel, E. R., & Patterson, L. E. (2005). *The counseling process: A multitheoretical integrative approach* (6th ed). Belmont, CA: Brooks/Cole.

White, M. T., & Weiner, M. B. (1986). *The theory and practice of self psychology.* New York: Brunner/Mazel.

Wilkins, P. (2003). *Person-centred therapy in focus.* London: Sage.

Williams, D. I., & Irving, J. A. (1997). Empathy. *International Journal of Psychology and Psychotherapy, 15,* 271–276.

Willison, B. G., & Masson, R. L. (1986). The role of touch in therapy: An adjunct to communication. *Journal of Counseling & Development, 64,* 497–500.

Wilson, J. M. (1982). The value of touch in psychotherapy. *American Journal of Orthopsychiatry, 52,* 65–72.

Wispé, L. (1986). The distinction between sympathy and empathy: To call forth a concept, a word is needed. *Journal of Personality and Social Psychology, 50,* 314–321.

Wispé, L. (1987). History of the concept of empathy. In N. Eisenberg & J. Strayer (Eds.), *Empathy and its development* (pp. 17–37). New York: Cambridge University Press.

Wolf, E. S. (1983). Empathy and countertransference. In A. Goldberg (Ed.), *The future of psychoanalysis: Essays in honor of Heinz Kohut* (pp. 309–326). New York: International Universities Press.

Wolf, E. S. (1988). *Treating the self: Elements of clinical self psychology.* New York: Guilford.

Woolfolk, R. L. (1998). *The cure of souls: Science, values and psychotherapy.* San Francisco: Jossey-Bass.

Wolowitz, L. (2002). The changing face of the ideal therapist. In P. R. Breggin, G. Breggin, & F. Bemak (Eds.), *Dimensions of effective empathy* (pp. 13–28). New York: Springer.

Worrell, J., & Johnson, D. (2001). Therapy with women: Feminist frameworks. In R. K. Unger (Ed.), *Handbook of psychology of women and gender* (pp. 317–329). New York: John Wiley & Sons.

Wyatt, G., & Sanders, P. (Eds.). (2002). *Rogers' therapeutic conditions: Evolution, theory and practice. Vol. 4: Contact and perception.* Ross-on-Wye, UK: PCCS Books.

Yalom, I. D. (2005). *The theory and practice of group psychotherapy* (5th ed.). New York: Basic Books.

Young, M. E. (2005). *Learning the art of helping: Building blocks and techniques* (3rd ed.). Upper Saddle River, NJ: Pearson Education.

Zausner, T. (2003). Humility, empathy, and rebirth: The dynamics of Ferenczi's metapsychology. *Journal of Humanistic Psychology, 43,* 46–58.

Author Index

S

T

U

V

W

Y

Z

Subject Index

P

R

S

T